Treating Trauma

Treating Trauma

Relationship-Based Psychotherapy with Children, Adolescents, and Young Adults

Edited by Toni V. Heineman, DMH,
June M. Clausen, PhD, and
Saralyn C. Ruff, PhD

JASON ARONSON
Lanham • Boulder • New York • Toronto • Plymouth, UK

Published by Jason Aronson
A wholly owned subsidiary of The Rowman & Littlefield Publishing Group, Inc.
4501 Forbes Boulevard, Suite 200, Lanham, Maryland 20706
www.rowman.com

10 Thornbury Road, Plymouth PL6 7PP, United Kingdom

Chapter 10 poems reprinted by permission of Cynthia Franco.

British Library Cataloguing in Publication Information Available

Library of Congress Cataloging-in-Publication Data

Treating trauma : relationship-based psychotherapy with children, adolescents, and young adults / edited by Toni V. Heineman, June M. Clausen, and Saralyn C. Ruff.
pages cm
Includes bibliographical references and index.
ISBN 978-0-7657-0982-0 (cloth : alk. paper)—ISBN 978-0-7657-0983-7 (electronic)
1. Psychic trauma in children—Treatment. 2. Psychic trauma in adolescence—Treatment. 3. Foster children—Mental health. 4. Child psychotherapy. 5. Adolescent psychotherapy. I. Heineman, Toni Vaughn. II. Clausen, June M., 1962– III. Ruff, Saralyn C., 1979–
RJ506.P66T745 2013
618.92'8914—dc23
2013021523

∞™ The paper used in this publication meets the minimum requirements of American National Standard for Information Sciences Permanence of Paper for Printed Library Materials, ANSI/NISO Z39.48-1992.

Printed in the United States of America

This book is dedicated to the clinicians who volunteer their time out of a conviction that healthy relationships can and do make the world a better place.

Contents

Acknowledgments

A group of clinicians in San Francisco, CA, created A Home Within thirteen years ago to address a gap in effective mental health treatment for children and youth in foster care. By 2006, organized groups of clinicians providing treatment within the "One child, one therapist, for as long as it takes" model were working in eight states across the country and some of them came together and produced a book, *Building A Home Within: Meeting the Emotional Needs of Children and Youth in Foster Care*, about this model of care (Heineman & Ehrensaft, 2006). Now, seven years later, clinicians in fifty-four communities in twenty-four states are delivering open-ended, relationship-based therapy to current and former foster youth.

This book presents the rationale for this approach to treatment, provides several case illustrations written by A Home Within clinicians across the country, and outlines the eight essential elements that form the framework underlying effective intervention with these vulnerable children and youth. We have been honored to work with the contributors to this volume, whose care in honestly portraying the joys and challenges has been astounding. They have each taken extraordinary care to use pseudonyms, change all identifying information, and paraphrase conversations. In addition, they have elected to present this as a group effort, rather than take individual credit for their chapters, as a further protection for their clients' privacy.

This book, though organized and edited by the executive director, research director, and training drector of A Home Within, with chapter contributions from twelve A Home Within clinicians, is the work of many in the organization. We are particularly grateful to staff members Rene Fay, Jade Hoffman, and Edith Del Pezo Vargas for their support. Wendy Von Weiderhold and Molly Saeger, co-directors of our local chapters provided thoughtful clinical insights and Dr. Diane Ehrensaft, founding and continuing board member, gave valuable feedback on both content and format. Rosana Aguilar, Ashley Plushnik, and Corie Schwabenland from the Foster Care Research Group at the University of San Francisco provided essential support in reviewing literature and organizing references; their work and that of many other research assistants who have participated in the research is essential to the evaluation of the work of A Home Within, the results of which are presented in this book. The work of the clinicians of A Home Within, together with the experiences of the patients served over the last thirteen years, provides the insight and rich information necessary to understand what works for foster youth, what doesn't work, and how to best survive, as a clinician or a patient, in a child welfare system.

We would like to express our gratitude to the many board members who have provided guidance over the years. They have helped us move from a grass roots group to a vibrant and growing organization. In particular, Linda Fitzpatrick, Kira Stiefman, and Michael Hansen have been steadfast in their commitment and leadership.

We are extremely grateful for the help of the many large and small foundations that have provided financial support and the wisdom of their program officers. In particular, The Draper Richards Kaplan Foundation and the Peery Foundation provided financial support and direction that allowed us to take our original idea to scale. Our particular thanks to Bill Draper, Robin Richards, Jenny Shilling Stein, and Anne Marie Burgoyne of DRK and Dave Peery and Jessamyn Lau of the Peery Foundation.

We also deeply appreciate the support of the Faculty Development Fund and the Jesuit Foundation at the University of San Francisco for the projects of the Foster Care Research Group over the last decade. Professor Colin Silverthorne, the late Professor Maureen O'Sullivan, Associate Dean Shirley McGuire, and Dean Marcelo Camperi have been particularly instrumental in support of the research group and the vision of A Home Within.

Of course, this book would not have been possible without the expertise and support of the staff at Rowman & Littlefield. In particular we extend our appreciation to Amy King, Kelly Blackburn, Stephanie Brooks, and Meredith Nelson who patiently and expertly guided us through the publishing process from proposal to production.

We would also like to thank those who have taught us so much: caseworkers, judges, attorneys, foster parents, and other organizations serving the foster care community have broadened our perspective. The therapists who bring their skills, knowledge, and questions to A Home Within expand our clinical horizon. The consultation group leaders offer professional development to those in their group, but also help extend organizational knowledge. Of course, our most important teachers are the children, teens, and young adults who have shared their stories of life in foster care. They have allowed us to know their minds and hearts and for this we are profoundly grateful.

REFERENCE

Heineman, T. V., & Ehrensaft, D. (2006). *Building a home within: Meeting the emotional needs of children and youth in foster care*. Baltimore, MD: Brookes Publishing Co.

Introduction

The Need for a Relationships Framework in Effective Trauma Treatment for Children and Youth

Children who experience abuse and neglect suffer consequences of trauma far beyond the initial physical and psychological injuries (Peckins, 2011; Rosenkranz, Muller, & Henderson, 2012; Trickett, Negriff, Ji, & Wilson, Hansen, & Li, 2011; Zielinsks, 2009). For many maltreated children and youth, the negative impact of abuse is exacerbated by their subsequent removal from home, school, and community and placement into foster care (Baugerud & Melinder, 2012; Wechsler-Zimring, Kearney, Kaur, & Day, 2012). And, for many who are moved to out-of-home placements, the instability, ambiguity, and unpredictability of the foster care system results in an even further worsening of the psychological consequences of the original trauma (Havlicek, 2011; Stott, 2012). These children, who have been ignored, abandoned, assaulted, exploited, and/or tormented by their parents or primary caregivers must now live in a world in which everything is unfamiliar and tenuous, in which they have little to no contact with their families of origin, and in which abrupt change recreates itself at a moment's notice, with no warning.

Any therapist who provides mental health treatment for a child in foster care must address the psychological consequences of the neglect and/or abuse the child experienced, as well as the loss of the family of origin. Clinicians working with foster youth must also attend to the trauma of unanticipated and often poorly executed changes in the care provided by the child welfare system, all within the context of the uncertainty and ambiguity of the child's life in out-of-home care. The child in foster care needs support in the process of grieving uncertain loss, a far more difficult task than the grieving of loss that is certain and unchanging. When a caregiver dies, children must eventually come to terms with the impossibility of a reunion; in contrast, children in foster care are often left with terrible uncertainties. They may have weeks or months—or sometimes even years—of visits with their biological parents with the presumed intention of the reunification of the biological family. Because of their uncertainty, these ambiguous losses are nearly impossible to mourn. While processing the impact of chronic and uncertain loss, the therapist must also address the mental health symptoms expressed by foster children as a consequence of their history and current context of ambiguity and insecurity.

Professional journals, newsletters, and conferences abound with reports of evidence-based treatments (EBTs) with demonstrated efficacy in treating a variety of mental health symptoms in children and youth (Chorpita, Daleiden, Ebesutani, Young, Becker, Nakamura, & Starace, 2011; Southam-Gerow, Rodríguez, Chorpita, & Daleiden, 2012); however, these interventions have only recently begun to be evaluated with children in foster care or with children who have experienced multiple traumas and present with a complex array of mental health symptoms. And, with the exception of information about oversight of psychotropic prescription guidelines for foster youth (Mackie, Hyde, Rodday, Dawson, Lakshmikanthan, Bellonci, Schoonover, & Leslie, 2011) and recommendations for relationship-focused approaches to policy and work with emancipated foster youth (Smith, 2011), few guidelines exist to assist therapists in navigating the unique challenges of providing treatment to a child or adolescent living in foster care who, by definition, does not have a reliable and continuous parent figure available.

The goal of this book is to begin to address the failure of the clinical and research literature to provide a theoretically sound and empirically supported framework for mental health treatment of traumatized children and youth in foster care. In the paragraphs that follow, we briefly summarize the EBTs that have been developed to date for use with children and adolescents, each of which has been found to improve mental health functioning in research samples. We discuss the limitations of these treatments with children in foster care and advocate for inclusion of EBTs, when indicated, within a relationship-focused therapeutic framework that is sensitive to the unique needs and context of children and youth in foster care. We present findings from an initial evaluation of Relationship-Based Therapy (RBT) with foster youth and describe the nature and mission of A Home Within, a non-profit organization that delivers this RBT approach to foster children throughout the United States.

EBTs such as Parent-Child Interaction Therapy (PCIT), Multi-Systemic Therapy (MST), Trauma-Focused Cognitive-Behavioral Therapy (TF-CBT), Functional Family Therapy (FFT), Multidimensional Family Therapy (MDFT), and Interpersonal Psychotherapy for Adolescents (ITP-A) have demonstrated efficacy in reducing disruptive behavior, externalizing behavior problems, the negative impact of sexual abuse, the consequences of exposure to domestic violence, juvenile delinquency, substance abuse, and depression in non-foster children (Cohen, Deblinger, Mannarino, & Steer, 2004; Henggeler et al., 2011; Liddle, Dakof, Henderson, & Rowe, 2011; Lyon & Budd, 2010; Mufson, Dorta, Wickramaratne, Nomura, Olfson, & Weissman, 2004; Waldron & Turner, 2008). These treatments have only very recently begun to be implemented and evaluated with clients who are in foster care (Dorsey, Kerns, Trupin, Conover, & Berliner, 2012; Farmer, Burns, Wagner, Murray, & Southerland, 2010; Timmer, Urquiza, & Zebell, 2006; Weiner, Schneider, & Lyons, 2009). EBTs should be employed in treatment of foster youth whenever appropriate, for example, when the foster child's diagnosis or presenting symptom(s) is comparable to the presenting symptoms of the youth who participated in the research studies and when the foster parents' ability and willingness to engage in treatment is comparable to that of the families of origin who participated in the research studies. However, as noted recently by child welfare researchers (Briggs & McBeath, 2010; Maher et al., 2009; Naccarato & DeLorenzo, 2008; Storer, Barkan, Sherman, Haggerty, & Mattos, 2012), therapy with foster youth must go beyond EBTs in order to effectively assist these children, who are not living with their parents, to process their traumatic past and survive the uncertainly and ambiguity of their present. In order to maximize the effectiveness of EBTs with the foster child client, the therapist must employ these tools within a sound clinical framework that is sensitive and responsive to the unique challenges of the child welfare system and the needs of a child in out-of-home placement.

Nearly all of the EBTs currently available substantially involve parents in the treatment; for foster youth, their parents are not available due to either incarceration, abandonment, or court restrictions on parent-child contact. Moreover, the future involvement of the biological parent in the foster child's life is uncertain and unknown. The availability and willingness of foster parents to participate in treatment varies. Even when foster parents are willing to engage in their foster child's mental health treatment, the utility of family-based treatment with the foster child and his or her foster parents may be limited. This is particularly true if the foster child's difficulties do not lie with problems in the foster family context or the foster parents' caregiving. Furthermore, the fact that most foster youth experience multiple and often-unplanned placement changes while in foster care (O'Neill, Risley-Curtiss, Ayón, & Williams, 2012; Unrau, Chambers, Seita, & Putney, 2010) often makes the involvement of foster parents in treatment untenable.

Children and youth in foster care, while often demonstrating symptoms which include the treatment targets of EBTs, rarely suffer from *only* those well-defined target symptoms. Research that supports EBTs typically excludes from study samples children and adolescents who also suffer from psychiatric, social, or developmental issues beyond the identified target symptom(s). The prototypical foster youth may present with depression, substance abuse, and disruptive behavior problems, each of which has been shown to decrease with the application of one or more EBTs when the parents are engaged in treatment or when administered in a school-based setting (Lyon & Budd, 2010; Mufson et al., 2004; Waldron & Turner, 2008); however, the foster child is typically also suffering from the consequences of attachment failures, chronic neglect and/or abuse, abandonment and loss, and the instability and uncertainty of foster care placement. EBTs, to date, do not include guidelines and techniques for intervention with these additional complexities. Thus, while EBTs should be utilized when indicated in the treatment of foster youth, effective intervention with these vulnerable children and adolescents must derive from a framework and structure designed to address their unique presentation of psychiatric symptoms, traumatic history, and current contextual uncertainty. EBTs with foster youth, the therapist's "tools" must be employed within the context of a theoretically sound and foster-care sensitive framework, the "toolbox" in order to be effective.

RBT is an evidence-supported approach to therapy with current and former foster youth that is based on the centrality of relationships as the key to psychological health (Bachelor & Horvath, 1999; Smith, 2011). A relationship with an experienced therapist provides the safety, stability, and containment required by these troubled children, youth, and young adults to work through their traumatic history and address their current physical health, mental health, educational, and adaptive problems. RBT pays close attention to childhood experiences and the ways in which these early experiences influence psychological development. In particular, the therapist focuses on the impact of traumatic experiences in childhood and their lasting influence on the individual. Relationships beget relationships; the stories of past relationships are played out in subsequent relationships. Reviewing and revisiting, in and through relationships, the remnants of the past, embedded in the psyche, can provide opportunities for finding new ways of understanding feelings, thoughts, and actions. Learning how to be in a healthy relationship with a therapist allows the foster child to develop and maintain healthy relationships with other adults and with peers.

Though the efficacy of RBT with specific populations of children and youth who suffer from clearly defined psychiatric symptoms has not been thoroughly evaluated, the effectiveness of this approach with foster youth is supported by preliminary practice-based evidence (Clausen, Ruff, Von Wiederhold, & Heineman, 2012). Data collected from A Home Within clinicians by the Foster Care Research Group at the University of San Francisco over the last ten years demonstrates significant reductions in depression, anxiety, dissociative symptoms, school problems, sleep problems, eating problems, unsafe sexual behavior, self-injurious behavior, aggression and violence, risk taking, peer relationship problems, and foster family relationship problems. The average duration of treatments studied to date is three years and includes current and former foster children, youth, and young adults. Though the findings are preliminary, as the methodology is limited by sample size, potential bias of clinician reports, and the lack of a comparison group, results are encouraging and suggest that the RBT approach is supported by the data.

Research has shown that children in foster care demonstrate high rates of mental health symptoms (Clausen, Landsverk, Chadwick, Ganger, & Litrownik, 1998; Landsverk et al., 2009; Pecora, Jensen, Romanelli, Jackson, & Ortiz, 2009), yet most foster children do not receive appropriate mental health services (Levitt, 2009; Marx, Benoit, & Kamradt, 2003; Pecora, Jensen, Romanelli, Jackson, & Ortiz, 2009; Unrau & Wells, 2005), particularly those who have experienced neglect or who are ethnic minorities (Blumberg, Landsverk, Ellis-MacLeod, Ganger, & Culver, 1996; dosRios et al., 2001; Garland & Besinger, 1997). The failure to deliver needed mental health services to these vulnerable children in our care is due primarily to limited and fluctuating state and federal support, together with high turnover among inexperienced mental health interns and providers working for community mental health and social services departments. When funding is available for mental health treatment, foster youth are typically seen in community mental health clinics or community-based non-profit agencies, which employ mental health interns who are assigned to the agency or clinic for only six to twelve months. Thus, the foster child suffering from a complex array of psychiatric issues with background replete with trauma and loss, located in an uncertain and ever-changing familial environment, is seen for a series of short treatments by a rotating series of clinical interns, during their first year or two of practice.

The material in this volume draws on the work of clinicians who volunteer their professional time and expertise through A Home Within to support the emotional growth and healthy development of current and former foster youth. This award winning organization is based on a very simple model: "One Child. One Therapist. For As Long as it Takes." Intentionally, the commitment is not time limited; by working with just one child, teen, or young adult, each therapist is in a position to truly focus his or her time and psychic energy on understanding and meeting the needs of that one client. The work of each therapist is supported by regular meetings with a consultation group. Senior clinicians volunteer their time to lead these groups usually composed of four to six therapists. These groups offer therapists the opportunity to think and learn together about the work they are doing; they also provide support when the work is stressful and a place to share triumphs when the work is going well. Each local chapter is coordinated by a volunteer clinical director who devotes approximately four hours of pro bono time each week to establishing and maintaining the local chapter. This includes recruiting and vetting therapists and consultation group leaders, developing relationships with referral agencies, and matching therapists and clients. Clinical directors participate in a Three Year Fellowship in the Treatment of Foster Youth, which includes an annual conference for training, professional development, and networking. A Home Within is open to clinicians from diverse backgrounds bound together by their belief in the essential healing power of relationships and their willingness to make an open-ended volunteer commitment. A Home Within is built on the premise that everyone has something important to offer, from the newly minted therapist to the most seasoned clinician. Everyone is paid exactly the same—absolutely nothing. However, those who give their time through A Home Within extract value beyond monetary gain. They enjoy and benefit from their colleagues and they have the satisfaction of knowing that their efforts have made things better for someone sometimes a little and sometimes a lot. Clinicians who volunteer through A Home Within repeatedly say that their lives have been immeasurably enriched by the people they have come to know through their experience, both colleagues and clients.

Nine case studies exemplifying RBT with a diverse group of foster youth are examined in the chapters that follow. In addition, three clinicians describe their experiences of working therapeutically in the context of a consultation group, made up of like-minded peers and a senior clinician who facilitates discussion. At the end of the book, in the concluding chapter, we summarize the work presented in the chapters by articulating the eight essential elements of RBT with current and former foster youth. These eight elements—Engagement, Empathy, Environment, Egocentrism, Enthusiasm, Evidence, Endurance, and Extending—are the keys to successful RBT. As we share these experiences through the chapters of this book, it is our deepest hope that our readers take this framework home as a part the clinical toolbox in which they keep their therapeutic tools, equipping all of us to intervene most effectively and most humanely with the traumatized youth residing in the foster care system who come into our care.

REFERENCES

Bachelor, A., & Horvath, A. (1999). The therapeutic relationship. In M. A. Hubble, B. L. Duncan, & S. D. Miller (Eds.), *The heart and soul of change: What works in psychotherapy.* Washington, DC: American Psychological Association.

Baugerud, G., & Melinder, A. (2012). Maltreated children's memory of stressful removals from their biological parents. *Applied Cognitive Psychology, 26*(2), 261–270. DOI: 10.1002/acp.1817.

Blumberg, E., Landsverk, J., Ellis-MacLeod, E., Ganger, W., & Culver, S. (1996). Use of public mental health systems by children in foster care: Client characteristics and service use patterns. *Journal of Mental Health Administration, 23*, 389–405.

Briggs, H., & McBeath, B. (2010). Infusing culture into practice: Developing and implementing evidence-based mental health services for African American foster youth. *Child Welfare: Journal of Policy, Practice, and Program, 89*, 31–60.

Chorpita, B. F., Daleiden, E. L., Ebesutani, C., Young, J., Becker, K. D., Nakamura, B. J., & Starace, N. (2011). Evidence-based treatments for children and adolescents: An updated review of indicators of efficacy and effectiveness. *Clinical Psychology: Science and Practice, 18*(2), 154–172. DOI: 10.1111/j.1468-2850.2011.01247.x.

Clausen, J. M., Landsverk, J., Ganger, W., Chadwick, D., & Litrownik, A. (1998). Mental health problems of children in foster care. *Journal of Child and Family Studies, 7*(3), 283–296.

Clausen, J. M., Ruff, S. C., Von Wiederhold, W., & Heineman, T. V. (2012). For as long as it takes: Relationship-based play therapy for children in foster care. *Psychoanalytic Social Work, 19*, 43–53.

Cohen, J. A., Deblinger, E., Mannarino, A. P., & Steer, R. A. (2004). A multisite, randomized controlled trial for children with sexual abuse-related PTSD symptoms. *Journal of the American Academy of Child & Adolescent Psychiatry, 43*(4), 393–402. DOI: 10.1097/00004583-200404000-00005.

Dorsey, S., Kerns, S. U., Trupin, E. W., Conover, K. L., & Berliner, L. (2012). Child welfare caseworkers as service brokers for youth in foster care: Findings from project focus. *Child Maltreatment, 17*, 22–31. DOI: 10.1177/1077559511429593.

dosRios, S., Zito, J. M., Safer, D. J., & Soeken, K. L. (2001). Mental health services for youths in foster care and disabled youths. *American Journal of Public Health, 91*, 1094–1099.

Farmer, E. Z., Burns, B. J., Wagner, H., Murray, M., & Southerland, D. G. (2010). Enhancing 'usual practice' treatment foster care: Findings from a randomized trial on improving youths' outcomes. *Psychiatric Services, 61*, 555–561. DOI: 10.1176/appi.ps.61.6.555.

Garland, A. F., & Besinger, B. A. (1997). Racial/ethnic differences in court-referred pathways to mental health services for children in foster care. *Children and Youth Services Review, 19*, 651–666.

Havlicek, J. (2011). Lives in motion: A review of former foster youth in the context of their experiences in the child welfare system, *Children and Youth Services Review, 33*(7), 1090–1100.

Henggeler, S. W., Halliday-Boykins, C. A., Cunningham, P. B., Randall, J., Shapiro, S. B., & Chapman, J. E. (2006). Juvenile drug court: Enhancing outcomes by integrating evidence-based treatments. *Journal of Consulting and Clinical Psychology, 74*(1), 42–54.

Landsverk, J. A., Burns, B. A., Stambaugh, L. F., & Reutz, J. A. R. (2009). Psychosocial interventions for children and adolescents in foster care: Review of research literature. *Child Welfare, 88*(1), 49–69.

Levitt, J. M. (2009). Identification of mental health service need among youth in child welfare. *Child Welfare, 88*, 27–48.

Liddle, H. A., Dakof, G. A., Henderson, C., & Rowe, C. (2011). Multidimensional family therapy for young adolescent substance abuse: Twelve-month outcomes of a randomized controlled trial. *International Journal of Offender Therapy and Comparative Criminology, 55*(4), 587–604.

Lyon, A. R., & Budd, K. S. (2010). A community mental health implementation of parent-child interaction therapy. *Journal of Child and Family Studies, 19*, 654–668.

Mackie, T. I., Hyde, J., Rodday, A., Dawson, E., Lakshmikanthan, R., Bellonci, C., Schoonover, D., & Leslie, L. K. (2011). Psychotropic medication oversight for youth in foster care: A national perspective on state child welfare policy and practice guidelines. *Children and Youth Services Review, 33*(11), 2213–2220. DOI: 10.1016/j.childyouth.2011.07.003.

Maher, E. J., Jackson, L. J., Pecora, P. J., Schultz, D. J., Chandra, A., & Barnes-Proby, D. S. (2009). Overcoming challenges to implementing and evaluating evidence-based in child welfare: A matter of necessity. *Children and Youth Services Review, 31*, 555–562. DOI: 10.1016/j.childyouth.2008.10.013.

Marx, L., Benoit, M., & Kamradt, B. (2003). Foster children in the child welfare system. In A. Pumariega & N. Winters (Eds.), *The handbook of child and adolescent system of care. The new community psychiatry.* San Francisco: Wiley.

Mufson, L., Dorta, K., Wickramaratne, P., Nomura, Y., Olfson, M., & Weissman M. M. (2004). A randomized effectiveness trial of interpersonal psychotherapy for depressed adolescents. *Archives of General Psychiatry, 61*(6), 577–584. DOI: 10.1001/archpsyc.61.6.577.

Naccarato, T., & DeLorenzo, E. (2008). Transitional youth services: Practice implications from a systematic review. *Child & Adolescent Social Work Journal, 25*, 287–308. DOI: 10.1007/s10560-008-0127-z.

O'Neill, M., Risley-Curtiss, C., Ayón, C., & Williams, L. R. (2012). Placement stability in the context of child development. *Children and Youth Services Review, 34*(7), 1251–1258.

Pecora, P. J., Jensen, P. S., Romanelli, L. H., Jackson, L. J., & Ortiz, A. (2009). Mental health service use for children placed in foster care: An overview of current challenges. *Child Welfare, 88*(1), 5–24.

Rosenkranz, S. W., Muller, R. T., & Henderson, J. L. (2012). Psychological maltreatment in relation to substance use problem severity among youth. *Child Abuse & Neglect, 36*(5), 438–448.

Smith, W. (2011). *Youth leaving foster care: A developmental, relationship-based approach to practice*. New York: Oxford University Press.

Storer, H. L., Barkan, S. E., Sherman, E. L., Haggerty, K. P., & Mattos, L. M. (2012). Promoting relationship building and connection: Adapting an evidence-based parenting program for families involved in the child welfare system. *Children and Youth Services Review, 34*, 1853–1861. DOI: 10.1016/j.childyouth.2012.05.017.

Stott, T. (2012). Placement instability and risky behaviors of youth aging out of foster care. *Child & Adolescent Social Work Journal, 29*(1), 61–83. DOI: 10.1007/s10560-011-0247-8.

Southam-Gerow, M. A., Rodríguez, A., Chorpita, B. F., & Daleiden, E. L. (2012). Dissemination and implementation of evidence based treatments for youth: Challenges and recommendations. *Professional Psychology: Research and Practice, 43*(5), 527–534. DOI: 10.1037/a0029101.

Timmer, S. G., Urquiza, A. J., & Zebell, N. (2006). Challenging foster caregiver maltreated child relationships: The effectiveness of parent-child interaction therapy. *Children and Youth Services Review, 28*, 1–19.

Trickett, P. K., Negriff, S., Ji, J., & Peckins, M. (2011). Child maltreatment and adolescent development. *Journal of Research on Adolescence, 21*(1), 3–20. DOI: 10.1111/j.1532-7795.2010.00711.

Unrau, Y. A., Chambers, R., Seita, J. R., & Putney, K. S. (2010). Defining a foster care placement move: The perspective of adults who formerly lived in multiple out-of-home placements. *Families in Society, 91*(4), 426–432.

Unrau, Y. A., & Wells, M. A. (2005). Patterns of foster care service delivery. *Children and Youth Services Review, 27*, 511–531.

Waldron, H. B., & Turner, C. W. (2008). Evidence-based psychosocial treatments for adolescent substance abuse. *Journal of Clinical Child and Adolescent Psychology, 37*(1), 238–261.

Weiner, D. A., Schneider, A., & Lyons, J. S. (2009). Evidence-based treatments for trauma among culturally diverse foster care youth: Treatment retention and outcomes. *Children and Youth Services Review, 31*(11), 1199–1205. DOI: 10.1016/j.childyouth.2009.08.013.

Wechsler-Zimring, A., Kearney, C. A., Kaur, H., & Day, T. (2012). Posttraumatic stress disorder and removal from home as a primary, secondary, or disclaimed trauma in maltreated adolescents. *Journal of Family Violence, 27*, 813–818. DOI: 10.1007/s10896-012-9467-8.

Wilson, K. R., Hansen, D. J., & Li, M. (2011). The traumatic stress response in child maltreatment and resultant neuropsychological effects. *Aggression and Violent Behavior, 16*(2), 87–97.

Zielinsks, D. (2009). Child maltreatment and adult socioeconomic well-being. *Child Abuse and Neglect, 33*, 666–678. DOI: 10.1016/j.chiabu.2009.09.00.

I

Holding the Hope

When children who have experienced foster care are referred for treatment it is often with enormous hope on the part of their caregivers and the other professionals involved in their lives. Sometimes, it is also with a profound, unspoken, expectation that the child is beyond hope and that the psychotherapy, like so many other things that have been tried, will fail. In these situations the child is often perceived as bad, willfully disobedient, unloving, and or unappreciative.

The therapist, then, is given the unarticulated and impossible task of both making the child "better" and demonstrating that any hope of that happening is misplaced. In these cases the parents, whether foster, adoptive, or relative caregivers, have often found themselves in unanticipated and difficult situations. A grandfather is called upon to raise a grandchild who has been mistreated by his own child; the difficulties the child brings to his life are a daily reminder of the ways he feels he has failed his child and his fears of repeating the story. A couple dreams of parenthood and the satisfaction of rescuing a child who would otherwise be parentless only to find themselves trying to maintain the safety of a child who is physically and emotionally out of control. A woman hears through her church that there is a shortage of foster parents and decides that she can help; the children placed in her care complain constantly about her and her cooking and her house, angrily protesting that they want to return to the parents she knows abused them.

Caseworkers who are charged with creating safety and permanency for foster children often fail to explain fully the extent of children's difficulties out of a fear that they will be unable to find a suitable home for them. Or they may downplay the problems in the hope and belief that if the child just finds a loving home the problems will disappear. Those hopes are often transferred to the therapist—not only the wish that the child will find relief from suffering, but the hope that the therapist will improve the child's behavior so that questions about whether the child will remain in the placement will dissipate.

Of course, foster and adopted children also begin therapy with unspoken and unarticulated hopes. Unsurprisingly, they hope that they will be reunited with their biological parents; even if they were abused and neglected while in their care, there is little to stop them from hoping that things could be different in the future. Whether consciously or not, it is often this hope that motivates children's defiance and misbehavior—they act badly in the hope that they will be returned to their parents. They also misbehave because they are afraid to hope—afraid to hope that someone actually does love and want them.

Therapists entering these worlds of swirling, ill-defined, unconscious, and contradictory hopes have difficult and complex tasks—not the least of which is finding and holding realistic hope for all. It is not realistic to hope that a traumatized child's behavior or demeanor will change merely by being placed with a loving adult. It is not realistic to hope that weekly psychotherapy will work magic in a few weeks or months. It is not realistic to hope that caregivers will not despair and when faced with children who continuously dash their hopes of feeling competent and confident.

It is realistic to hope that if all of the important adults in the child's life can find a way of working together to support each other, over time, the child's relationships and behavior will improve. It is realistic to hope—though difficult to maintain—that the adults will resist the impulse to blame each other (publically) and themselves (privately) for the misery and chaos in the child's life. It is realistic to hope that the self-perpetuating cycle of despair and defeat can gradually be transformed into a cycle of optimism and success.

The chapters in this section describe the painful outcomes of cases when therapists were unable to keep hope alive, despite their best efforts. They each had the hope of connecting with the child, a realistic hope for a therapeutic relationship. However, that was not enough to offset the unrealistic hopes that the child's behavior arising from past trauma could quickly change as a result of therapy, or that all questions about whether a child would follow in his wayward parents' footsteps could be erased, or that the fact of adoption would magically transform a child's sadness and selfishness into happiness and generosity.

Molly's parents want the therapist to make her better, but they don't want to form the relationship that would promote that end. Juan's aunt approaches his therapy with the unspoken and disavowed hope that she could have her needs met, leaving her to experience the therapist's overtures as demands, rather than offers of help. All of Lilly's caseworkers' hopes for keeping her in her foster home are placed squarely on the shoulders of the therapist who is doomed to fail in meeting the unrealistic expectations set for the therapy without any input.

Despite the premature endings of these three therapies, in a most basic way they were not treatment failures. Each of these young people formed a relationship with the therapist and began to be more comfortable "in their own skin"; in other words, they were off to a good start when forces beyond their control brought the interpersonal relationship to an early end. However, in this context, it is important to remember that relationships are something created not only between people, but also within people. Both therapist and child will carry the other with them. Ending the treatment will not necessarily destroy the work that they did together, but it most likely will introduce a note of caution into the next relationship.

Ironically, by bringing an early end to the treatment the caregivers were also able to demonstrate what they had unconsciously hoped to show—that the child was beyond help. These children did not show enough improvement according to the external measures that had been established by the caregivers. However, all three did demonstrate progress not only in the context of therapy, but also in their relationships at home and at school. This raises the possibility that it was precisely because the success of the work was beginning to show, that it had to be brought to an end. Reaching the stated therapeutic goals would have undermined the unspoken belief that these children could not be helped—by the therapist, but more importantly, by the caregivers.

The final chapter in this section tells a therapist's story of fearing unknown relationships. Initially, rather than hope that the consultation group might be helpful, the therapist attempts to avoid the possibility of disappointment by avoiding the relationships offered by the group. Eventually, in the company of like-minded professionals who could see and know aspects of the treatment before the therapist could, the support and comfort provided by the group become evident.

Chapter One

Molly

INITIATION OF TREATMENT

The first time eight-year-old Molly walked alone into my office I was nervous. Although she was in third grade, Molly's diminutive size made her look more like a kindergartener. And small though she was, this little girl had such a history! Feeding disorder, sleep difficulty, extreme acting out behavior both at home and at school . . . I was not at all sure I was up to the task of addressing all these. There were also questions about underlying neurological issues.

I was new to private practice. Based on the information I had received about this child, I felt her therapy would need to occur over a long period of time, a frame likely to be measured more easily in years than in months. Molly lived some distance from my office and I worried about the toll the weekly drive would take on the family.

As part of our evaluation process, I had discussed with Molly's father, Dave, the reality of the distance to my office and the extended period of time this work might take. The fact that my office was in a location distant from their home would also make collaboration with her school and other professionals in Molly's life much more difficult. I was truthfully quite surprised that Dave would want to drive so far. In fact, my experience of Dave around his children was that he didn't particularly enjoy spending time with them. His role seemed to be almost one of drill sergeant, shepherding them from place to place and making sure they were properly enrolled in each activity they participated in. Still, he acknowledged understanding of the various issues inherent in treatment so far from home and wanted to proceed. I concluded that Dave, who was the primary parent in this gay couple, seemed somewhat conflicted about the therapy, but could also understand intellectually, if not psychologically, the importance of follow through with treatment. Looking back, I am not sure he understood the possible length of treatment and I am not sure I made that completely clear. I am also not sure that he had thought through the ramifications of driving so far every week.

I was less concerned, going in, with the fact that I work primarily with adults in my practice. I thought that my experience as a parent myself and my work with children in other settings would stand me in good stead. But I was mindful that this process was to be therapeutic. And Molly was still so little on top of being so symptomatic—simply talking with her about life probably just wasn't going to work. I was pretty sure about this. My experience hovered somewhere between wondering and panic that first day. I thought to myself, "Sure, we'll probably talk some. But what are we going to *do*?" All things being equal, as I prepared to start work with my new tiny client, this was my most pressing concern. It turned out, at least on that first day, my anxiety was well placed.

After she strolled in, Molly pulled a book out from under one arm. She immediately sat down and read . . . to herself. I looked on, questioning silently whether this could possibly be construed as therapeutic. After a few minutes of quiet in the room, I gave voice to the question that had been weighing heavily on my mind since I first agreed to work with this adorable but challenging little girl. "Hmmm. I see you are reading a book. I wonder what *I* am going to do." I waited hopefully for a moment. Molly's big brown eyes remained downcast and her tiny finger continued to skim across the page. I could see where this was headed and took matters into my own hands. I stated, with just a bit of a question in case I was making the wrong move, "Maybe I will read, too." With no reaction forthcoming, I found a magazine in a small stack of mail on my desk, glad that I hadn't yet put it in the waiting room. I opened it up and also skimmed with my finger and turned page . . . after page . . . after page. Within a couple of minutes, I finished my "reading" and glanced again at Molly, suddenly aware we had each kept one eye on the other the entire time. I felt the faintest glimmer of hope—she was interested. I pushed the envelope a bit. "You know, if you don't want to talk with me or visit in here, you don't have to stay. It isn't my job to make you do anything you don't want to do. If you want, you can go back to your father in the waiting room." The reply came instantly in a barely audible voice, "No, I want to talk." This was followed by an immediate return of her gaze to the page, her little mouth silently forming syllables as her finger continued to follow the words. Ahhh, now I was starting to catch on. I got up and walked to the window, musing aloud again about what I might do next while she was finishing her book. I wondered in a bright voice about the things I saw outside. After a bit she joined me at the window, and this led to our taking note of each thing we saw outside—our first documenting together of a view we would evaluate again and again over the next several months. I realized not too long after she left my office that day that I had passed a test. Molly and her adoptive father, Dave, struggled constantly over power and control. My having relinquished power to Molly during the passing of our session together was indeed therapeutic. What's more, it gave her an idea of what she could expect of her time in my office.

And so it went with this little girl. My fears about what we would do never materialized again, after that first session—running out of time to do it all quickly became the bigger problem. In the early weeks, she carefully inventoried everything in my office, examining each object she found, occasionally asking for information about what it was used for, then going back later to incorporate a variety of these items into imaginative play. Six tiny wooden birds were often turned into a gaggle of six children. The two birds that were the prettiest in Molly's opinion were outfitted with luxurious sleeping quarters fashioned from small wooden puzzle boxes and layers of folded tissues. The others were sometimes hidden under a couch cushion or simply ignored. My attempts to discuss the meaning behind some birds having more value than others were met with silence. I soon learned that if Molly did not wish to address a particular issue, she would simply ignore me. This happened quite frequently in those early days. I was often frustrated, early on, eager to make some sort of measurable progress in treatment. In the quiet emptiness that would hang in the air after I made a comment or asked a question, I sometimes imagined that at home, Molly was perhaps also subjected to more than her fair share of lessons in frustration tolerance. I suspected projective identification might be at play. This primitive defense mechanism, proposed initially by Melanie Klein (1949) describes the way in which the patient forces the therapist to experience what the patient herself is experiencing (Mayes, Fonagy, & Target, 2007).

As I learned more about Molly's life, I realized that many things about her time at home were difficult for her to tolerate. As an example, it seemed that Dave preferred a quiet and clean environment. In order to facilitate this, he would not allow the children to store toys or books in their rooms—these items were kept in one central location. Every night, each child was allowed to choose one item to bring to bed. Molly was often up for hours in the middle of the night, a possible side effect of one of her medications. Molly often struggled to choose between a book or toy to distract her and a stuffed animal for comfort. I had trouble understanding why her parents felt that the children could not have more than one source of comfort. Having myself grown up as an avid reader, just like Molly, but with well-stocked bookshelves lining a full wall of my room and a closet full of toys, I could not imagine such a dilemma. I came to realize that the frustration I felt in my weekly session with Molly was only a tiny fraction of what she experienced on a daily basis.

Initially in our sessions there were numerous invitations to involve me in power struggles, sometimes over which things Molly would play with, or how she might utilize them. This was perhaps another example of projective identification—Molly's father seemed to regularly engage Molly in these. I felt I needed to step carefully away from them—I did not want to become simply one more source of frustration. I learned to put away things that I didn't want her to use, rather than make them available for a potential battle. Other items I simply replaced when they ran out. Tape and correctional fluid, tissue and sticky notes, highlighters and stationary pads—these were all supplies which Molly loved to use in abundance in her play and drawing activities. I imagined that in her adoptive parents' neatly controlled world, such "waste" would likely be frowned upon. I have to confess it sometimes bothered me a bit, too, but I stayed quiet.

Molly was also quite physically active initially. In the early months of treatment, she would frequently turn herself upside down in a stuffed chair that sat in the corner. As she did a headstand of sorts, her shirt would often zoom downward, falling around her chin. Rather than tell her this made me uncomfortable and I would prefer she not do that in my office, I would instead physically turn away, saying, "I'm not going to watch while you do that, because your chest is a private part of your body and it is not for other people to see." For the first few months of treatment, we really struggled over this—she would turn upside down, and I would turn around. While I wanted to offer Molly an environment where she could be completely herself, I was also extremely uncomfortable at the prospect of her exposing any parts of her body that might be considered private. I think my discomfort over these actions was rooted in my experiences in other work settings with very strict guidelines about what parts of the body are private. Eventually we came to an agreement that before she turned herself upside down, she would tuck her shirt in. In return, I would keep my attention focused in her direction.

Leaving my office was quite challenging for Molly in those early months; she simply did not want to go. She would say she wished she could stay forever and she suggested hiding under the couch so other clients wouldn't see her. One time she curled herself up as small as she could and fit herself into a cabinet. Frequently when it was time to go, she hid behind a chair. I felt a lot of dismay during this phase—feelings of inadequacy, shame, and fear were all present and terribly uncomfortable. I was somewhat scared of Dave from the beginning and I knew it would hurt his feelings if he knew Molly didn't want to leave. Molly seemed to know this too and to the best of my knowledge, she never shared this information with her father. By the time Molly opened the door, all of her hiding and begging had already taken place. I had reciprocated with verbal empathic responses of various sorts though I usually finally had to resort to telling her that if she didn't come open the door to rejoin her father in the waiting room, I would need to do it. Yet, all Molly's father saw was little Molly trotting out to join him. If he noticed at all the resigned look, or the sadness, he never commented. For a time during this phase of treatment, I worried that I was somehow facilitating Molly's feeling so sad and that I was forcing her to tolerate a treatment that was too difficult for her to accept at such a young age. I brought this up in my consultation group and even considered aloud whether Molly might be better served by my becoming credentialed with an organization like Big Brothers, Big Sisters and being in her life in that way, rather than as her therapist, who saw her for only an hour each week. Through the processing of the group, I was able to see I was caught up in a counter-transferential hope that could never be realized. I recognized the impracticality of such a plan—both time and logistics would have made it impossible. But I still wondered if by limiting my availability instead of offering a relationship that was more integrated into her daily life, I might be asking her to take on a more abstract relational concept than she was developmentally prepared to handle.

I will never forget the day that I stepped into the room next to my office to put a cup away as part of our cleanup process and found, when I turned back around, that Molly was gone. I hadn't heard the door to the waiting room or the hallway open and I was hopeful she hadn't scooted past me into the hallway because this led to other rooms and doors, as well as to elevators and stairs which led to the ground floor and exterior of the building. I walked back to the middle of my office and stood very still, wondering how many seconds I should realistically allow before opening the waiting room door and admitting to her father that I had no idea where she had gone. About another five—very long seeming!—seconds passed before a little head popped out from behind a chair. Molly grinned and giggled and I concentrated on calming the frantic beating of my heart. As charming as this little girl was, I had to grudgingly admit that sometimes she could be quite a challenge. This was one of the few times I felt I had to risk angering her by drawing a boundary and I explained that her hiding like that had worried me greatly. I asked her to not do it again—and she didn't.

BACKGROUND AND FAMILY

According to Dave's report, Molly's outbursts and impulsivity were likely due to her exposure to drugs in utero. She had joined their family as a "foster-adopt" child at nearly four years of age. She came into care after she had been found wandering the streets with her older sister and inebriated father. Molly's family of origin included her father and two older siblings. Little is known about her living environment prior to coming into foster care, but her new family remains in sporadic touch with the siblings, who are struggling to make their way in the world. Molly was the only child to be adopted—the others remained in foster care.

Dave was in his early twenties when he and his partner Brian adopted twins through a private adoption and then, several months later, adopted Molly. So, from the start, Molly competed with two younger siblings in her adoptive home for attention. Perhaps at least partly because she was the oldest, Molly had taken on the role of the most difficult child. She was a climber and prone to impulsive behavior and Dave reported that she was frequently found climbing on bookshelves and furniture to dangerous heights. Molly often refused to eat the food that was offered at meals, insisting on just a few perennial favorites. Molly was punished for her misbehavior by having to sit alone in the pantry with the lights off and her back to the door. She could hear what was going on, but not see the family activities. This only intensified her anxiety and usually resulted in her having an outburst and an even longer time out.

I often wondered about the motivations of these young men in adopting three young children when they were still so young themselves. When I finally found an opportunity to ask, many months into treatment, it turned out that Dave had always wanted to have children, but had worried that it might not be possible for him as a gay man. Part of his attraction to Brian was his willingness to become a parent. This still did not explain satisfactorily to me the push to adopt multiple children so early in their relationship. Dave struck me as somewhat rigid and well defended, finding safety in order and routine. He seemed to be hanging on to his dreams of a perfect adopted family—even though one, and then another, of the children frequently behaved in ways that threatened the fantasy in a manner that he had probably never dreamed possible. I knew that as the years went on, he and Brian would likely face even more challenges. Brian's role in the relationship seemed to be as both financial provider and friend, rather than disciplinarian. The children roughhoused with him on weekends and Molly reported she enjoyed his coaching her soccer team. She often spoke fondly of him. I was surprised that in nearly two years of working with Molly, although he was always explicitly invited to parent conferences, he never once appeared in my office.

I also was not able to get to know Dave well, at least not during that first year. We communicated via email and, occasionally, text messages. He usually brought Molly for treatment, though occasionally a visiting grandparent or sitter took on the task. Whoever accompanied Molly always had at least one but usually both of the other children along. Molly's younger sister in particular was also demanding and attention-seeking, so whichever adult remained in my waiting room usually had their hands full.

Because of Dave's schedule it was difficult for us to meet in person with no children present. Despite my consistent offers to find times that were convenient for him, nothing seemed to work. We first found time during one school vacation. At that time Dave seemed eager for suggestions that would be helpful in his relationship with Molly and indeed, all the children. I offered some suggestions for books on parenting and initially Dave seemed interested and engaged. He instituted some of the ideas he read about, but only for a brief time.

Even though I often felt Dave's rigid approach to parenting was not serving Molly well, I knew that she and her siblings could each, on their own, be very difficult. No doubt, as a threesome they must have sometimes seemed impossible. At one point, in a meeting near the end of the first year, I said, "You know, raising children is never easy. And these children have complex and difficult histories. Their behavior isn't your fault. You are both doing the best that you can." This last thought I absolutely believed to be true, though I wondered sometimes whether their best could possibly be enough for all three of these youngsters. I was shocked at Dave's response—this normally extremely collected and well put together young man quietly wiped tears from his eyes. It seemed, at least for a while, after this meeting that we moved into a more collaborative position in working to help Molly.

This increased collaborative alliance with Dave was important because Molly clearly needed psychotherapy. In fact, it seemed to me that despite the initial reports, she was medically a pretty healthy little girl. She didn't sleep or eat much—but I suspected attention deficit hyperactivity disorder (ADHD) medication was contributing to these issues. As for her reported impulsivity and recklessness, I noticed that in my office from the very first day, she was careful with every object she touched. Over time she made use of many small items she discovered through the course of her play—a number of them fragile. She handled each delicately and always put everything back exactly where it belonged. Yet, in addition to her home and school struggles with food and following rules, both likely made more difficult by her parents' clear and unwavering expectations, Molly struggled with social issues. When around other children, she would make scary noises and faces that alienated them. She offered to demonstrate in one of our early sessions. "I can be really scary, wanna see?" I responded, "Why, you certainly can! That's quite impressive." I otherwise remained impassive about this display, sensing it was important not to recoil like her classmates and to also not express disapproval like her parents. Molly studied me for a moment and a look passed between us. She then went on to something else and, though we discussed this behavior much later in one of our conversations about the things she did when she was younger, she never again demonstrated this behavior in my office.

Molly also had a history of lying and stealing from other children in her school classroom. According to Dave, if Molly saw something she wanted, she simply took it. Any attempts to discuss this with Molly in the early months of treatment were met with resistance. Initially, this came in the form of silence and often switching to another play activity. Later, she would say, "I don't want to talk about that." Unfortunately Dave usually wanted to report to me as he was dropping Molly off, talking to me in a whisper that was loud enough for her to hear, "Molly had a very bad week at school. She took a puzzle from one child and a book from another." Although I felt terribly uncomfortable with these reports, there was something about Dave's attitude that let me know that any direct suggestion from me would be taken as a most unwelcome confrontation. Over time, I was able to model a clearer and more direct way of communicating about children, though I was never sure if my message—that children are simply small people worthy of respect and needing to be treated as such—was getting through.

SETTLING IN

There was a lot to address in this family and with Molly, whose behavior was the area of focus whether warranted or not. But before Molly and I could get down to business, we had to address the issue of whether I could be trusted. When Molly was still in foster care, she had briefly participated in play therapy. This therapy had terminated when the therapist unexpectedly had to relocate for personal reasons. Inexplicably, Dave chose to remind Molly frequently of this loss. Perhaps because of this, Molly asked numerous times throughout those early months if I was married and if I planned to move. I usually responded to the marriage question with a question of my own: "what do you think," or "what would you like for the answer to be?" To the question of moving I always responded with the truth, "No, I am not planning to move away." After several months, when the marriage question came up a number of times during one particularly trying session, I pointed out, "You know, right now you can always have the question. And I am not completely against answering you, and someday I'm pretty sure you will come to know the answer. But keep in mind that once you have the answer, you can never have the question again." A knowing look passed between us and she stopped pestering me about my marital status. I was coming to see that underneath all the difficult behaviors, this was a bright and psychologically savvy little girl.

Inevitably, we navigated our first missed session because of my vacation. We talked about it ahead of time. I was curious to see what might happen upon my return. When I did return, for the first time since our initial session, Molly entered the consulting room with a book. She sat down in my overstuffed side chair—a favorite of hers—and proceeded to read, again mouthing the words while tracing over them with her finger, as I again watched. Perhaps halfway through I commented, "I like Paddington Bear, too," but got no response. I was initially puzzled. She usually enjoyed using markers and crayons and different kinds of paper, modeling clay, blocks, some abstract wooden 3-D puzzles, and a small number of other toys and games. After our first meeting, she had not shown any further interest in reading, preferring instead to play with the various things I had on hand. So I put myself in Molly's place and tried to figure out what might be motivating this change in routine. Finally I said, "I think I understand. I made you wait to see me, so now you will make me wait to see you!" Molly said nothing, and the finger continued its tracing. But a small smile played at the corners of her mouth. When she turned the last page, she finally looked up. "May I get some more books out of the waiting room?" I smiled slightly too and nodded, and perhaps also groaned inwardly a bit as I realized that understanding the consequences of my absence was going to come with an additional consequence. I did not acknowledge this and instead said, "Of course, it is your time to do with as you wish." Molly returned with more waiting room books and read each one carefully as I sat patiently and waited. At the end of the last book, she returned to exploration of the toys in my office, never again resorting to reading alone during our time together, though we did sometimes share books together. When she left that day, I felt we had negotiated one more hurdle.

Another early topic for Molly was naturally the subject of families. She was ambivalent about whether she had ended up in the right one. She enjoyed many material benefits in her adoptive family, but she did not feel that she was loved unconditionally just for being Molly. I, too, sometimes wondered what her life would have been like in different circumstances. This, of course, is the fact of adoption—it could just as easily have been another family as this one.

She seemed to understand that it wasn't possible to go back to her family of origin, as this came up, briefly, only once or twice. While in my office she spent significantly more time considering other options. First, for a period of many weeks, she tried to determine if I might be a suitable fit. I fielded a number of personal and invasive questions about whether I had a yard and a pool (which Molly didn't have but very much wanted), whether she might be able to still see her siblings on occasion if she lived with me, and even what sorts of movies I liked to see. I did my best to not hurt her feelings with my refusal to offer most of the information she desired while at the same time keeping details about my life to myself. The struggles over knowledge about me and my life intensified until I finally one day, somewhat exasperated, said as kindly as I could, "Look, Molly. You have parents. I can't be your parent—that isn't the role we both need for me to play in your life. What I can offer you is this"—and at this I swept my hand around my room. "It's a safe space for you to come and play and talk and figure things out about yourself, your life, and the world. That's what I have to give you." She didn't reply and as it was nearly time for the session to end, she collected her jacket and artwork and rather uncharacteristically, left the consulting room with little protest. For the next few weeks, a quiet and perhaps pouting Molly showed up for our sessions. She sat very quietly, the first week after I declared that I could not be her new mother, drawing pictures which she took home (previously, she nearly always left at least one drawing in my office). My attempts to engage her in conversation were ignored. Finally, around the fourth week, she returned to a more effervescent presentation. I realized the mourning period for her fantasized life at my house was ending. Not for the first time, I felt relief at having rounded another corner. Next, a neighbor child's family was deemed perhaps to be a fit. We pondered together the pros and cons of making a move to this home. Molly was pretty sure, initially, that there would be lots of positives and didn't seem aware of any possible negatives. I agreed that certainly some of the things on her list sounded pretty good—for instance, the neighbor child kept a number of toys in her room, while at Molly's house toys were all kept in one central play area and all shared equally. I wondered with Molly about rules next door that might be in place and a moment of quiet passed as she considered this. I asked Molly if there was anything she might miss about her own family if she were to follow through with such a move. I mused whether she might have some favorite foods cooked for dinner and I mentioned her grandparents, of whom I knew she was extremely fond. She became quiet for another moment as she thought. Finally she reported that she wouldn't really like to make the move, mainly because the neighbor family was going through a divorce and there was not even one dad in that house. Molly very much enjoyed Brian, but he was not the primary parent and I think that Molly sensed that if her parents separated, he would be the one to leave. After this day, she seemed to settle into an awareness that she would be staying with her adopted parents.

Several sessions followed in which elaborate play unfolded that placed her birth parents far away—not surprisingly, in keeping with the "family romance" that children frequently create to manage their disappointments with their actual families, they were sometimes conceptualized as royalty (Frosch, 1959; Heineman, 1999). One day, about nine months into treatment, they were placed across an ocean, represented by the space in my office that stretched between my sitting area and the door. As Molly pointed out, there was no way to get to them across that massive expanse of emptiness. We were able to talk that day about the difficult choices people make in life and we explored the reality that the judge had actually made the final decision that Molly would live in another home with a different set of parents than the ones who had birthed her. She seemed surprised by this, having apparently assumed, as so many adopted children do, that her parents had simply not wanted her in their lives any longer. She seemed to assimilate this new information thoughtfully. In another session around this time, which was near to Halloween, she drew tombstones which represented each of her biological family members. The references to her birth family decreased over time and finally the day came when she spoke of them no more.

We spent our first few therapeutic months together in a mostly companionable silence or engaged in small talk, but slowly she became more willing to talk about the things that were bothering her. Her promotion to the fourth grade felt like a big accomplishment, though it was a tenuous one. The school personnel had considered holding her back a year and conducted an evaluation to determine whether she needed special services for children with learning disabilities. It was recommended that she begin tutoring to help her with organizational skills—which are a challenge for many children diagnosed with ADHD. Her parents arranged for tutoring which, not surprisingly, led to more power struggles over whether her tutoring homework would be completed in a timely fashion.

BREAKTHROUGHS

One day, toward the end of the first year, we were reading a book on adoption together. Molly's behavior was still pretty out of control. Her father was driving a long way for her to see me each week. We were both feeling a bit hopeless about Molly's continued misbehavior, and Dave had mentioned once or twice that he was not excited about continuing the long drive with three children settled into the back of the minivan, with so little demonstration of improvement. That day, Molly chose to read a few of the books I had in my office on adoption. Midway through one of these, there was a discussion of the different ways adopted kids sometimes felt about their birth parents. It noted that some kids wondered why their birth parents couldn't keep them. Molly looked up and said softly, "I wonder that all the time." This was the first time she had so genuinely verbalized such heartfelt pain and, of course, I didn't have a ready response. The long silence that passed between us that day, and the accompanying look, seemed to say it all—there are some things that happen in life, to even the smallest among us, which are simply not explainable.

Not long after that day, I was trying without much luck and at Dave's behest to engage Molly in a discussion about the ongoing struggles at home and at school. Molly finally commented that it did not really matter what she did. I considered this for a moment and I then exclaimed, "Are you doing all this misbehaving so that your parents will hurry up and throw you out of this family in the same way that it feels your first family did?" Her eyes widened and she met my gaze—a phenomenon which, I was sure I was not imagining, was happening more and more often. She looked astonished as she responded with, "How'd you know?" I was finally feeling comfortable in our interactions. I held her gaze and solemnly responded, "It makes perfect sense." Again, the knowing look.

It was around this time that Dave announced that he had reached his limit. He once more mentioned his dissatisfaction with the fact that there was very little progress seeming to occur where Molly's behavior was concerned. He asked about a timeline for "wrapping this up." I felt some mild panic welling inside—in our months together, Molly and I had become attached to each other. I knew that her brief hour with me each week was a bright spot for her—a time when she could do what she wanted and not be judged or controlled or teased. I asked Dave to give me some time and said I would talk again with Molly to see if we could come to some sort of agreement about her behavior. I reminded him of Molly's attachment to visiting me and my office and said that termination of treatment would be something which would have to be done carefully and slowly. Though I didn't say it, I additionally felt it would be quite important for Molly to have some voice in when and how it happened. Not for the first time, I realized I had very little control over what actually would occur.

At the time of my next meeting with Molly, I initiated a discussion with her which I forever after remember as "The Day I Read Molly the Riot Act." She walked into my office as usual and said, "I wonder what I want to play with today." I replied perhaps a bit sharply, "First, we need to talk." This was huge—I had never made any particular demands on Molly as to whether we talked, when, or what about. I hoped we had enough of a solid foundation built together that I wasn't seriously crossing a line. Still, I kept my voice serious and said, "Sit down," patting the couch cushion next to me. Molly, seeming to sense this was important, sat. I went on, "You know I try to talk in here with you sometimes about your misbehaving, and you usually don't really want to talk about it. But today we have to talk about it. Your Dad is pretty upset that he is driving so far to bring you here, with the idea that you will start behaving better because of all this work you are doing in here with me, and you are still behaving the same as you were before—in fact, lately he says you have been even worse. He is doing his part to drive you here, and that is hard for him because he has three kids to take with him everywhere and traffic is awful and this office is a long way away from where you live. I am doing my part by making this time available for us to spend together so we can meet each week. We need you to do your part by cleaning up your act a bit—do you know what that means? It means you have got to start working on behaving better so that you can still keep coming here, if that's what you want to do." Molly nodded and said, "I do still want to come here." I asked, "So does that mean we can count on seeing some improvement?" She didn't answer and though she was somewhat subdued for the rest of the hour, she played as usual and we did not talk further about difficulties in her behavior. When she left my office that day, I crossed my fingers, said a silent prayer, and hoped for the best. We had some interesting conversation about this session in my consultation group. In the group, we were really tackling this case from a psychodynamic perspective. On this day, with little warning, I had suddenly pulled a bit of a social work move and the group was not sure how to receive this or to provide feedback on it. As a person who is practical to a fault in real life, I struggle with leaving this essential part of me out of the treatment room—and on this particular day it obviously won out. The consultation group leader seemed to feel this was not an action he would have taken, but he was respectful of my having decided to go in that direction. I sometimes wonder still how things might have turned out differently if I hadn't delivered my challenge, but ultimately I feel it is likely that treatment would have ended around this time if significant behavioral changes had not taken place quickly and dramatically—so I felt somewhat backed into a corner in terms of having to make such a bold move.

In Molly's classroom, there was a reward system. Children received "stars" for good behavior. The week after "the riot act" talk, Molly practically skipped through the door of my consulting room with a big grin on her face, clutching a star-filled chart. Her face flushed with pride, Molly held the chart out for me to inspect. For the first time, Molly had earned a week's worth of positive marks in school. I heaved an inward sigh of relief . . . another hurdle overcome. In the following weeks, Molly mostly behaved well in school and she continued to accumulate stars. Her grades began to improve and she put forth effort even in the tutoring assignments that she hated. Gradually, instead of stubbornly refusing to do her work in time for family activities, she could complete the assignment and join her family.

It was not as simple to learn if Molly's behavior at home with her siblings was improving because Dave was usually much quicker to report problems than progress. However, I was able to note changes in Molly's behavior toward her brother and sister when they came to my office. Molly's relationship with her sister was particularly tumultuous when we started working together. This little girl would ask to visit my office, but Molly wouldn't allow it. Once I had ventured to wonder aloud about how little Abigail might be feeling about being shut out and at the time, Molly ignored me. Her sister had long since become accustomed to the idea that she would not come into my office. But one day some months into treatment, Molly sat down to draw a picture and when it was completed she said, "This has a princess on it and Abigail really likes those. I want to give it to her." And she went to the waiting room, carrying her gift for her little sister. Another day she spent the entire hour making drawings for her brother and sister and a neighbor child who had become her friend. Through these exercises, I saw that Molly was starting to reach out to the other youngsters in her life. Finally the day came when she allowed Abigail into the consulting room for a quick look around before showing her back out to the waiting room. It was lovely to see glimpses of traits like kindness, empathy, and generosity emerging in this previously self-absorbed little girl.

Because of summer travel schedules and Dave's continuing reluctance to drive so far, we met on a reduced schedule during the school break. Dave also became more vocal about desiring suggestions for interacting with Molly. This always surprised me somewhat because when I did offer ideas, they didn't seem to be well received. I had made numerous suggestions of parenting classes, books to read, ideas for handling various situations at the house, for example, and these were mostly ignored. I often wondered whether Dave needed these children to be difficult. More than once I wished he would enter his own therapy, but that clearly was of no interest to him.

END OF TREATMENT, AT LEAST FOR NOW?

As I write this, Molly and I are getting close to wrapping up our work together. Dave has continued to voice distress over the drive and the various after school commitments for all three children. He has expressed some interest in family therapy so that all of the children could be seen at the same time. I had suggested this previously in the hope that Dave and Brian would gain parenting skills and become more flexible in their approach. I am hopeful that family therapy could be helpful for his interactions with Molly and indeed, all the children, but I am worried about Molly's adjustment to either decreased time in my office or termination. When I met with Molly after her parents let her know that they were considering making this change, I asked her how she felt about the news. She immediately met my gaze with a solemn look and said, "Very, very, very sad." Her eyes widened as she went on, "Did you know that I cried for an hour last night! A *whole hour*." She looked away. My attempts to get her to discuss this further were met with resistance. "I don't want to talk about this because I don't want to cry." I reminded Molly that the idea behind the work we were doing is that she and I could meet for "as long as it takes." I told her this meant that even once she became an adult, she could contact me and I would see her again at any time. My practical side kicked in and I smiled at the thought that she would contact me so many years in the future. I gave her a card with my name and phone number on it. I, too, felt hopeless and helpless and angry and sad—desperate even. My interactions with Molly in that hour did not feel like good ones. I tried again and again to get her to talk about it, but she wouldn't. We finally agreed that it might be a good idea for me to meet with both her parents to discuss further the idea of a transitional phase and what it might look like. At the end of the hour, I spoke briefly with Dave and said it didn't seem like Molly was ready to make a change. I did not tell him that I felt tricked—in a recent e-mail to me Dave said Molly liked the idea of changing to someone who would work with her parents too, and that they wanted to free up time so Molly could take swimming lessons. I asked Molly about these things and she said she did not say she liked the plan and she further reported she had not been told about the possibility of taking any lessons. I wondered with Dave whether we could make a gradual transition to the family therapist. He agreed to meet with me to further discuss what this might look like, but that meeting never took place. I so often wished that I had been able to form a bond with Dave; I could only hope that he would allow himself to take in more from the new therapist than he had been able to take from me. I am also hopeful that work with a therapist closer to home will permit for a more collaborative effort that could include Brian, teachers and staff from Molly's school, and other treatment providers. As I said good-bye to Molly it was with the hope that she would take from our time together the capacity to connect and grow with others.

I have been so thankful throughout the time I have worked with Molly to have the holding and containing safety of the peer consultation group. It is a small group so Molly and I have been able to benefit from the collaborative nature of the work we have all put in on her behalf. Because of the group, I have been able to understand much better the importance of my role in Molly's healthy growth and development and to consider the multiple factors at play from a variety of angles. If there has been one thing I have learned as a result of my work with A Home Within, it is that it truly takes a village to raise a child.

REFERENCES

Frosch, J. J. (1959). Transference derivatives of the family romance. *Journal of the American Psychoanalytic Association*, *7*, 503–522. DOI: 10.1177/000306515900700306.

Heineman, T. V. (1999). In search of the romantic family: Unconscious contributions to problems in foster and adoptive placement. *Journal for the Psychoanalysis of Culture & Society*, *4*(2): 250–264.

Klein, M. (1949). *The psycho-analysis of children*. London: Hogarth Press.

Mayes, L. C., Fonagy, P., & Target, M. (2007). *Developmental science and psychoanalysis: Integration and innovation*. London; New York: Karnac.

Chapter Two

Juan

HEAT OF THE MOMENT

Maria, running a bit late for her appointment, pulled her notepad out from her big, rugged purse, announced as she barely finished her last breath, "This is not gonna work." This sounded familiar. I recalled our last phone call a few days ago, when she complained that I did not do anything after knowing that her nephew had cut himself.

It was an ambiguous phone message that she left last Friday after work hours, in which Maria said her fifteen-year-old nephew, Juan, was "cutting" and that his school counselor with whom she consulted was not concerned. I did not receive this message until the following Monday and was not immediately alarmed, thinking Juan might have cut one or two of his classes. I returned Maria's message in a calm mood, thinking I would check in with her and see if she had found out why he did not attend his classes. "This is not gonna work," Maria said with a frustrating voice. "Not gonna work? What's not gonna work?" I thought to myself. How would cutting classes make anything not work? His grades? Juan has been doing exceedingly well, having only recently transitioned from a mediocre middle school in a rough neighborhood to the current high school with more than two thousand students. In fact, he received mostly As and Bs in his classes last term. What's not going to work? Juan has been doing well since I began to work with him about a year ago, despite his long history of behavioral problems that most notably included food-stealing from the house and fire-setting at school. In my full confusion, I began to feel my anxiety and wondered if there might be something I did not understand, something much worse. I gathered my courage and inquisitively inquired Maria, "How do you mean?"; she could not believe I asked such a stupid question: "You gotta be kidding me?" I was left with even more confusion and anxiety. I asked her once again, "I'm not sure if I'm understanding." Maria, as much as she tried to hold her frustration, began to tell me, with despise, how she did not think Juan's therapy with me has been working, especially after having discovered a few superficial cuts on Juan's arm last week. She was in disbelief about how lightly I took it without an immediate response last Friday. I was speechless and embarrassed by such an oversight.

Before I even knew how to respond, Maria demanded a collateral meeting for the next day in lieu of Juan's regular session time. I agreed to meet with her but felt a strong need to protect Juan's time and suggested we meet either before or after his session. "Why can't we meet at four o'clock?" she protested. I expressed my desire to maintain Juan's time with me and felt it might be better to meet at an alternate time. "Fine"; she eventually agreed to meet immediately after his session.

WARMING UP: HOW DID THE HEAT BUILD UP?

My meeting with Maria the next day was our first collateral meeting since nine months earlier, when Maria was very upset with me for not providing subway fare for Juan to return home. It was a session immediately before my month-long sabbatical, during which I spent my time overseas for my annual teaching assignment. Juan spent most of the session pleading for five dollars from me so that he could fix his skateboard. It is not my usual practice to give money to my clients and thus I explored a few times whether he could wait until he saved up enough or borrow the money from his aunt, especially his birthday was soon approaching. "She wouldn't let me," he replied. Juan went on and began to lower his bid to three dollars, one dollar, and finally, 75 cents, changing his story and claiming that he had lost his subway pass, and desperately trying to get something from me. In addition to my discomfort with giving money to him, I especially felt uneasy about being manipulated and asked to participate in something about which I had no idea. I resisted his pleas, letting him know how helpless I felt about his requests. The session ended without my giving him money and I left the office shortly thereafter to get ready for my flight later that evening.

About 30 minutes later, I received a fairly upset phone call from Maria, asking me why I had not given her a call about the missing subway fare and left Juan stranded near my office. She questioned why I would not lend 75 cents to him that could have spared her from making a trip to my office to pick him up. I apologized somewhat reluctantly and told Maria that I had no clue whether he in fact had lost his subway pass. "Why didn't I call her to confirm?" I began to question my decision and was speechless in response to her questioning. She could not hear my impression of the session and ended the phone call bitterly, which left me with much guilt and regret; I spent the next fourteen hours ruminating about this on the plane.

Upon my return, I made multiple attempts to invite Maria for a collateral session but was unsuccessful. When I connected with her by phone, she responded coldly and would not say a word more than needed to communicate the most basic information, such as rescheduling Juan's session. Very often Maria would not pick up my calls despite how approachable she had been in the past. At times, she would let Juan answer my calls instead. Her obvious coldness, bitterness, resentment, and avoidance left me with a feeling of tremendous helplessness and hopelessness. As much as I believe in having parental involvement in treatment, there was no way to engage with her. I could not help but feel as if, like a child, I was grounded and left deserted by my parent for a single "mistake." I felt I never could regain her trust and recover our broken relationship—the same way Juan was not often trusted by Maria because of his poor track record.

THE EMERGENCE OF JUAN

In the beginning of treatment, Maria demanded that I call her before and after sessions to notify her of Juan's arrival and departure from therapy sessions. It seemed a small request, but it created a strong, inevitable presence and monitoring of Juan from this dedicated aunt. After Maria's self-exclusion from the therapy process, my relationship with Juan gradually grew and trust developed between us. Her absence created space in probably both of Juan's and my mind during sessions. As we enjoyed our time in the office, without the sense of Maria's hovering presence, Juan's sense of self became more readily felt.

Juan, a fourteen-year-old Hispanic freshman, was referred to A Home Within by his previous therapist who was ending her role at her agency. At our initial meeting, his paternal aunt, Maria, raised concerns over his behavior, most notably his lack of control over food, stealing, and lying. She offered an episode that encapsulated her concerns. She complained that Juan had taken several cookies despite her clear instructions that he could only take two. He, like most children, lied to avoid punishment, about which his aunt was much concerned and angry. Maria also provided Juan's long history of behavioral problems which included bringing a knife to school and threatening a teacher, and setting fire in the school restroom. Additionally Maria noted Juan's difficulty with separation. She mentioned that Juan often seemed too clingy to her and had difficulty doing things on his own or spending time outside the house without her on the weekends. She also added that Juan had some difficulties separating from his previous mentor and the previous therapist.

Despite Maria's initial warning of Juan's separation anxiety, I was content with the progress we made in our relationship. Initially Juan came to sessions consistently and often early. He skateboarded in front of my office, making just enough noise to remind me of his presence. In this early stage, he would begin sessions rather mechanically and report his week with little interest in my feedback. When I commented on this, he said he was told by his aunt to report about his week. He also said it was what he used to do with his previous therapist of about two years. After running out of things to report to me, he would invite me for a game, most typically the Game of Life, Stratego, Connect 4, or the pickup sticks. His rigidity usually softened during play, when he gradually became energized, more spontaneous, and even playful. His playfulness peaked when he could not resist cheating in the games. He would creatively come up with reasons to justify his cheating and why I should not make a fuss about his tactics. With my best efforts to provide my observations and insights about how he might need to cheat, Juan continued to play in this manner—as if cheating was inevitable.

Initially I had a difficult time holding my urges to stop him from cheating, thinking that it was important to maintain a structure for him. Following the advice I received from my A Home Within consultation group—a space that is provided for affiliated therapists of A Home Within to process and discuss our clinical work with this challenging population—my anxiety about the lack of structure began to loosen. Like Maria, I was also worried that Juan's dishonesty and lack of frustration tolerance would one day cost him his future. I wondered whether I should be correcting him, rather than letting him play. As my anxiety was contained by the group, I slowly allowed myself the freedom to celebrate the brilliant twists and creative reasoning he used to defend his cheating, while giving no hint of displease. This openness that I demonstrated gradually lessened his anxiety and his urge to cheat. Juan slowly became more aware of his need to cheat and was even able to resist it at many occasions.

Our relationship shifted again in subsequent months. Juan began to play board games (e.g., Chutes and Ladders, Candyland) that are usually of little interest to adolescents. In addition, he started to enjoy the simplest fun with me. Sometimes a deck of cards allowed for "target practice," as he carefully aimed and tossed them into an empty vase. With less control he would toss all of the Game-of-Life bills into the air and watch them slowly fall to the floor—as if he had won the lottery. Having my own needs for orderliness, I initially had a difficult time tolerating this. I thought of stopping Juan and saving myself from having to pick up the cards or bills, but I refrained. My heart instead melted for him and I wondered to myself when I had last watched a fourteen-year-old having a good time tossing paper bills into mid air or throwing playing cards into a vase? I felt sorry for Juan and could imagine how his stern aunt would have stopped him from doing something this "meaningless" that would create a mess for her. In my reverie, I felt as if I was playing with my own child—a young toddler, who finds these simple games gratifying. In these moments, I found myself letting go of my therapeutic stance or urge to make any profound interpretations or interventions and simply enjoyed letting myself soak into this purest form of father-child relationship that I had never anticipated experiencing with Juan. This is a feeling I do not always feel with my other child clients.

YOUNG NEEDS AND DEPRIVATIONS

My evoked reverie, in retrospect, was highly relevant to Juan's family background. Juan's father lived a chaotic life and has been in and out of the jail since Juan was born. Juan's relationship with his father had been estranged and their only connection came when he occasionally visited him in the jail or when his father called the home. Juan's mother was a drug addict who had also been uninvolved in Juan's life since birth and maintained rare contact with him. Maria was Juan's father's older sister and had helped raise Juan's father when he was young, When it became clear that neither of Juan's parents were available, Maria once again came to her younger brother's rescue and eventually decided to become Juan's foster parent, despite being divorced and financially strained.

At the outset of therapy, Maria seemed to be quite disturbed by Juan's insatiable need for food and theft of her belongings. She reported that he would fail to follow her instruction and consume half dozen of the cookies or other treats that she brought home instead of two pieces that he was allowed to have. On another occasion, Juan took a small decorative box from his aunt's room without permission. When asked about why he had taken the box, Juan said he was curious about it and was planning to return it later. Unfortunately this act did not seem to amuse his aunt, who decided to ground him because it was an important keepsake for her. While these might be reasonable expectations for some families, it was striking that there seemed to be little room for playfulness in Maria's approach to these rules, for example, laughing together that, indeed, sweets are sometimes irresistible or suggesting that they shop for a treasure box for him. Instead it seemed that her rules needed to be mechanically obeyed—concretely and thoroughly.

In our play, Juan similarly expressed his deprivations, for example, in the Game of Life. His goal for the game was clear—to make as much money as he could. He cheated almost every time to become a doctor, who earns the most money in the game. He often re-spun the wheel enough times to make sure he would land on a favorable spot in order to maximize his earnings. After being able to tolerate his cheating, I began to register that his needs for resources also bore a sad tone. In particular, he deliberately tried to have as many children as possible in the Game of Life so that, at the end, he would receive a "compensation" of $1000 from each child. This strategy—to have multiple children in order to earn more money bore an uncanny parallel to Juan's life. Maria told me that she had decided to become Juan's foster parent, in part, to receive tax relief for her own benefit. I felt utterly sad for how, in Juan's mind, children were used for monetary purposes.

Both literally and metaphorically, Juan was a hungry, deprived adolescent who looked for every chance to fill himself, either with food, material possession, or money. His mind was incredibly preoccupied with ways to feel resourceful, as seen in his approach to the Game of Life, his insatiable interest in food, his desire to keep his aunt's keepsake box, and his attempts to get money from me. Similarly he tried his best to resist feeling empty, as seen by his cheating in games to avoid losing. The need to feel filled in the stomach arises from the infant's most basic need for survival. As development proceeds this unmet hunger is often experienced as a need for material resources—such as money or property—or more metaphorically, in the need to win at all costs.

My observations of Juan's unmet needs from earlier developmental periods seemed to correspond with my paternal feelings toward him, which were probably brought forward in response to his yearnings for his unavailable parents. According to Ogden (1997), clients often communicate unspeakable and unconscious needs to the therapist in forms of images, feelings, and fantasies. The therapist's ability to metabolize and understand these dreamlike images and fantasies allow the therapist to get a glimpse of what cannot otherwise be communicated by the client. From what transpired in our sessions and in my reverie, I could not help but wonder if Juan was, unconsciously, trying to communicate his longing for a paternal connection—something that he did not experience growing up with an absent father.

THE NEED TO BE HELD

Shortly after birth, Juan's aunt assumed the role of his parent and provided care for him. As a divorced and lone foster parent, Maria had always been the sole breadwinner for the household with very limited income. From my early meetings with her, it was clear that she was under suffocating stress financially and, perhaps, emotionally as well. In my early attempts to schedule Maria for collateral meetings, she often raised concerns about having to make extra trips to my office and the additional costs for gas, despite living only a few miles away. Many of her complaints about Juan (e.g., his lack of compliance, being called by the school regarding his problems there) centered on managing his behavior so that her anxiety as a parent could be eased. This overwhelming stress seemed to have stripped Maria of her capacity to attune to his emotional needs. For example, in a seemingly ordinary afternoon, a distressed-looking Juan came to see me in the office. He reported that his shirt was torn into pieces by a few of his peers at school because they thought that he had deliberately and aggressively thrown a ball into their game. When the school notified Maria about the incident, she was only angry at Juan, demonstrating no sympathy for him in the face of this humiliating and potentially injurious incident.

With her resources stretched thin, Juan's emotional needs were often not held in Maria's mind. As shown through her complaints, Maria's main goal was to find ways to manage Juan's behavior so that her burdens could be minimized. It was not the torn clothes, lack of subway fare, or possible humiliation from being bullied that were of primary concern to Maria. Rather it was the burdensome calls from school, the additional time to meet with me, the cost of extra gas that troubled her. Ultimately, she just wanted the elimination of Juan's lying, stealing, and other difficult behavior. Juan's emotional needs were often uncharted in the mind of this overwhelmed aunt, who was preoccupied with preserving her resources.

Maria's lack of attention to Juan's needs unfortunately translated into Juan's sense that his needs were unacceptable and shameful. His adult-like and controlled demeanor while reporting on the events of each week at the beginning of each session, for example, contrasted sharply with the creativity, spontaneity, playfulness, and even silliness he displayed in later sessions—behavior that a younger child typically enjoys. She was too worried to have this kind of fun with him and thereby, inadvertently, deprived herself of many of the pleasures of parenting, leaving Juan with the feeling that he had little capacity to bring pleasure into their relationship.

Several months into the treatment, Juan noticed the license and diploma of my colleague on the office wall and asked me about him and about the office arrangements. I explained that I rented time in the office from him. Later in that session, Juan seemed to project his discomfort with deprivation onto me, commenting that he felt sad for me that I did not have my own office or furniture, and that the only things that I could afford to buy for the leased office space were the board games and playing cards "that are not worth more than a hundred dollars."

Often times client's needs are reluctantly expressed until there is enough safety in therapy. In Juan's case, it was not until I held an open, non-critical space that ultimately provided a chance for his unacceptable, negative, developmentally younger needs to emerge. The non-attacking space that I sustained (e.g., allowing him to play games that are more suited for younger children, remaining non-critical of his cheating), together with the concentrated focus I maintained on Juan's needs, or in Winnicott's (1965) words, "primary maternal preoccupation," where I also suspended my needs—ranging from wanting to keep the room clean, to interpret or to intervene—

resembled a "holding environment" (Ogden, 2004; Winnicott, 1965), in which the notion of otherness, that is, what is "not-me," was insulated from Juan. In a simpler example, such dedication is best shown by how parents are able to suspend their needs for sleep and get up in the middle of the night to feed their young infant. The holding environment that I sustained allowed for Juan's uninterrupted psychological development, or "going on being" (Sweet, 2010; Winnicott, 1965), in which the focus was all about himself—his needs to feel gratified in his way (e.g., throwing playing cards into mid-air). With the holding environment, Juan's needs could then be expressed freely without having to keep my or his aunt's needs in mind or to worry about upsetting me or her (Ogden). Juan was also able to grow in his ability to observe his urge to cheat in games as a result. He was able to stop his cheating and occasionally joke about it. It is important for the mother/therapist to hold her child/client's needs in mind while keeping her own needs at bay to allow for the child/client's uninterrupted development (Winnicott, 1965).

FACING THE HEAT AND BEGINNING TO UNDERSTAND WHAT FUELED THE FLAMES

Despite having made significant progress with Juan in a relatively short time, I now had to face an angry aunt who had agreed to meet with me in order to terminate my relationship with Juan—or to "terminate" me, which was what I was dreading. At the beginning of the final collateral meeting with Maria, I did not need to try very hard to connect with my anxiety. She retrieved a list of complaints from her notepad and began to announce my repeated failures as Juan's therapist. She accused me of not having made contact with the psychiatrist, being late to a meeting at Juan's school, and having suggested the involvement with a youth empowerment program when she had already rejected that with the previous therapist.

Most importantly, she was distraught that Juan was not yet "fixed," as shown by his consistent lying, argumentative manner, overall disobedience, and now cutting himself. In those moments of heat as she piled up the complaints, I felt as if I was quietly sweating bullets. My heart was pounding as I helplessly hoped that she would run out of venom. I was also astounded by how she had begrudgingly held these incidents in mind and the extent to which she had carefully tallied my mistakes in order to give me this embarrassing "report card." My memories of the angry phone call about the subway fare re-surfaced as her litany of complaints continued. I could not help but feel that I had failed miserably and felt embarrassed by the shortcomings she listed. Despite my strong sense of success with Juan, her seemingly endless complaints and frustration quickly overshadowed and dominated my sense of achievement. Her displeasure evoked feelings of discomfort, anxiety, helplessness, guilt, and incompetence that I normally do not experience with clients. These intense feelings left me with little choice but to begin to wonder if I had failed my job as Juan's therapist.

As I prepared to meet with Maria I found myself flooded with anxiety. I entertained the thought of defending my efforts, for example, explaining that the psychiatrist's voicemail was always full, which was why I hadn't spoken to her, or reminding her that I told everyone at school that I would have to be late for the meeting to discuss Juan's placement. More importantly, I wanted to tell her that there had been important movement in the therapy, as shown by Juan's regular attendance, his trust for me in showing his young, unfulfilled needs, and his improved ability to monitor his urge to cheat in our sessions. However, as I revealed my own understanding of "cutting," Maria was, again, in shocked disbelief and contemptuously responded, "Well, I thought this is how it is called in your field!" Following her strong reaction, I decided not to try to explain myself. I was convinced that her sense of frustration, disappointment, and anger was something that needed to be registered, quietly contained, and not denied, as it is often the case when feelings show such impenetrability (Ogden, 1977a; Winnicott, 1971). Resisting the urge to defend myself was not easy, but it became possible with the belief that her forceful and desperate communication of these feelings carried meanings that I had yet to know.

Instead of rebutting, I retreated to these awful feelings and began to wonder about them. Epstein's idea of "bad-analyst-feeling" came to mind and I became curious about what feelings Maria might have split off, finding them too unbearable, overwhelming or even threatening. Perhaps she needed to expel them from her awareness and project them into me (Casement, 1991; Epstein, 1987). The aim of such projective process, as Epstein commented, is to "urgently rid the psyche of the painful affects and unwanted self and object parts that would give rise to unbearable and potentially disorganizing experience" (Epstein). In Maria's case, I began to wonder if my negative feeling, or countertransference, was reflective of such process, through which she discarded her terrible feelings of frustration, disappointment, incompetence, and the sense of failure as Juan's sole caretaker. Her anxiety as a caretaker was apparent and it peaked especially when Juan's behavior worsened, for example, as he experimented with cutting himself. It must be noted that her anxiety about being a good, successful mother/caretaker was often fueled by her conviction that Juan was doomed to follow his father's path and becoming a criminal. Any slight reminder of such a possibility (e.g., Juan's lying or stealing) became concrete evidence that she had failed as a parent and raised her anxiety. In addition, Maria faced the urgency of "fixing" Juan before he reached the age of eighteen in four years, fearing that "it would already be too late" if improvements did not become obvious soon.

In accordance with Epstein (1987), such painful affects and unwanted parts of herself create unbearable and disorganizing experiences for Maria. Through the process of projective identification—the recipient of the intolerable feelings is usually caught by surprise, often experiencing the projected feelings as foreign—as belonging to someone else (Casement, 1991; Ogden, 1977a). Spotnitz and Meadow (1976) state: "in this way, the patient attempts to make the analyst into a defective person, more like himself, and, therefore, a person more comfortable to be with." Epstein (1987) continues "the patient . . . because he is haunted by feelings of badness—which are heightened and perpetuated by his nullifying destructive interactions—simply cannot allow us to enjoy feelings of goodness. The better he allows us to feel about ourselves, the worse he would have to feel about himself."

Epstein's ideas aptly captured what also transpired in the collateral session between Maria and me. As she asked for my feedback regarding Juan's therapy, I naively reported to her that I believed the therapy had been effective and that Juan had been able to trust me and enjoyed coming to see me. In reaction, Maria contemptuously rolled her eyes, obviously trying to stifle a spiteful laugh, as if I had just fabricated such a positive relationship. Clearly Juan would have never enjoyed a relationship with this terrible therapist. More importantly, it would have been a threatening idea to have allowed such possibility of my being a good, effective therapist, while leaving her feeling like a terrible, failing aunt who had yet to learn how to parent Juan.

PERCEIVED ABANDONMENT

My positive report of the therapy was clearly upsetting to Maria. I believe that what distressed her, in retrospect, was my inability to attune to her underlying anxiety and sense of incompetence as a parent at the time of the collateral meetings. This lack of attunement created a heightened sense of abandonment as perceived by the projector—in this case, Maria, about which she was upset (Epstein, 1987; Ogden, 1977a). This sense of abandonment particularly peaked on the eve of each of my sabbaticals, during which I became unavailable. For example, Maria ended the second collateral meeting, which took place shortly before my second absence, with a sarcastic parting comment, "Have a *wonderful* vacation," and left my office without making any more eye contact. I think that Maria felt similarly abandoned at my first sabbatical some months earlier, which started immediately after she was left alone to rescue the stranded Juan because I had not offered subway fare. Instead of absorbing her sense of failure and incompetence, this perceived abandonment, intensified by my physical unavailability, highlighted these awful feelings that she had yet to find a way to process.

In the months following my return from the second sabbatical, Maria continued to avoid my attempts to establish contact with her while Juan attended several sessions in the midst of his busy summer. One day, I received a call from the A Home Within office that Maria had officially requested a transfer to a new therapist. At last I had an opportunity to meet with Maria, who essentially confirmed that it was my inability to attune to her frustration and pressure as the lone caretaker of Juan that ultimately prompted her decision to end the therapy.

DISCUSSION: WHY TREATMENT ENDED

As a foster parent, the work of raising a foster child is emotionally and financially challenging and exhausting. In this case, because she was also the paternal aunt, Maria bore the additional pressure of ensuring that Juan would not follow in the hopeless footsteps of his father—the other "child" she failed to parent in the past. Her anxiety, frustration, disappointment, hopelessness and perceived incompetence loomed as Juan grew to become a teenager who still was not "perfect." The urgency to "fix" him before he turned eighteen became a vivid concern for Maria, who was heavily invested in avoiding repetition of her worst nightmare.

Maria's attempt to find help from therapy bore the hope that Juan would have a chance to alter his fate and reroute the course of his life to become a success. Unfortunately, as this treatment progressed, a series of events that marked my empathic failure—such as my withholding the subway fare and lack of urgent concern for Juan's cutting—had led Maria to perceive me as cold and insensitive, not only towards Juan but equally importantly towards her as the lone caregiver for him. This perceived coldness and lack of sensitivity had two levels of significance; on one level, it highlighted my inability to attune to and embody her painful, frustrating, and anxiety-provoking experiences as a foster parent who tried to avoid failing again. My lack of attunement and understanding, I believe, created intense feelings of intolerable separation and abandonment in Maria, leaving her feeling furious. On another level, my imperfect work unfortunately heightened her anxiety that the supposed curative hope from me, the therapist, was absent.

The uncanny timing of the incidents of subway fare and cutting, each happening shortly before my sabbaticals is also worth noting. These incidents of misattunement highlighted the distressful separateness of my experience from hers. This distress peaked particularly on the eves of my departures, which essentially and somewhat concretely emphasized the loneliness that she had always suffered as Juan's sole caretaker and the loneliness that none other could seem to grasp.

An important, communicative aspect of the process of projective identification is the projector's unconscious wish to communicate her emotional experiences to the recipient so that he could be able to attune to her and to be effectively at one with her to counter the painful feeling of loneliness. Paraphrasing Ogden, the engendered feeling in the recipient of the process of projective identification is *exactly* the same as it is with the projector (Ogden, 1977b; Sweet, 2010). It is essentially an unconscious attempt to bridge the differences between self and other, so that on an affective level, the two end up feeling the same, as if the projector's actual feeling has been transplanted to the recipient (Ogden, 1977b). Viewing our interactions through the lens of projective identification, Maria's massive complaining could be viewed as an unconscious wish to forcefully influence my feelings to such an extent that I began to register how deeply incompetent, hopeless, and anxious she exactly felt as a concerned parent. The concept of projective identification then illuminates Maria's unconscious wish for me to feel exactly the way she felt, in the hope that I could sympathetically join her experiences and provide support and understanding. Without my understanding, she experienced a sense of abandonment and ultimately the unbearable loneliness that she dreadfully tried to avoid re-experiencing.

Epstein states that, in working with someone like Maria who evokes the "bad-analyst-feeling" in therapists, it is important that therapists "learn how to function competently while feeling incompetent" (Epstein, 1987). In the end stage of projective identification as Ogden defines it, the recipient of the projection needs to metabolize the disowned feelings from the projector before he can return these feelings, experiences, and aspects of self, in a more tolerable form or manner, back to the projector (Ogden, 1977). In this case, it was crucial for me to process Maria's anxiety, frustration, helplessness, incompetence, and loneliness that she created in me, despite having felt confident about the progress in the treatment of Juan. In doing so, I needed to function competently while feeling incompetent, thus re-joining Maria's painful experiences, becoming her understanding and empathic ally, and minimizing her perceived abandonment and loneliness. Unfortunately this sense of abandonment and loneliness was too unbearable for Maria and she had to terminate from this treatment and transfer to another therapist with the hope, I postulate, of finding an ally on whom she could depend.

CONCLUSION

In this chapter, I have illustrated how the use of projective identification allowed for an intricate understanding of the unconscious, unspeakable, and unbearable experiences of a foster parent, who desperately tried to communicate these experiences to me to avoid feeling frustrated, helpless, and dreadfully alone. I believe that it was also her unconscious hope that, upon my attunement and processing of her awful feelings, there would be a chance for her successfully to finish the task of raising this foster child with help from an ally. In forming such alliance, her loneliness as the only caretaker for the foster child and her vivid anxiety of failing as a parent would also be absorbed, borne, and digested, thereby lending her space and freedom to function as a parent with manageable burdens to become once again lively. Paradoxically, Maria also needed to keep me at a distance in order to keep me from really getting to know her. She treated my offers to meet with her as evidence that I did not understand the extent of her burdens and the limitations on her time and energy. Although she endowed therapy with the power to "fix" Juan, she persistently treated me and the process with contempt, making it clear in many ways that she found me useless. When I review my interactions with Maria, I remind myself that it is difficult to get to know someone who, fundamentally, is terrified of being known, lest she be found to be as bad as she believes herself to be.

Successful work with foster parents is a complicated art. The stress, challenges, needs, and loneliness of being a foster parent are often impossible to verbalize and thus are out of awareness. However, the foster parent's urge to communicate these needs and struggles as well as the need to form an alliance with the therapist who can bear this weight of foster parenthood are always present. These needs are often communicated through the intricate and communicative process of projective identification. To effectively make use of this unconscious process, the therapist must be attuned to his/her own reverie and eventually process the evoked feelings and fantasies generated from this process. What makes it a form of art is the paradoxical and nearly symmetrical nature of this avenue of communication between two separate minds. Despite having used words and language to attempt to describe such complex, intricate process in this chapter, the process of projective identification manifests itself in unique shape and form within each dyad and it takes a distinct process of exploration and musing about ideas to begin to grasp the significant meanings that are being communicated. It is precisely the purpose of this chapter that this clinical illustration serves as an inspiration to others who work with foster parents and not as a fixed, unalterable template that other therapists can apply. This kind of communication demands a lively navigation of ever-changing feelings and thoughts to keep it vital, energizing, useful, and hopeful.

REFERENCES

Casement, P. (1991). *Learning from the patient.* New York: Guilford Press.

Epstein, L. (1987). The problem of the bad-analyst-feeling. *Modern Psychoanalysis, 12*(1), 35–45.

Ogden, T. (1977a). Issues of technique. In *Projective identification and psychotherapeutic technique*. Lanham, MD: Rowman & Littlefield.

Ogden, T. (1977b). The concept of projective identification. In *Projective identification and psychotherapeutic technique*. Lanham, MD: Rowman & Littlefield.

Ogden, T. (1997). *Reverie and interpretation: Sensing something human*. Lanham, MD: Rowman & Littlefield.

Ogden, T. (2004). On holding and containing, being and dreaming. *International Journal of Psychoanalysis*, *85*(6), 1349–1364.

Spotnitz, H., & Meadow, P. (1976). *Treatment of the narcissistic neuroses*. New York: Manhattan Center for Advanced Psychoanalytic Studies.

Sweet, A. (2010). Paranoia and psychotic process: Some clinical applications of projective identification in psychoanalytic psychotherapy. *American Journal of Psychotherapy*, *64*(4), 339–358.

Winnicott, D. W. (1965). Primary maternal preoccupation. In *The maturational processes and the facilitating environment*. Oxford, England: International Universities Press.

Winnicott, D. W. (1971). The use of an object and relating through identifications. *Playing and reality*. Oxford, England: Penguin.

Chapter Three

Lilly

THE BEGINNING

Hearing voices moving toward the waiting room, I opened my office door to find an expectant Lilly and her foster mother, Mrs. Jay, who announced that Lilly had had an accident in church and wasn't wearing any panties underneath her dress. As I crouched down to say hello, I immediately noticed a lovely six-year-old with blue eyes, light olive skin, and braided dirty-blonde hair clutching her wet underwear in a paper towel. After saying hello, I excused myself to rummage though my things in search of a plastic bag in which she could place her sodden clothing. I thought to myself that those panties could have been left in the car and in fact, *should* have been left in the car. I wondered to myself why she had to be shamed this way. This "carrying of the wet panties" amplified my concern regarding Mrs. Jay's apparent lack of empathy and shame inducing discipline. I had learned something about her parenting style when we had met the previous week in order for me to garner a better understanding of the family dynamics and her concerns about Lilly before my actual meeting with Lilly.

Lilly came from a wonderful blend of African American, Caucasian, and Native American ethnicities. She was fifth in a family of eight, ranging in age from three to twenty. All of the children under the age of eighteen had been placed in foster care and for the previous two years Lilly and her ten-year-old brother, Bobby, had been living with Mrs. Jay. I had met Bobby the previous week when he accompanied Mrs. Jay to our appointment. When Mrs. Jay asked him to stay in the waiting room, I realized that he had nothing with which to entertain himself. Without meeting my gaze, Bobby mumbled his gratitude in response to my offerings of drawing materials, puzzles, and an invitation to knock on the door if he needed us.

As Mrs. Jay and I settled onto the couch in my office, we began to discuss her concerns about Lilly. When I asked how I might be able to support the family, she immediately expressed her preference for Lilly over Bobby, openly stating her lack of interest in adopting both children. She said that she got along better with Lilly, whom she experienced as physically warm and affectionate, while Bobby, who was more likely to verbalize his feelings, made it difficult for Mrs. Jay to overlook his pain. Mrs. Jay proceeded to report on the children's nightly bedwetting and how each morning she had them strip their beds and wash their sheets. When I asked why the children were responsible for their soiled sheets, Mrs. Jay replied with seeming disgust and surprise that those were *their* dirty sheets with *their* pee and she would not touch them. I felt sad at the thought of the two young children, shamefacedly washing their own sheets and pajamas each morning.

These two children, who had already experienced enough trauma and pain in their short lives to cause them to have nightmares and enuresis (Sempik, Ward, & Darker, 2008), were now living with a woman who found their symptoms disgusting. I also wondered to myself if Mrs. Jay had been prepared for the challenges of raising two children who had been so traumatized. I knew that she had not been trained as a therapeutic foster parent, but I also had the feeling that she hadn't expected to have foster children who presented with so many difficulties.

THE SIBLINGS

Mrs. Jay's expressed concerns for Lilly focused on the fighting between the siblings. She wanted me to reduce the number of battles Lilly had with Bobby, as she simply and understandably wanted peace in the house. I learned that Bobby was seeing his own individual therapist. When I inquired, Mrs. Jay said that Bobby's therapist hadn't given her any suggestions about how to reduce the conflicts.

Although I could sympathize with the challenges of living with regular bickering, I also understood that fighting, in various ways, was what these children knew. This was likely the communication style they had learned from their family of origin and they hadn't yet discovered other ways of expressing themselves physically, emotionally, and verbally. Until someone patiently, lovingly, consistently, and bravely demonstrated a new form of communication, the children were going to speak the language of their people. I could appreciate that Mrs. Jay did not understand the complexity of Lilly's history and its subsequent effects on her behavior. I understood there would be a need for regular communication between Mrs. Jay and myself in order to help her better empathize with Lilly (and Bobby). Additionally, I recognized the need for collaborative treatment with Bobby's therapist and made a mental note to contact the caseworker to get releases.

My goal is always to include parents in the therapeutic process because it is very difficult to effect change with a young client without the support of the family. I believe therapy with children and youth demands a holistic approach, working as a team with other community members such as teachers, tutors, or pediatricians who share in the child's care. As I began my work with Lilly, I called Mrs. Jay on a number of occasions only to be met with short, unengaged responses. The result was that the therapeutic process with Lilly seemed to be in a vacuum, as collaboration with important people in her life was virtually nonexistent. My continuing attempts to engage Mrs. Jay seemed only to increase her annoyance with me. In retrospect, I think that my calls felt to her more like additional burdens rather than offers of help.

THE HISTORY

Lilly had five different caseworkers during my two-year tenure with her. Barry was the first to have worked with Lilly's family of origin and had remained their worker for enough time that he understood the complexities and challenges of the whole family and was able to empathize with and advocate for the rights of all the children. Prior to meeting Lilly, I had heard from Barry that Lilly was an incredibly intelligent child whose challenges lay more in the emotional realm. The written report I had initially received listed Lilly's symptoms at the time of intake as severe tantrums, aggressive behaviors, enuresis, uncontrolled diurnal encopresis, frequent nightmares, psychological distress, great reactions to past traumas/triggers, and regressive behavior.

Lilly and Bobby had been removed from their parents' home following allegations (that were later substantiated) of sexual abuse by an older brother. They had also reportedly been living in squalor, suffered emotional and physical abuse by their parents, and witnessed domestic violence. Their biological parents accumulated nearly one hundred reports to Children's Protective Services and, despite the absence of current reunification plans, the children continued to have monthly supervised visits with their parents.

I was aware from Barry that Lilly's biological parents were smart, determined, and armed with an understanding of the system. This meant that they fought hard to reunify with their offspring but, for a variety of reasons, fell short of meeting the established goals. Yet, because they often came just close enough to meeting reunification goals, the court granted them extensions, thereby creating an enduring uncertainty for the children and their potential adoptive parents.

For both Lilly and Bobby, stability would prove to be an elusive goal. Over the course of my treatment with Lilly, Mrs. Jay moved from wanting to adopt Lilly, but not Bobby, to not wanting to provide permanency to either of the children. In an attempt to reignite the possibility of adoption for Lilly, Bobby was removed from the home. The hope was that in his absence, Lilly's tantrums and aggression would decrease, and Mrs. Jay would respond to the greater peace at home with a reconsideration of keeping Lilly. Unsurprisingly, quite the opposite transpired. Lilly's distress over losing contact with her brother only served to escalate her tantrums, encopresis, and enuresis.

THE FOSTER PARENT

Overwhelmed by Lilly's behavior, Mrs. Jay suggested that she might want to have Lilly removed as well. Yet, even though Lilly was living in a home with a parent who did not understand her special needs and had no training to help her, all efforts seemed directed at keeping Lilly in that foster home.

Lilly had entered foster care with very disturbing symptoms, which had only increased over her time in the system. Three imperatives dictate plans for children in foster care: first is the assurance of their safety and well-being, second is the preference to keep siblings together whenever possible, and third is promoting permanence. None of these imperatives were met for Lilly after she was removed from her family of origin and the prospects for her future did not look bright.

THE TREATMENT

As a non-directive play therapist, in order to create a sense of safety, nurturance, consistency and an *almost* anything goes environment, I allowed Lilly to control the play. Within reason, Lilly was permitted to dictate the social rules and roles within the sessions, while I reflected, commented upon, and redirected her when necessary. The fundamental goal of therapy was to provide corrective and reparative experiences, in order to offer the child an experience of safe and appropriate interactions that engender a sense of safety, trust, and well-being (Gil, 1991).

In the first couple of sessions, I found Lilly to be sweet and charming with an ostensibly quick attachment to me, shown in hugs and affectionate notes. Securely attached children are taught to be wary of strangers and to approach them with curiosity along with some level of self-protection, which means they do not attach deeply in a short period of time. Traumatized children, on the other hand, can often demonstrate a pretense of happy, excited and affectionate behavior that hides underlying feelings of insecurity, shame, fear, anger, sadness and loss. I expected that I would soon see another side of Lilly.

By the third session, Lilly demonstrated more controlling behavior in her play. She created games in order to stay in command and avoid the possibility of losing, and consequent feelings of vulnerability. If she perceived that she might not win, her agitation and anxiety would increase as she "lost interest" and moved onto a different game or activity. She would constantly change the rules while we played in order to stay ahead of me. I would reflect the challenge in playing games I didn't understand, as I imagined it might mirror her life in which she lacked both understanding of the rules and any control.

An opportunity for a therapeutic intervention arose spontaneously when both Lilly and Bobby arrived at my office together. Lilly invited Bobby in to play and Mrs. Jay reluctantly agreed, then said she'd stay in the waiting room in case the session went awry and I needed her. The session began cooperatively with Lilly eagerly showing Bobby around a place that was especially hers and introducing him to the games she enjoyed each week. They picked a game that only the two of them could play, thereby putting me in the outside position of referee or mediator, if necessary. They played, sharing turns, laughing and encouraging one another. I noticed that Bobby was in charge of their interactions, allowing me to see a very different, more obsequious Lilly. When Bobby grew tired of that game, he shifted to a new one and I watched as a vulnerable Lilly asked Bobby to slow down and explain the rules to her, even complimenting him by reminding him that he knew more than her. The sibling interactions intrigued me. Bobby did not explain the game, but forged on, seemingly indifferent to Lilly's level of participation. Anxiety and frustration rising, Lilly physically and verbally lashed out at Bobby, who did not retaliate, but moved away to cower against the wall, crying. Lilly, looking contrite could not change direction and what seemed like vacillating feelings of guilt, anger, anguish and sadness moved like shadows across her face. Knowing Lilly was unable to contain herself, I commented on her behavior and likely feelings as I tried to help her regain control.

As she heard the rumpus and before I could explain, Mrs. Jay immediately blamed Bobby. We eventually calmed Lilly enough for them to leave and it wasn't until I closed the door and took a deep breath that I noticed the wet stain on the floor where Lilly had first become anxious. I don't know which came first, her anxiety over the vulnerability while playing with Bobby or her discomfort over wetting herself. I imagine both had an effect on her inability to contain herself and accept redirection.

The impact of the reparative experience depends on many external factors, such as the degree of continuity in the therapeutic setting, how well parents or caretakers cooperate, and how rigorously social service agencies and courts plan for the child's future (Gil, 1991). The only way I could imagine making a lasting impact was to let Lilly be herself, which at times meant allowing her to be controlling and harsh. She would tell me to do something, then tell me I did it wrong and would repeatedly chastise me for "not getting it." The following is an excerpt from my notes on one of our sessions:

> Lilly came running into room and immediately picked up all five decks of cards and began organizing them by color and size, the way she had in the previous session. As she stacked, she demanded I do the same. Again I didn't understand her goal or intention. She expressed frustration when I asked her to explain and also when I asked specific questions. I then asked her about school, which apparently she'd missed that day due to her having a doctor's appointment. After not answering a question regarding her ailment, she very directly asserted that she didn't like to be asked any questions. I told her I knew that and when she asked me how I knew, I replied, "You've told me and because when I do, you get this look on your face (I mimicked her and she laughed). What don't you like about questions?" Exasperated, Lilly nearly shouted that everyone is always asking her questions. I explored a little further, wanting to learn more about all these people asking all these questions.
>
> Remaining silent for a couple of long moments and continuing to stack the cards, she eventually blurted out in a frustrated voice that I had no idea what she hated. I gently assured her that I truly wished to know what she hated and encouraged her to share. Without missing a beat in her card stacking, tears began rolling down her saddened face.
>
> "Oh Lilly," I said, "What is making you so upset? I'd really like to know why you are crying." Unable to answer me, I continued to gently coax an answer from her, until she shouted an accusation of my not understanding anything. It was clear that she was outwardly referring to the game. Having asked her to help me understand, Lilly complained that she had instructed me on how to place the cards and I had failed to follow her directions or get it right and then she angrily demanded to know if she had to take care of everything, due to my apparent lack of comprehension.
>
> Repeatedly declaring her frustration for my ignorance, she became increasingly impolite. Dropping my pursuit of apprehending the source of her abhorrence to questions, I finally encouraged her to use "please" and "thank you" and to ask nicely when she wanted my help. She shifted her mood and became playful again. She predominantly played the game by herself only occasionally inviting me in. Toward the end we came together—at her behest—and finished the "game" where she made the rules up as we went along. Playing unfairly and mostly by herself, as her rules demanded that she have turn after turn.
>
> She was ready to leave when it was time to clean up, which she did after repeated requests. When we were done, she commented on her own behavior being good, so I gave her a sticker. She wanted two. I held to the limit of one.

In the year and half that I worked with Lilly, our sessions were inconsistent and challenging, replete with tears, controlling behavior, angry defensive language, and acting out. Mostly, they were not fun and I found myself simply not enjoying my work with this child. I felt guilty and disconnected from my authentic self because, though I feared to admit it, I wondered if I even liked this little girl. It took me a considerable amount of time to warm to her, which wasn't my experience with other children in my practice. My supervisor understood how hard Lilly was for me and validated my feelings, yet I still felt that as the adult, the professional, I "should" have a better outlook on this case. I felt that I "should" like her because she was a child with a disproportionately traumatized beginning. The fact that she usually smelled, had an unpleasant skin condition, urinated in my office, slapped me across the face not once but twice, kicked me, threw things around, damaged items in the office, yelled at me, and generally was not particularly nice to me did not improve her odds of endearing herself to me.

THE THERAPIST

Throughout our work together, I constantly questioned if I was doing right by Lilly. Seeking consultation and support, I wondered how I could provide a more useful therapeutic environment and process for her. Should I be pressing her for more information? Was there another therapist that could engage her better, differently, effect more significant change, help her to open up and truly express herself and all the traumas she'd experienced in your short life? I wondered if I was doing anything useful with and for her at all. Both my supervisor and my consultation group reminded me that I was providing safety and consistency, which was fundamentally more intrinsic to her survival than anything else I could offer. It would lay the groundwork upon which she could build an emotionally healthy life. Despite my frustration and negative outlook on both Lilly and my work with her, I wanted to believe them, so I tried to accept their support and feedback. But my feelings of incompetence and frustration persisted.

Over time, I learned that the more Lilly acted out in my office, the safer she felt. She tested me at every turn and in response, I was consistent. I was the rock in that office. She could and did expect to find me with the same toys and the same four walls and the same temperament and personality each week. In retrospect, I have more appreciation for what I offered her, but during the process, I was filled with doubt and uncertainty.

After a little more than a year, I noticed a change in both Lilly's play and her demeanor. She appeared relaxed and comfortable, sharing just a bit more. Lilly would come into my office smiling, outwardly happy to see me, and ask *me* what we should play. She might ultimately choose the game, but she asked me first and that was a change. She also engaged *me* in play and didn't seem as reactive to losing. Of course, she still liked to win, but if she didn't or suspected she might not, she was calmer and could finish the game, letting me win and joking about it.

THE DISRUPTIONS

At about this point in our treatment, Barry, the first caseworker for the family and the one who had been the most involved in Lilly's case, had to transfer the case to another division. The subsequent four caseworkers, with whom I barely had contact, were in and out of Lilly's life so rapidly that they never had an opportunity to invest themselves in the case.

Upon the arrival of the fifth caseworker, Lilly began to experience significant disruptions in her young life, which inspired a change in her play with me. The caseworker told Lilly that she would be seeing her parents less frequently and that she would not be returning to live with them. This was also the point at which Bobby was removed from the home. The caseworker reported that Bobby was "happy" about the move, which didn't surprise me in some ways as he had been living with a foster mother who expressed disdain, frustration, contempt, and coldness for this little boy. Although the siblings fought often and bitterly, I had also experienced them as loving, sweet, and playful with one another. I believed that in a different foster home in which both children were fully accepted along with their behavioral and emotional challenges, Lilly's relationship with her brother may have developed in a healthier manner.

I learned of Bobby's removal from the foster home two months after it occurred, when the caseworker called to complain about Lilly's escalating regression. She refused to obey Mrs. Jay and the frequency of her enuresis had increased. When neighbors saw Lilly sitting outside the house in the dark in only a nightgown and called the police, the caseworker arranged for Mrs. Jay to have in-home parenting support.

Lilly's symptomatic behavior was escalating, rather than abating. Not so curiously, as Lilly's acting out behavior increased, so did Mrs. Jay's doubts about keeping her. Although the relationship between Lilly and her foster mother was not good, removal from the home could have been a significant loss. I assumed that this was the reason that the caseworker was directing all of her attention to preserving the placement, rather than looking for a potential adoptive home for Lilly.

THE TERMINATION

As Lilly's aggressive behavior increased, I learned from the caseworker that Mrs. Jay was at a loss as to how to manage her and that she blamed me for Lilly's deteriorating condition. The decision to have Lilly begin anger management work with a new therapist was made, apparently without any consideration of having her continue in therapy with a mental health professional she had already grown to trust. I strongly advocated for Lilly to continue working with me, so as to ensure constancy and safety rather than creating another potentially avoidable transition in her life, especially when so much was unstable. The caseworker stood firm that the course of action that she had initiated was in Lilly's best interests, but did agree that Lilly could have one more session with me if we could find a time that did not interfere with the next week's scheduled appointment with the new therapist.

In that next session, Lilly announced her dislike for the new caseworker. She was under the impression that she wouldn't be seeing her parents as often because seeing them made it hard for her to obey her foster mother. Lilly's sharing this kind of information with me was new in our relationship. Lilly was going to lose me just as she was feeling safe enough to talk to me. I felt immobilized. I continued to hold out hope that Lilly and I would continue our work together. I knew that her caseworker was planning to tell her about the new therapist at the beginning of the next week. I found this frustrating because if the decision to transition Lilly was set in stone, then I wanted to begin preparing her as soon as possible in order to minimize the impact.

I was confused about why Lilly was being transferred to a new therapist. Having endured Lilly's tirades, I certainly understood that she needed to learn to control her anger. Yet, she had good reason to be filled with fury. She had endured an onslaught of losses; had been physically, sexually and emotionally abused by people who were supposed to be safeguarding her and when she was moved for her protection, she was placed in the care of a woman who met the symptoms of her distress with disgust. I struggled to see how the new plan was in Lilly's best interests or how it offered protection to a person desperately in need of being kept safe. The abrupt transition seemed to be for the convenience of the adults, rather than a transition that would help Lilly. We had worked for almost two years to create a relationship upon which Lilly could rely and I had grave concerns that an unexpected termination would attach itself to the list of Lilly's traumatic losses. Conversely, I sincerely hoped that if Mrs. Jay could feel more connected to a new therapist, her relationship with Lilly might improve.

In the end, due to my insistent reminders of how damaging a sudden transition could be within the therapeutic process, the caseworker decided that Lilly and I could have three sessions to say our goodbyes. I also arranged for the new therapist to participate in the final session in order to help ease the changeover. When Lilly arrived at the first of the final three sessions, I learned that Mrs. Jay had told her that this would be our last session. In her new spirit of cooperation, Lilly instigated a game of catch. Initially, Lilly had no comment about the anticipated change in therapists. I explained that we would have two more sessions after this one and that the new therapist would join us for part of that meeting. I also told her how sad I was that she would no longer be coming to see me and described the many ways in which I had seen her grow in our time together. She asked many questions, which was very much unlike her, about what I'd miss and seemed to enjoy hearing how she'd changed and grown over our months together. Her interest in my feelings and thoughts about her and the conversation in and of itself was representative of Lilly's significant transformation. Midway into the session she expressed her desire not to change therapists and mentioned missing her previous one.

As we played, Lilly asked me to pick up some balls. When I didn't immediately get them, she began yelling at me for not doing what she asked and not listening to her. Her verbal harangue quickly regressed to a physical expression of throwing things, and shouting about how unfair all of this was. She left my office and began running up and down the hallway, slamming doors, and sitting on the stairs that led to the front door, clearly unsure of what to do with all of the feelings running rampant within her tiny frame.

Just as suddenly as her rage had taken flight, Lilly's emotions shifted to howling tears and heart wrenching sobs. It was hard for her to accept my comfort. As I attempted to soothe her verbally and physically, she hit and kicked me, but remained in my lap. Then she'd jump up, push me away, and run out of the room. Finally, when Lilly had calmed down enough, I reminded her she would be returning the following week, as today would not be our last visit. She seemed both relieved and anxious at the thought, understandably, as there was too much emotion wrapped up in this process—too much for a little person.

I closed the door behind Lilly and cried. I was angry at the caseworker for not better preparing Mrs. Jay about how to proceed as a team with what I knew would be a sensitive and frightening transformation for Lilly. I was frustrated because I felt alone in wanting to create a safer reality for this child. This whole situation was surreal. I had the distinct feeling that the caseworker felt that the termination sessions were a favor to me, rather than helpful for Lilly. I was outraged and wanted to shout, "See? This is what the change is doing to her!! How dare you think so little of her to not seriously consider how this unnecessary transition would adversely affect her! I'm furious that her needs are not being prioritized!" But there was no one to listen.

The next week I learned from Maggie, who would be Lilly's new therapist, that Lilly had come close to being hospitalized the evening after our last session. Her level of distress regarding the upcoming therapeutic remodeling was demonstrated in her loss of bowel and bladder control and her inability to be calmed until a crisis level mental health team was called into the home. It was heartbreaking to hear how frightened, anxious, unsafe and out of control this little girl felt. During this conversation, Maggie expressed alarm and deep concern for Lilly's mental health. She also voiced her apprehension about commencing work with a client who had not been properly transitioned within the therapeutic boundaries of professional care. Due to Lilly's unsafe departure from her therapeutic experience with me coupled with her innumerable encounters with loss, Maggie understood she could be facing an angrier, more guarded, potentially more explosive, untrusting version of Lilly. She wondered if it might be possible for Lilly to continue with me, and meet with her for anger management and said that she would talk with the caseworker. Yet, she was also unable to preserve Lilly's relationship with me.

Lilly arrived for the next session with a fresh wet circle on the back of her dress, clearly just having had an accident. She asked to go for frozen yogurt, a special treat we'd shared in the past on particularly difficult days. I explained to her that I wanted to have an adult conversation and if and when she reached her limit, to tell me, and I'd stop. I told her that I had talked with Maggie and liked her. "I think she's kind and you might like working with her." Lilly interjected with her positive impressions of me being kind. Appreciating the unforeseen compliment, I let her know that Maggie and I were working together to make this passage as easy for her as possible, by decreasing the speed of the transition and allowing Lilly to have a few more sessions with me. I showed her the impending schedule and encouraged her to participate in the decision making process. We then spoke about the previous weekend and how in crisis she'd been. I reflected how difficult it could be to have all these people making determinations for you without having any input. She was nodding her head in agreement. I offered that sometimes both children and adults don't know how to handle that feeling of powerlessness and will kick and scream to let themselves be heard. She again nodded and explained that that was what it was like for her. The progress in our work was amazing and I was profoundly disturbed by its premature ending. Lilly was finally communicating with her words and engaging in conversations about her own behavior and feelings. It was truly extraordinary.

The third termination session was not as productive as the previous ones, to say the least. Lilly immediately and loudly rejected all suggestions that had anything to do with saying goodbye. She escalated quickly, tearing apart my office, upturning furniture, throwing shelf items, running in and out of the room, repeatedly slamming the door, hitting and kicking me and doing everything she could to get my negative attention, impervious to redirection. Repeatedly screaming, "I don't care" at the top of her lungs, she was unmanageable, defiant, and furious. As she crossed every previously established boundary and broke all of the rules, I found my anger skyrocketing and simply wanted and needed her to ceasefire! I wanted her to stop screaming, running, hurting herself, hurting me, destroying the room. I, too, was exceptionally angry, frustrated, and frightened by her alarming behavior and my own helplessness in this situation. Despite my fierce efforts to protect this little girl, I felt I had failed her. The people who had made this decision were not on the receiving end of her torturous pain. I was. She blamed me, yelling that I didn't do enough to help her, that I didn't do enough to keep her. I felt ineffectual and powerless to shelter her, and with tears of frustration and despondency welling up inside of me, I eventually came undone.

I oscillated between keeping my voice low, steady and consistent in my redirections, reflecting the depth of her feelings, ignoring the behavior, grabbing items from her before she ruined them and ultimately raising my voice to make myself heard. I tried desperately to use the "safe hold" I'd learned in a group home. Filled with despair, overwrought with the words "Get out" silently screaming in my head, bouncing off the walls of my insides and drowning out calming reason, I had reached my limit and wanted, needed her to leave. I wanted the session to be over. It needed to end, because we were both hurting so deeply and I barely had the strength to calm myself.

When Lilly at long last departed, I was overcome by waves of shock, confusion, grief and vulnerability. I knew I must have been sharing at least some of what Lilly was feeling. But she was only eight and therefore unable to care for herself or make any important decisions about her life. I had truly believed that I could advocate for the mental health and well-being of this child AND be heard. In this instance, I was wrong. I felt as powerless as Lilly.

THE FINAL SESSION

For our final session, undeterred by my fear that this would be a repeat of the previous weeks' maelstrom, that I would be on the receiving end of Lilly's deeply rooted pain, I prepared for our goodbye by buying Lilly some mementos of our work together—a deck of cards, a favorite dessert, and an incredibly soft stuffed bear, which I hoped could provide some comfort to her. I also wrote a card specifying the extraordinary developments I'd been witness to during our two years and all that I would miss about her.

I opened the door to find a smiling Lilly. I sighed a little with relief, but didn't bask in it, as she hadn't entered the room yet. I acknowledged that it was party day and I gave her the presents. Handing me the card, she hid behind the window curtain while I read to her. She beamed as I enumerated all of her wonderful attributes and successes. Then we played while she ate her very chocolate cupcake. When I reminisced about our time together, affirming my enjoyment of seeing her each week, she looked at me earnestly, knowingly and said, "But not last week." Surprised that she mentioned the oppressive session and grateful because I had wanted to address it, I thanked her for bringing it up. I agreed that the session had truly been tough for both of us and then apologized for yelling and not being able to help her. I explained that I too, felt heavyhearted and would miss her greatly.

We then discussed how the new therapist, Maggie, would be joining us for a game of Lilly's choosing. I encouraged Lilly to ask any questions or not—to do what was comfortable for her. Trying to wink, Lilly asked me to tell Maggie that she did NOT make the honor roll, and that she was actually very stupid. When I asked why she wanted me to lie to Maggie, Lilly clearly and wisely replied that she didn't know or trust her yet. Fair enough, I said.

When it was time for Maggie to join us, Lilly jumped up to check the waiting room. Lilly opened the door, smiled into the ethers and then promptly closed the door. I playfully admonished Lilly for not inviting Maggie into the office. She smiled, opened the door and very politely welcomed Maggie, who then joined us on the floor. Lilly played with the cards by herself, so I took the opportunity to let Maggie know of Lilly's intellectual shortcomings. Lilly kept winking at me, or least attempting, as she didn't really know how, so she'd comically and endearingly blink both eyes at me while smiling broadly. Our little secret, said her face. Maggie didn't call us on the joke, which caused Lilly to beam with delight. After a few minutes, Lilly turned to me and asked if we could speak alone. Once the door closed behind Maggie, Lilly nonchalantly inquired after my feelings regarding Maggie with an offhanded, yet unequivocally earnest, "So, whadya think?" I smiled, again surprised by what she was showing me after all this time, and said, "I think she seems very nice. I liked her." Standing upright with her shoulders back and her head nodding ardently, Lilly responded very maturely as she expressed how kind she found Maggie to be. Smiling more broadly, I encouraged Lilly to be brave and openhearted as she got to know Maggie.

Lilly invited Maggie to return for the end of the session and despite her smiles, while laying across my feet in a way that I could feel the wetness of her freshly soaked pants, she revealed her unfathomable fear and anxiety as she faced another loss. In those few moments of waiting to see what she'd do next, Lilly picked up the cards and instructed us to start stacking them. Sadness crept in as I witnessed Lilly's protective play, control, reveal itself once again. She knew we were watching her, patiently waiting on her to let us know what was next. So, we dutifully did as we were told. Lilly marched around, checking our work, ensuring we were listening to her demands. When we put everything away and were saying goodbye, Lilly gave a little wave and an offhanded goodbye, as if she'd see me the following week. I asked her for a goodbye hug and before flying into my arms, wrapping her legs around me and hugging me fiercely, with "See you later, alligator," she reminded me that it wasn't "goodbye." She got down, started to walk away, then turned around and did it again. Parting with the sweetest of sorrows, I wiped tears from my eyes.

My consultation group reflected that my apology to her in this last session might have been the first of its kind for her. They supported me in understanding that I had been there for Lilly in every way I knew how; that, despite the therapist having a connection with the client, the caregiver system was unable to make a connection to the therapist, thereby negatively impacting the work and the therapeutic relationship. My hope is that the consistent, nonjudgmental, and reassuring way in which I showed up for her, recognized and acknowledged my own behavior, and modeled an appropriate and healthy goodbye would stay with her as she journeyed on her path. I had felt a little disappointed to have to share her in our final moments, but I also felt more lighthearted than I had expected as I watched her turn toward the future. I also felt protective as I knew she was gearing up to challenge Maggie and start all over with forging a new alliance with yet another new adult, who probably would not be in her life for too long, but who would, ideally, provide some level of consistency and continuity.

Upon reflection, it is hard for me to understand how the goals of the child welfare system—safety, well-being, and permanence—were promoted by the decision to end Lilly's therapy with me. Collaboration among all of the important adults in Lilly's life might have helped to support the relationship, avoiding the anxiety and trauma Lilly experienced as a result of the abrupt and improperly prepared termination. The rapid turnover in caseworkers made it hard for me to know them and for them to know me or, more importantly, Lilly. Certainly, these changes might also have been unsettling for Mrs. Jay, who was trying to manage the very disturbing behavior of two traumatized children.

The foster care system is unfortunately, in many ways, set up in a manner that deters the workers from thinking. There is a level of unconsciousness that is unconscionable. Due to exorbitantly large caseloads and the need to be in seventeen different places at once, while keeping official notes on all activities of all children and families in their care, despite the best intentions of the caseworkers, there just simply isn't enough psychic energy to breathe, let alone make a decision that may or may not be in a client's best interests. Also, with the level of horror that caseworkers regularly face, it would be almost impossible not to become numb. It is imperative to change the system, if for no other reason than to give the caseworkers room to calmly and insightfully make good decisions based on careful analysis of the evidence.

Barry, the caseworker who knew Lilly the best, referred her to A Home Within precisely because he wanted her to have the possibility of an ongoing therapeutic relationship. Sadly, that relationship ended just as Lilly was beginning to trust me enough to open up. It is understandable that if caseworkers feel that they have to choose between the possibility of a permanent home for a child and an ongoing relationship with a therapist, the home will prevail. In this case, it was not at all clear that Mrs. Jay would become Lilly's "forever family." In retrospect, I think that the new caseworker came to this case when the family was falling apart and may have felt compelled to make decisions that inadvertently yet directly impinged upon the immediate safety and well-being of this child. Changing Lilly's therapist might have seemed like the most expedient course of action and for Lilly's sake; I can only hope that the caseworker's decision was a good one. I do know that I was important to Lilly, as she was to me, and I hope that we are both able to hold on to one another and what it means to fight for those we care about. My deep-rooted wish is that she is in a safe, loving and supportive environment, receiving the nurturing care, both professionally and personally, that she so deserves—as all children do.

ADDENDUM: AFTERTHOUGHTS

I did not imagine that the writing of this chapter would be challenging. When I first sat down to write, I stared at the screen and then out the window for a time before I got up, distracting myself with other, easier tasks. Aware of the deadline, I forced myself to return to the empty screen and picturesque window view, only to surprisingly discover my brain devoid of any case details despite it having ended just a few months before. It did not occur to me that the depth of the trauma I had experienced was the reason for my lack of focus. As hard as I tried, I sincerely felt immobilized mentally, in that I could not recall her face, the specifics of her life, or our time together. Ultimately, I took out my case notes and only then was my memory immediately flooded with the gruesome and painstaking particulars. The beginning of the chapter, in terms of describing Lilly and providing her case history, was more easily accessible and therefore easier to write about. When I arrived at the point where I needed to describe the events shaping the conclusion of our relationship, I found myself, once again, stuck, namely because I felt unsure of what or how much of this story I should share for this chapter. How deep or specific should I get? The unmistakable decision was an unleashing of floodgates, a howling release of pain and vitriol and anguish and powerlessness all encompassing my truth. My trauma paralleled Lilly's in the depth of our impotence. I thought, believed, that working outside the system safeguarded me from being hurt by the weaknesses I'd previously experienced within the system. In effect, it was almost a double dose of my feeling incapacitated, ineffective and voiceless because it was so unexpected. Through the many varieties of edits and the process of getting the story out of me, like cleaning up the debris left by my war torn experience, I now recognize the profound impact this case has had on me and I'm grateful to have had the opportunity to use the writing of this chapter as a spiritual, emotional, and professional catharsis. This has enabled me to begin work with another client in need of safe and consistent long-term mental health care.

My hope is that the reader of this chapter is able to recognize this as an opportunity for growth and understanding. For those who are presently or will in the future work within or around the foster care system, I implore you to always, *always* do what is needed in order to stay grounded, present, empathic and focused on the basic needs of the children, who by no fault of their own, find themselves exposed to a system that is not always able to represent their *best* needs.

REFERENCE

Gil, E. (1991). *The healing power of play: Working with abused children.* New York: Guilford Press.

Chapter Four

Joining a Consultation Group

Right out of college I got a job as a caseworker for foster families. About four years later, a Master's degree, and two dollars more an hour, I began working for a state-funded program to provide clinical services to high-risk foster kids. I remember the woman who interviewed me said that no one had ever questioned her so rigorously during an interview before, or seemed so cautious about taking a job. Years later, after she became my boss and trusted mentor, I confided in her: "It's because I was so scared."

For the next ten years, I worked as a psychotherapist and later as a clinical supervisor for this foster care program. Its motto, "Whatever It Takes," was steeped in the understanding that the trauma for foster children of multiple placement disruptions is often compounded by concurrent, multiple therapeutic disruptions. Consequently, the program's contract stipulated that the therapist would sustain the therapy despite placement disruptions, ensuring the continuity of the treatment. However, over the years, I learned that promises made are not always kept. The unfortunate reality of the program was that its good intentions were often diluted by fiscal or other concrete constraints. "Whatever it takes" morphed into "Whatever it takes, so long as it's within our catchment area" or "Whatever it takes, so long as it's accomplished within a two-year timeframe." I spent years saying goodbye to kids before it was time, and I learned how it felt to be complicit in a system that I knew to be inadequate by even a "good enough" standard.

Years later, I was thrilled to learn about A Home Within, a program that not only gave me the opportunity, but also the necessary supports, to do "whatever it takes" to meet a foster child's need for one reliable, consistent adult. I had learned a long time ago that the hard part wasn't figuring out what foster kids need; rather it was the creation of a working environment with the necessary supports to provide it. A Home Within offered me that chance and, with almost no hesitation, I joined.

I learned that the consultation group involved a few A Home Within therapists meeting twice monthly for ninety minutes with a consultant (Heineman, 2008). I initially attributed my growing and unexpected reluctance to join the group to the fact that the meeting times/days were not compatible with my schedule. I began to contemplate the idea of meeting privately with my own consultant, with the inherent benefit of fewer meetings and greater control over my schedule. I also started to feel hesitant about entering into a collaborative relationship with strangers, with potentially radically different or even opposing philosophical bents. Finally, I began to reminisce about my old trusted supervisors, consultants, and mentors who had safely shepherded me through hundreds of cases in the past; surely I could bring one of them with me into this new venture in a private consultative fashion? With these thoughts/fantasies in mind, I telephoned the clinical director to explore the possibilities.

After listening patiently and thoughtfully to me for several minutes, he acknowledged my concerns but also challenged me to think about why I might be pushing back so hard against the consultation model. After just a few minutes fleshing out the matter with him, I understood the role of my fear of the unknown in driving my resistance. Grateful for his wisdom and the steady hand by which it was delivered, I hung up the phone and scheduled my initial meeting with the consultation group.

With new and clever ideas whirling around me as we discussed a colleague's case, I spent much of my first meeting feeling in awe of my good fortune. The members were all strong, experienced psychotherapists with bright minds, who shared my commitment to improving the lives of foster children. And ironically, I discovered that I already knew of couple of the group members, including the consultant, a psychiatrist who had been my teacher and supervisor when I was a student years ago in a child and adolescent training program.

While my familiarity with some of the members surely eased my transition into the group, I still struggled to get my footing on this new ground. I wrestled with some generic "new kid on the block" issues like how much and what of myself to reveal to others, and the requisite process of titrating the exposure. By the third meeting I was feeling quite comfortable with the landscape, and I volunteered to present my case to the group. As a solo practitioner, I was grateful for the opportunity; a few conundrums in the case had left me feeling ill equipped and outright alone without the benefit of a sounding board. I presented the case of my thirteen-year-old, Latino male client, Aurelio.

Aurelio presented in the initial session as a slender but muscular young man, his neat clothes and remarkable composure signaling his pride in his outward presentation. Seemingly as unsure of himself as he was about being in treatment with me, he said, "[My foster parents] sent me here because they think I need help adjusting," but added he didn't need help or want therapy because "I'm fine." In what I understood as a possible projection, he added that his ten-year-old brother is "not fine," as he is quick to anger and "will get out of control—like when he has trouble letting things slide." I was beginning to get the idea that he was all too familiar with the inherent danger in feelings that accidentally "get out of control."

Aurelio spoke with exquisite guardedness about his mother's longstanding drug abuse problems that culminated in his removal and growing estrangement from her, as he defended mightily against the attendant feelings. He also identified himself as a strong wrestler a sport in which "you need to be in total control always." He underscored that he hates wrestling girls, since he is "uncomfortable with them" and also "because it's inappropriate to touch a girl." I wondered to myself what it was like for him to be in treatment with me, a female therapist, in anticipation of a kind of emotional wrestling and intimacy. I also wondered whether he might be introducing what would later become one of his hallmark treatment issues: his emerging adolescent sexual development.

Aurelio assumed many of the caretaking responsibilities for his four younger siblings until age nine, at which time he entered foster care (and a series of foster homes) following substantiated allegations of neglect. He has no contact with his biological father. He and his ten-year-old brother, Marco, were placed six months ago in their current, pre-adoptive foster home. And shortly after my treatment began with Aurelio, a third foster child, five-year-old David, was placed in the home in a pre-adoptive capacity.

I informed my consultation group that David (the new foster child) had been placed almost as matter-of-factly as the foster parents had alerted me, three days beforehand, to his impending arrival in the home. At the time the foster parents shared this news with me, I recall thinking it was odd, or at least significant, that I was only just then being informed of the major change in family structure. In fact, the foster parents and I had met the previous week and they made no mention of their intent to adopt another child. With wide eyes and open mouth I gasped, "Really? I had no idea!" conveying both my disbelief and disappointment at not being told earlier. Surely, I thought, the foster parents must have understood the breadth of my intended role in the case, and my potential usefulness to them and Aurelio as a vehicle for contemplating or preparing for such a profound shift in the family. Moreover, I wondered if their choice not to include me in the decision or in the planning process signified some sort of personal and/or professional devaluation.

My colleagues were also alarmed by the seeming quickness and ease with which the foster parents decided to pursue yet another adoption. As the discussion evolved into a critical analysis of their intra-psychic motives for pursuing permanency with another child at this time, perhaps involving rescue fantasies or a mindset of "the more the merrier," I interjected my escalating concern and regret that I had somehow misrepresented them and in turn subjected them to such harsh scrutiny. The sharp tone of my voice betrayed my subconscious feelings of irritation and defensiveness.

One of my colleagues turned to me and bravely asked a question so obvious, yet somehow still so elusive, to us all in the moment: "Wow, what just happened here?" Relieved, and grateful for the opportunity to understand how I had become so unwittingly mired in my own countertransference, I was able to take a close-up look at the complicated and intense dynamics at play within me, and the group as a whole. In a strong identification with my client, I felt threatened by a new child in the family whose needs (I fantasized) could upset the delicate balance of supply and demand in the home and in turn jeopardize Aurelio's placement. But perhaps due to my wish to preserve an idealized image of the foster parents, I was inhibited in my ability to confront my anger at them and rather projected it onto my colleagues in a displacement. My colleagues functioned as a substitute outlet for my repressed anger at the foster parents. After all, not only did I have more to lose through my disappointment in Aurelio's foster parents, since his permanency was ostensibly riding on them, but it seemed somehow easier or safer to be angry with my colleagues, who via their professional training I imagined were better equipped to tolerate my hostility.

Another colleague theorized about the role of parallel process via my defensive stance against intruders, suggesting parallels between my resistance to the inclusion of a new foster child into the family, and new members into my consultation group. Indeed, I had just verbalized my ambivalence about the news that a clinician from a different consultation group in the area intended to transfer into our group, with the hope that it would be a better fit for his needs. Upon learning of this clinician's plans to terminate with his current consultation group as a result of some disappointment with its consultant, I became flooded by years of memories, as a therapist, consultant and supervisor, of so many child treatments truncated by premature terminations in the wake of unrepaired empathic breaks or unexplored and unmet needs; broken relationships, discarded rather than repaired, with the unfulfilled promise of new treatments and beginnings that could somehow outrun the awfulness of the old feelings of disappointment, hurt and anger. Bewildered by my countertransference, I was grateful for my colleague's invitation to understand better the convoluted dynamics at play within and around me.

In a continuation of my case-presentation at the next consultation group meeting, a colleague asked me to comment briefly on the nature of the caretaking dynamic in the therapeutic relationship, given Aurelio's historical role in his biological family as a caretaker for younger siblings. By way of illustration, I recounted an unfortunate incident several months into the treatment in which I arrived at the office with the wrong set of keys and could not gain access to the treatment room; nor was I successful with my impromptu efforts to secure a different office space for us within the same office complex. As I watched Aurelio become increasingly despondent with the dawning awareness of our "homelessness" and inability to meet, I listened to the stinging sound of the inadequacy of my own profuse, repeated apologies and felt the horribleness, not only of my mistake, but also of how it feels to be in such a strong identification with the bad (neglectful) mother (Woodard-Meyers, 2007). As Aurelio muttered consolations to me like, "Don't feel bad," and "It's ok, don't worry about it," I was struck by the degree to which we were in uncharted, new territory; indeed I could not recall ever having been in this position before of Aurelio functioning in the role of my caretaker.

I commented that I found my client's lack of proclivity towards caretaking in the treatment surprising, given his historical propensity for adopting a significant caretaking role within his family-of-origin. Fortunately, a psychologist in our group offered that she had written her dissertation on children who serve as primary caretakers for younger siblings. She noted that these children often choose later in life not to have children or to have only one or two children, as they have already fulfilled their caretaking responsibilities and satiated these drives.

Indeed, Aurelio later told me he imagined he would get married someday, but he did not want to have any children. "I've been down that road before," he said with a strained laugh. "I've had more than enough of kids," he said, referring to his experience as a small boy caring for his smaller siblings. He spoke with remarkable depth and length, and a whisper of anger, about his profound sadness as a young child charged by default with the task of filling the immense void left by his mother's emotional unavailability and limited parenting capabilities. Holding his tears at bay, and with the shame of a confession of his guiltily held secret that his badness had driven his mother away, he confided in me, "You know, I know now that my mom is never going to be able to parent me." In the next session, he called his foster mother "Mom," rather than by her first name, alluding to his mother-fantasies.

At the consultation group's next meeting, I recounted the following vignette as further illustration of Aurelio's mother-fantasies:

The week after our "missed" session due to my office key mishap, Aurelio said to me: "I just remembered what I've been wanting to tell you." Then lowering his voice and eyes, as if ashamed about what he was about to say, he admitted: "There's something really wrong with me. I can't talk to people . . . mostly kids at school . . . especially about myself." As we carefully folded back the layers of his secret, he described his despair at expending energy getting to know people time and time again, and then "having to let go of them" with each placement disruption. "I don't know how long I'm going to be here [in the current home], if I'm even going to stay. I'm really getting to make a lot of good friends and *if I left them I would be broken.*"

We talked about all of the important people that he has had to leave behind with each placement change, including his mother, siblings, and close friends. As we spoke about his profound losses, I noticed him beginning to rub his foot back and forth on the ground. He seemed to be almost digging his feet into the rubber soles of his shoes. With a smile, he commented that it just occurred to him how "squishy the rubber" was on the soles of his tennis shoes. "It really reminds me of something," he said, "something really big but I can't describe it. Besides, I can't think of it anyway and I know how silly the whole thing sounds." Hopeless about the prospect of having to remember and understand, and ashamed at his childlike, playful regression, he continued with a little encouragement from me to "go on."

Much to my surprise, he suddenly pulled off his shoe and took a big whiff of its rubber sole. As a humongous grin spread across his face, he said, "I remember now what the rubber reminds me of." "What?" I asked, with not even a vague idea of what he might say. "It reminds me of the baggers (long pause) in grocery stores (long pause), they wear rubber gloves [to handle] produce and put it in the plastic bags," he responded. Confused, I asked him to elaborate. He said he remembered once being in a grocery store and seeing baggers with rubber gloves. Still unsure of what he was trying to tell me, I encouraged him to say more.

With a just little prompting, Aurelio told me a story about a time years ago. He was a young boy with his mother and grandmother in the grocery store a couple blocks from his home; his mother and grandmother were buying fresh produce to make dinner that evening. Initially confused and embarrassed by his overwhelming affect associated with what seemed to be such a trivial memory, he was ultimately able to understand his association to his mother and grandmother feeding/nurturing him as a representation of the family that he has had to leave behind. He said, "I miss my mother so much and I just want to be with her. The truth is I don't really like [my foster parents'] cooking very much. . . . Well actually it tastes kind of ok but it's just not as good as my mother's."

After my colleagues and I explored at length Aurelio's longing for "home" embodied by his mother's (home)-cooking, and bolstered by critical insights and the group process by which they became available to me, I raised another pivotal dynamic in the case—the emergent problem of potential triangulation. The foster parents had expressed their profound disappointment with Marco (Aurelio's ten-year-old brother in the home), the intractability of his problems, and his treatment. Marco was in treatment with a different A Home Within therapist, a member of the other A Home Within consultation group in my area. On numerous occasions, the foster parents insinuated to me that they were thinking about terminating Marco's treatment, a threat they ultimately followed through with months later. I reminded them each time that entrenched, serious problems such as Marco's often necessitate longer-term treatment. I also implored them to be speaking directly with Marco's therapist about their concerns rather than repeatedly bringing them to my attention, a third-party with the potential, via triangulation, for conflating the communication problems rather than resolving them. Finally, I briefly explored with them whether they might also be communicating indirectly to me about some dissatisfaction on their part with Aurelio's treatment (which they denied).

On another occasion, the foster mother telephoned me to express her concerns about the viability of Marco's placement, given some of his recent acting-out behaviors, and his likely need for residential treatment. I indicated that I was not knowledgeable enough about Marco or the situation to make placement recommendations and implored her to speak directly with Marco's therapist. However, I did interject my opinion that based upon what I knew of the situation, I had no reason to believe that Marco currently required residential placement, and that there were likely still many avenues to explore that would ensure all the children's safety while enabling Marco to remain in the home.

After I hung up the telephone, I began to second-guess not the content, but rather the delivery of my message. I co-opted the group here to explore the question of whether or not I had been somehow too confrontational or dismissive with the foster mother. While my colleagues ultimately legitimized my intervention, they also noted that I was likely feeling disconcerted by our interaction; surely I feared that my treatment- or worse yet, Aurelio- could be the next target of the foster mother's disappointment, and in turn, possible rejection. Thankfully, the group had become a safe stomping ground for me, wherein I could readily explore my old, familiar worries about being a "good enough" therapist—surely for any client but particularly for society's most vulnerable members such as children, and even more so for foster children, where the stakes for basic human needs such as family and home are so high. Just as I needed the group's affirmation about my treatment, I fantasized about a kind of guarantee from the foster mother that I would be safe from the threat of being terminated or "kicked out" like Marco's therapist: A fantasy evocative of the hopeful promise within Aurelio, and all foster children, that for at least one person they will be good enough to keep.

Reflecting on my experience with the consultation group in writing this chapter, I developed a renewed respect for the clinical director—who via his keen clinical insights and skills helped me understand and move through my initial resistance to joining a group. The consultation group has proven to be a critical learning tool for me. Unlike a traditional dyadic supervision, it affords me access to multiple, interdisciplinary perspectives and their invaluable interplay. I have also come to appreciate how lucky I am to be afforded the luxury of a professional "home." Like all comfortable homes, the consultation group is a place where I know I can stay and grow professionally for as long as it takes in order that I might be a "good enough" therapist for Aurelio and, likewise, where I can be myself without regard for whether I will be deemed good enough to keep.

REFERENCES

Heineman, T. (2008). "The network is down": Building an alternative network to address the multiple disruptions in clinical work with foster children and youth. *Journal of Infant, Child & Adolescent Psychotherapy*, 7(2), 145–150. DOI: 10.1080/15289160802165052.

Woodard-Meyers, T. (2007). When the helper becomes traumitized: Take care of you. In R. E. Lee & J. B. Whiting (Eds.), *Foster care therapist handbook* (pp. 469-484). Arlington, VA: Child Welfare League of America.

II

The Heart and Soul of Psychotherapy

When we ask therapists to work with a current or former foster child "for as long as it takes," our intention is to open the door to a therapeutic relationship that will allow therapist and client together to determine "for how long and for what purpose." Sometimes people approach therapy with clearly defined concerns. A child may say, "I want to make more friends." An adolescent may ask for help with anxiety because, "I'm driving myself crazy." A young adult may bring worries about what the future holds: "I'm afraid I'm going to be just as mean as my father."

More often, particularly with children and teens who have been told, "You need to go talk to someone," things are less clear. In response to "How can I help?" the response is likely to be along the lines of "I dunno," or "Get my foster mother off my back," or "Just make it better." In these situations it may take some time to define the emotional landscape underlying the reasons someone believes that psychotherapy could be helpful.

Whether clients come of their own accord or are referred by another, they come to therapy because of one or more symptoms—something that they are feeling or thinking or doing is distressing to them or to those around them. They understandably want relief from symptoms that make life difficult. However, they often want more—they want to know themselves more completely. They want to develop a fuller understanding of who they are and why they act and feel as they do in different situations, especially when their actions and feelings make no sense to them and seem to cause them unnecessary trouble.

"Who am I?" "How did I get to be this way?" are natural, more abstract extensions of the young child's "Where did I come from?" Our innate curiosity about ourselves is amply demonstrated by the multitude of choices human beings have created to enhance self-knowledge. Some look to the skies, hoping to learn about themselves through astrological charts. Some look inward, anticipating that solitary meditation will reveal personal truths. Others seek out "talk therapy," believing that insight will come through conversations with a professional.

People often begin psychotherapy in a state of tortured confusion. They are unhappy but don't know why. They don't understand others' reactions to them. They don't like the way they act, but feel unable to change their behavior. They may have worries that they know to be ill founded, but can't contain their anxiety. Typically, the troublesome behavior and feelings have arisen as unconscious self-protective efforts. And, while they might have been useful defensive strategies at a particular time or in a particular situation, when, over time, they are woven into personality structure, they can cause misery of all sorts.

For example, if a child is moved from one foster family to another he might need to learn all the new rules and follow them faithfully and without question in order to try to protect himself from being moved again. In another setting this rigid adherence to rules might interfere significantly with learning or work that requires flexibility in thinking. In another instance, foster teens in a group home might develop different strategies for managing the group dynamics—one always calling attention to herself in order not to be overlooked, another fading into the background in order to stay out of trouble. In other settings someone who always needs attention can quickly annoy others, making relationships difficult, and someone who rarely speaks up is unlikely to get her needs met.

The three cases in this section demonstrate how unconscious defensive strategies that have continued beyond their original usefulness can be understood in the context of the therapeutic relationship. "Lucy" keeps herself at a distance from relationships rather than lose them as she has before and expects that she will again. "Michael" continues to go to great lengths to command attention long after his adoption by very attentive parents. "Isaiah" becomes a caretaker to others as a way of managing his own wishes to be cared for. These young people, ranging from children to a young adult, developed these defenses under extreme circumstances, but were unable to set them aside when their circumstances changed such that they should not have had to work so hard at protecting themselves. These case studies allow us to see how the therapeutic process gradually helps them to relax a bit and begin to enjoy themselves and those who care for them.

The chapter that describes interactions among therapists in a consultation group that has been together for several years also allows us to appreciate the ways in which our unconscious defensive strategies come into our work and into our relationships with colleagues. The material also helps us understand how interactions among people who respect and care deeply about each other can help each other loosen those defenses, allowing them to think openly and creatively together in ways that enhance their relationships with each other, the group process, and ultimately their relationships with their clients.

When considering how heart and soul contribute to therapeutic change it is important that we not overlook the importance of the mind. It is the convergence of the three that allows for the creative, reflective thought and attuned responsiveness from which change emerges. Of course, clinicians' capacity to think and to call on their education and experience is an important component of therapeutic work. However, especially in the case of foster children, the therapist's interest in them and in holding them in mind—even when they are not in the office—is of monumental importance. The knowledge that you exist in the mind of another is fundamental to building relationships and an essential part of the work described in these chapters.

Chapter Five

Lucy

When I met Lucy, she had been in foster care—for the first time in her life—for about three months. A cerebral thirteen-year-old, Lucy was Caucasian, with brown curly hair and horn-rimmed glasses. She tended to dress in jeans and t-shirts, appearing tomboyish and slightly "alternative." Prior to foster placement, Lucy lived with her father, his girlfriend, and her younger brother. Lucy had required multiple psychiatric hospitalizations over the course of the preceding year for explosive behavior, self-injury, and suicidal thoughts. There was additional concern during this time that Lucy's thinking might be psychotic because when she became upset at home, her behavior sometimes became disorganized and her perceptions distorted. During her most recent hospitalization, Lucy had revealed her father's (previously unidentified) neglectful and abusive behavior to the nursing staff and, as a result, was placed in emergency custody and ultimately discharged to a foster family. Her foster parents[1] were a married, middle class couple in a town about fifteen miles from Lucy's home. My office, as it happened, was situated in a community roughly midway between Lucy's father's home and her foster home. And, I had some prior professional experience with foster children and foster parents.

For me, as well as for the members of my A Home Within consultation group, my work with Lucy raised moral and existential questions about the nature of parenthood, in particular parental rights and responsibilities. It also forced us to confront our own assumptions regarding a child's "best interest." As Lucy and I faced her rapidly and dramatically unfolding life circumstances together, many themes arose. These included notions of freedom of choice, loyalty, grief, rejection, forgiveness, truth, lies and distortion, dreams and reality. Many clinical concepts came to life for me in the year that I saw Lucy, among them cultural and professional notions regarding parent-child attachment, the etiology and treatment of "mental illness," and the power of unconscious forces to influence thought and emotion and motivate behavior. My work with Lucy also demonstrated for me, and the members of my consultation group, the crucial role of communication and collaboration among the myriad adult players that inevitably comprise a foster child's family and professional care network. By way of introduction, I will describe Lucy's psychiatric history, in particular the nature of her multiple hospitalizations prior to the start of therapy with me, and also the family circumstances, identified during her final hospitalization, that led to Lucy's removal from her father and stepmother's home.

Lucy's documented psychiatric history began when she was twelve. Her father had initiated outpatient treatment for Lucy that ultimately included some family meetings. Their presenting concerns were that Lucy's behavior at home was frequently out of control. In particular, she was prone to temper tantrums and angry outbursts that would last for several hours at a time. Following these tantrums, she would typically "isolate" herself in her room for extended periods, refusing to speak. The psychotherapist diagnosed Lucy with severe anxiety and referred her for a psychopharmacologic evaluation at a local hospital-based clinic. In that evaluation, the psychiatrist referred her for inpatient admission due to the her revelation of increased self-injurious behavior including scratching, clawing, and biting herself, as well as suicidal ideation, aggressive behavior and extreme tantrums at home, and eating problems. He also raised the question of a thought disorder.

During this first hospitalization, Lucy's father reported that she was an extremely difficult child whose emotional problems began very early in her life. He described Lucy's late achievement of motor developmental milestones as her being "unwilling, not unable" to walk and needing help to learn to do basic movements and tasks. He reported a series of chronic troubling behaviors including Lucy's binging on food from their family's pantry, hoarding food, eating food from the garbage, lying, stealing from other children, and engaging in physical aggression toward her brother, other children and animals. Lucy's father and girlfriend presented hospital staff with an extensive bibliography of advice books on how to manage explosive and emotionally disturbed children. They appeared to be trying to demonstrate how diligently they had tried to address Lucy's "difficult" behavior at home, albeit without success.

Lucy's father also presented developmental and family history. Lucy's mother became pregnant with her at age seventeen. Lucy's parents then married and subsequently had a second child, a boy (also unplanned) a year or so later. They separated when Lucy was approximately two years old and shared custody of both children. Lucy's father reported his strong suspicion that Lucy was emotionally and physically abused/neglected while in her mother's care during the next couple of years. He described Lucy's mother as a sexual abuse victim who had been prone to promiscuity, substance abuse, and erratic, dangerous behavior. He reported that Lucy's mother moved out of state suddenly when Lucy was four, relinquishing custody of both children to him.

At the time of Lucy's first hospital admission, her father described Lucy as having "fits" lasting up to six hours at a time, during which she would become non-communicative except for screaming, mumbling to herself, and clawing, hitting and biting herself to the point of bleeding. She was expressing wishes to die and thoughts involving "knives." Also, in an apparent "suicide attempt," Lucy had consumed a large quantity of energy bars that her grandmother had warned were "poisonous." During this initial two-week psychiatric hospitalization, evaluators considered differential diagnoses of psychosis, dissociation, and anxiety. Both an anti-depressant and an anti-psychotic medication were prescribed. Lucy was discharged to her father's home and returned to her local public middle school.

Lucy was hospitalized again five months later, after reporting a plan to hang herself. During this extended stay—almost a full month—clinical staff observations and Lucy's eventual revelations revealed a complex and concerning picture of the home environment and thus the context for her distress. The hospital admission notes indicated that Lucy was underweight, anxious and kept to herself. She told the staff that she and her father do not get along and that he and his girlfriend like her younger brother better.

The hospital staff filed a child abuse report, based on Lucy's hesitant description of mistreatment at home and her nearly emaciated condition. Her weight was charted daily. She almost immediately began to gain weight and within a short time her weight was in the normal range for her age and height.

Hospital notes also indicated that Lucy displayed neither the eating disorder nor temper tantrums and loss of control described by her father. Lucy was discharged to a specialized foster home placement with a recommendation that she begin tapering off anti-psychotic medications as soon as she was settled into her foster home.

Shortly after Lucy was placed in foster care, her social worker referred her to A Home Within, through which she was assigned to me for individual therapy. Upon meeting Lucy, I promptly learned that she was an avid reader and in particular a consumer of Japanese comic books, or "manga." One of her compelling interests throughout the time we worked together was a weekly, animated manga series, "Naruto." This program happened to air new episodes on the evening following our weekly meeting, so Lucy was always eagerly anticipating watching it when we met. Sometimes we would look up information about this program on my desktop computer. Eventually, Lucy's foster parents generously equipped her with an iPod so she would occasionally bring videos of the program to watch in the waiting room or during our sessions. Not yet familiar with the Japanese genre, I needed to time to orient myself to the storyline. In the year that Lucy and I worked together, I did come to grasp the basic premise of this particular narrative.

> Many years ago, in the hidden village of Konoha, lived a great demon fox. When it swung one of its nine tails, a tsunami occurred. The fourth [village leader] (Hokage) sealed this demon fox inside a boy in exchange for his own life. Naruto was that boy, and he grew up with no family, and the villagers hated him, thinking that he himself was the demon fox. Naruto's dream is to become [village leader] (Hokage), and have the villagers acknowledge him. (Kishimoto, 1999)

As I came to know Lucy, I began to understand her experience of "badness," derived from successive abandonment by of each of her parents. The treatment she experienced by her father and the girlfriend—in which they labeled her as the "bad" child and her brother as the "good" child who could be unduly influenced by her—left Lucy feeling that there must be something bad inside her. It was not hard to imagine how Lucy reached this conclusion; her father and his girlfriend mistreated her to a degree that required her removal from their home yet, even following the state's thorough investigation of the family, they were deemed good enough parents to her brother for her brother to remain in their home. Later, Lucy would enact this identification and family drama with her foster parents through her internalized identification with the demon fox—by becoming dangerous and attacking of them, in a wholly unconscious attempt to provoke their exclusion of her, the same way that Naruto in the television program had been excluded but longed to be included.

As soon as Lucy was placed in foster care, her caseworker located and contacted her biological mother, whom Lucy had not seen since she was four. By the time Lucy and I began working together, her mother was settling into regular contact with Lucy's caseworker regarding Lucy's situation. Lucy's mother was now living in a distant state, was recently remarried, and had a new baby. She expressed great interest in re-connecting with Lucy and Lucy's caseworker immediately began working to establish the foundation for their reunion. To this end, about three months after I began treating Lucy, I was asked to speak with her mother on the phone, both to describe Lucy's current state and to begin to assess the advisability of contact between them. When I first reported to Lucy during one of our sessions that I had spoken with her mother, she glazed over to such an extent that I wondered whether she was dissociating. When Lucy returned to conscious focus, we discussed how sometimes when feelings overwhelm her she "leaves."

The following week Lucy arrived at our session wearing headphones, watching the "Naruto" series on the iPod. She offered me her headphones so I could watch the beginning of the episode myself. I watched the young male protagonist waking up in his bed, rubbing his eyes, and saying, "I had a dream." I listened and watched on Lucy's iPod for few moments, then took the headphones off and suggested that I download it on my computer later so that we could watch together at some other time.

Subsequently, Lucy told me that she herself had two recurring dreams. In one of the dreams, she is beneath a pile of clothes that has built up and is weighing her down. In another, she is in her home neighborhood where animals (such as alligators) are being let loose on the streets. People are on the rooftops, trying to stay safe. In the course of discussing her dreams, Lucy recalled a story she was told about her mother taking her, as a very young child, to the basement apartment of a boyfriend, where there were live alligators and other animals crawling around. She did not think she had her own memories of this incident, nor was she even sure the story was true. Like much of what her father and paternal grandparents had told her about her mother, this tale had always been somewhat mysterious and puzzling to Lucy. I wondered aloud about Lucy's reaction to my speaking with her mother, noting that perhaps I should have asked her permission before doing so.

Lucy responded that she didn't care—that I had contacted her mother, or about her mother at all. She then quickly acknowledged, "Well, okay, I do care about her."

She went on to describe a number line, with +20 at one end, and -20 at the other. She said that her feelings for her mother fell at neither end of the number line, but rather right at "zero," indicating no feeling in either direction.

I said she had a really interesting way of putting it, but wondered if maybe her feelings were not exactly the average of the two "twenties" but actually both extremes: the positive AND the negative—and maybe even every number in between.

Lucy agreed that this was probably the case. She recalled that she had scary memories in her head about her mother—both memories of her own, and things she had been told. She thought she remembered the boyfriend with a "zoo" in his basement, where her mother gave her a snake to hold, and that there was an alligator. She also recalled that her mother took her to get her ears pierced when she was only two.

Lucy said that she probably missed her mother at first, when she was five or so, but that by the time she was seven, she had thrown her feelings [about her mother] "in the trash." She continued that there is no point in having dreams if you can't make them happen. She went on to talk about not fitting in at her new school, feeling that she has a few acquaintances but no real friends. She added that sometimes she wants to shout at the other kids and tell them about what she is going through.

After a while she mused that she could not be sure about the circumstances surrounding her mother's departure. She remembered her [paternal] grandparents telling her that they begged her mother to stay, offered her material incentives, like jewelry, but she wouldn't stay.

A month after Lucy began therapy, her mother visited her for the first time, under the supervision of Lucy's social worker. A month later, she returned and took Lucy out for dinner and a brief shopping excursion. They began to correspond through e-mail and instant messaging. Her mother explained to Lucy that she was living with her new husband and their one-year-old son. She had finished college and was working as a hospital nurse.

During this time it was also becoming distinctly apparent that Lucy's father would not be seeking her return to his home. Not only had he stopped attending visits, he was also moving to prevent Lucy's brother from seeing her. State law mandated regular visits between separated siblings; on one occasion, Lucy's father dropped Lucy's brother off for a visit but chose not to enter the office himself. Lucy was horrified to learn from her brother that their father was telling him that Lucy was a bad influence on him and a destructive force within their family. Lucy perceived—I believe accurately—that her brother was terribly torn between his love for Lucy and his love for and dependence on their father. Lucy seemed to grasp intuitively that her brother was in an untenable psychological position in which he could not afford to question their father's position. Lucy felt that her brother, too, was now slipping away from her. In fact, she would see him only a handful of times after this visit. Meanwhile, Lucy's mother was actively working with Lucy's social worker and consulting mental health professionals in her home state about how she might approach reunification, including plans for Lucy to eventually join her and her husband in their home.

In the coming months, Lucy had several visits of increasing length with her mother, at first near Lucy's foster home, and later through travel to her mother's home. By spring it was clear that Lucy might very well move to live with her mother permanently, though Lucy never initiated discussion of this possibility with me. I received updates through Lucy's attorney or caseworker that plans were moving in that direction, and then introduced the issue into our conversations. On numerous occasions, the other professionals involved with Lucy asked whether I could ascertain whether Lucy in fact wished to move in with her mother. The best answer I could provide was that I did not believe Lucy could really know what she wanted, but that she was not objecting to the prospect and, frankly, she did not feel she had a better option. While her foster placement was positive and stable in many ways—and many of us had the impression that her foster parents might well have considered adopting her—Lucy was clear she did not consider it a permanent option. She felt that in many respects, there was nothing worse than being a "foster child."

At this point, Lucy's father, who had attended several social worker-supervised visits in the previous months, started canceling weekly visits. He often did so at the very last minute, offering vague excuses as to why he could not get to the social services office that day. He also expressed little, if any interest in Lucy's well being, often taking a long time to return the caseworker's phone calls. Lucy's caseworker, attorney, and I agreed that Lucy would not be told about visits very far in advance because her father seemed so likely to cancel. I was alarmed and deeply troubled by this development. Lucy had already been abandoned by her mother at a very young age; so her father seemed, at that moment, like her only option. Despite my own intense reactions, which were echoed and underscored by the members of my consultation group, I felt I had to remain invested in the possibility that her father might be able to take Lucy back. Lucy had only been out of the home for six months. Understandably, she routinely expressed her assumption that she would return to her father's home, her brother, her friends, and her middle school. What made this predicament especially wrenching to witness was the degree to which Lucy perpetually blamed herself for the deterioration in her family situation; the adults in her family had repeatedly told her that she was bad, mentally ill, and toxic. They took no responsibility for their role in Lucy's necessary removal from their home—and in fact, never would.

One day, when I greeted Lucy at the start of our session, I was surprised to find her accompanied by her lawyer, Nancy, whom I'd never met in person. Apparently, she had driven Lucy to my office. Lucy and Nancy had stopped at a bookstore during the drive to my office, where Nancy had bought Lucy a manga book. In front of Lucy, Nancy said that they were supposed to meet at her office, but Lucy's father had cancelled the visit.

Nancy let me know that Lucy's foster mother would pick her up at the end of the session. When Lucy and I sat down in my office moments later, Lucy began bouncing back and forth, pushing her body against the back of the chair.

When I asked Lucy how she was feeling, she replied that she was fine, but kind of "hyper." I wondered if she had any particular feelings about her dad canceling. I suggested that it might be upsetting.

Lucy replied that she didn't care, that she was expecting it. Again, I wondered if it might still be upsetting, maybe. She responded that she got really stressed out and then when she found out he wasn't coming, felt like it was just a waste to get nervous in the first place.

I sympathized that it was hard, because she wasn't always sure she wanted to see her dad, but it could still hurt her feelings that he can't get his act together to follow through with the visit.

Lucy went on, as she often did, to update me on the happenings of her school day. She had been chosen to be a helper at the parent-teacher conference night that evening. She was troubled that a boy at school had grabbed her papers and books, thrown them all over hallway, and laughed. We laughed together as we shared ideas about our favored tactics for revenge on her classmate.

She offered that she would get yelled at for having violent thoughts in her father's home. I added that she still feels critical of herself for even entertaining those kinds of thoughts. Lucy added that sometimes it seems like there are two of her: a "devil Lucy," and an "angel Lucy."

Eventually, Lucy was able to talk about her getting "hyper" as a way to avoid feeling sad. She also discussed—as she would many times over the course of the year—her deeply held conviction that there must be something wrong, something devil-like about her; otherwise why would her father seem to hate her so much?

Meanwhile, foster placement was quite successful in numerous respects. Her foster parents treated Lucy as cherished member of their family. She was the only child in the home and their attention focused on her adjustment to their home, her new school, and the community. They faithfully delivered her to weekly appointments with me and were conscientious about keeping me apprised of developments at home or school. As was the case on the inpatient psychiatric unit, Lucy did not demonstrate aggression, tantrums, or any unusual eating behavior in her foster home. At school she was a compliant and pleasant, if somewhat isolated and anxious student. A somewhat "quirky" teenager with her avid interest in Japanese anime, Lucy was out-of-place in the conventional, somewhat parochial public middle school in her new community. She felt like an outcast as a new seventh grader but, most of all, as a self-described "foster child." When a new friend impulsively revealed Lucy's status to a group of classmates, Lucy felt betrayed and ashamed. While she found her foster parents supportive, benign, and relatively stable, the very notion of being in foster care remained quite devastating to her.

As much as her mental status had improved since her removal from her father's home, Lucy longed to return to the family and to the home she knew. Though she acknowledged she had been mistreated at home, Lucy routinely minimized the effects. Because there had been little physical violence—but rather deprivation, neglect, and psychological manipulation—it was perhaps easier for Lucy to underestimate the gravity of her family situation than if she had been assaulted and/or injured. For the same reasons, she frequently blamed herself for the fact that she had been mistreated and supposed that if only she had behaved differently "none of this would have happened." Lucy also expressed significant regret that she had confided in the staff at the psychiatric hospital, as her revelations to them had been the impetus for her eventual removal from home and placement in foster care. At this time Lucy did not talk about missing her father or his girlfriend. It was never clear to me whether she was protecting herself from their rejection by avoiding her feelings of loss, or whether her attachment to them was not that deep. However, Lucy often talked about missing her brother a great deal and worried about how her brother was faring without her.

Eight months into our work together, there was a dramatic disruption in Lucy's foster placement. The "honeymoon" period ended abruptly and Lucy's attitude and behavior toward her foster parents transformed into what in retrospect appeared to be a repetition or "enactment" of the trauma she had endured within her family of origin (Huber & Whiting, 2007). Lucy had been placed in this foster home for almost a year. During this time, Lucy had started a new school, virtually lost contact with her father and brother, and reconnected with her biological mother. During the weeks just prior to this disruption, Lucy learned through her attorney and social worker that her father planned to relinquish his parental rights, meaning that Lucy would never return to his home. Around the same time, she also learned of the prospect of longer-term placement with her biological mother. By then, Lucy had visited with her mother several times under the caseworker's supervision and was anticipating traveling to her mother's home for the first time to spend part of the upcoming school vacation with her mother, her husband, and their one-year-old child. Up to this point, Lucy's stance toward her foster parents had been one of quiet, tentative acquiescence. At times, Lucy's agreeable, complacent attitude had puzzled and frustrated her foster parents, who wanted very much to know what *she* wanted, but often found that she was reluctant to tell them even when asked directly.

Between sessions, Lucy's foster mother contacted me to report that Lucy had spoken with one of her social workers the previous week about how she feels nothing is hers. She told the social worker that she believes her foster father "owns" her and "can do whatever he wants with [her]." She also voiced concern that if she were to go to live with her biological mother, she might not be able to take her cat, purchased for her several months before by the foster parents, with her, which would represent a major loss. A few days later, the foster parents received word from Lucy's caseworker that a "mandated reporter" had filed a child abuse report, indicating that the foster parents were feeding Lucy nothing but junk food and sometimes withholding food from her altogether. Lucy also complained to the mandated reporter (later revealed to be a teacher) that her foster mother was sometimes late picking her up from the school bus stop. The foster parents learned that a social worker would be visiting their home to investigate this claim. At the same time, Lucy had begun to vacillate between retreating into her bedroom and issuing threats to her foster father. She said that if he was mean to her cat while she was out of town visiting her mother, she would report it to her caseworker. When, following a minor disagreement, Lucy's foster mother began to walk out of the store where they were shopping, Lucy threatened to call her caseworker if her foster mother did not come back inside immediately.

This scenario was reminiscent of several themes within Lucy's family of origin. Taking into account both the early history—her mother leaving when Lucy was four, never to be heard from again—and the more recent history/immediate context in which Lucy was removed from her father's home following her revelation of their mistreatment of her, I was aware of the repetition of certain questions and dynamics, including—what and who do we believe? Who is/are the victim(s)? Who is/are the perpetrator(s)? Lucy's behavior also seemed to serve at least two functions—to threaten and dominate the foster parents and, if "successful" and taken to logical conclusion of her removal from their home, to ultimately deprive her of their care and support. One might construe her behavior as a loyalty "test"—would her foster parents reject her like each of her biological parents had? Was she truly "bad" and therefore unlovable? Yet, Lucy's behavior was far beyond her conscious awareness or control.

In response to e-mail messages from the foster parents regarding these escalations, I called the foster mother's cell phone and left a message suggesting that we speak. Somehow, she never received my message. The following day, I received an upsetting e-mail message stating, "We were really surprised by your recent silence with us. We usually hear right back from you. Lucy continues to threaten us and act out. We are dealing with it day by day. Let me know when we can call you. Thank you." My emotional reaction to the e-mail was to wonder immediately what I had done wrong. I felt not only accused, but also momentarily quite guilty—as if I had in actuality responded to their pleas for help with silence and indifference. Only when the situation resolved a few days later was I able to reflect on the fact that the silence, withdrawal, and profound misunderstanding Lucy had experienced both with her mother's departure early in her childhood and her father's recent abandonment might be reflected in the foster parents' momentary experience of me. In this instance, parallel interpersonal dynamics and emotions seemed to occur on multiple levels simultaneously—between child and foster parents; between child, foster parents, and child protection agencies; and between foster parents and me.

I wrote back to the foster parents immediately and we arranged to confer over the telephone the next day. Before the time we were scheduled to talk, Lucy's foster mother reported to me via e-mail that the foster care agency supervisor had contacted her husband: "Although it is still up in the air, they spoke to him about the strong possibility of a new placement for Lucy. My gut feeling, knowing [the agency], is that they are just trying to ease us into it." When we finally spoke, I learned that, though exasperated and confused, the foster parents very much wished to keep Lucy in their home. They were frightened of the possibility that the agency would remove her, despite the fact that, of course, the investigator planned to dismiss the complaints against them as totally unfounded. Apparently the agency felt the foster placement had become "toxic" and thus no longer viable. I explained to Lucy's foster parents that clearly the "honeymoon" had ended and that they were now seeing Lucy's natural, inevitable reactions to the maltreatment and loss she had endured at the hands of her biological parents. The foster parents were exceptionally quick to entertain—and accept—the notion that Lucy was displacing her anger at and mistrust of her own parents onto them. They even entertained my suggestion that this turn of events might represent a form of psychological progress, in that Lucy was now comfortable enough in their home to show her true feelings and more of her real self.

The following morning, the foster parents affirmed with Lucy's caseworker that they wished very strongly to keep Lucy in their home. They sent me the following e-mail message: "Just wanted to thank you for the conversation . . . it puts things into perspective for us. We now agree that we have to be more compassionate with Lucy. We've just been so weary from all of this and in self-preservation mode. We bought Lucy a nice travel bag with lots of girly products for her trip [to visit her mother], which we know she will love. She thanked us for it, but hasn't opened it yet. I told her caseworker that I'm feeling a bit renewed and ready to take on the rest of the week, and whatever happens with Lucy. Lucy has come out of her room and is doing some talking and playing with the animals. It is so good to see." Once Lucy's foster parents spoke with the caseworker, the agency immediately reversed course and determined that Lucy would remain in her foster home. Lucy seemed relieved at this decision. She stopped most of her challenging, antagonistic behavior toward her foster parents She also began talking more routinely and contentedly about her daily life with them; for example, anticipating relaxing activities like watching movies together, or visiting her foster father's nearby relatives.

In the ensuing months, Lucy's team of social service professionals, as well as her attorney and I, collaborated in evaluating whether her biological mother might be awarded custody of Lucy. In my consultation group, we debated the psychological, moral and existential questions the placement dilemma raised. My consultation group members leaned in the direction of wanting Lucy to remain with her foster parents, who had already demonstrated their commitment, stability, and capacity for providing for Lucy's basic needs. Lucy's social worker was inclined to place Lucy with her mother, even though it would require and out-of-state move and even though the two had been out of contact for almost ten years prior to their recent reunion. Lucy herself seemed afraid to express a preference or a wish. Or perhaps she simply could not begin to contemplate making such a complex decision about her own life. There were no clear answers, no guarantees. Ultimately, the social service agency and the court agreed that Lucy would move to her mother's home. Lucy's father had already agreed to relinquish his parental rights in exchange for not being prosecuted for child neglect. And Lucy's foster parents, while reluctant to see her go, understood and supported this decision.

When Lucy's mother arrived in town to fly back home with her, she came to my office for a separate appointment while Lucy was in school. The woman before me was still very young, but presumably much more mature and self-possessed than she had been almost ten years before. I found myself asking her the question that Lucy, and I, and perhaps every person who had heard Lucy's story, wanted to ask about how and why she left her young children: "What happened?" The story Lucy's mother told me put some of the memories and mysteries in context, or at least into perspective. She had been a very young mother whose life deteriorated pretty quickly after Lucy and her brother were born. She stated that she and Lucy's father separated when Lucy was about three, a year later than reported by Lucy's father, and initially shared custody of the children. Shortly thereafter, uneducated and without psychosocial support, she decided to move to another state where she could live with extended family and attend college. Though she left her children, she had a plan to return. She sent letters and gifts to them and called regularly on the telephone. Gradually, Lucy's father started limiting the length of the phone calls and eventually, avoiding the calls altogether. When Lucy was about six, her mother received a letter, apparently from the father's attorney, informing her that because she had abandoned her parental duties, her parental rights were being terminated. She perceived this letter to be fact. Lucy's mother did not give a clear explanation, in our single meeting, of why she did not pursue her children after that point. When she was contacted by Lucy's caseworker—when Lucy was placed in foster care—she responded immediately and began to work toward reunification. By this time, she had earned a nursing degree, was employed at a hospital, and was remarried with an infant son. At present, there would be no perfect answers and no guarantees about the future—only a second chance for both of them.

Lucy and I have stayed in touch sporadically since she moved over one year ago. Her mother arranged for Lucy to receive mental health services in their community, but it has been difficult for them to find a consistently available provider, in large part because of the small town in which they live. Lucy and I have sent occasional e-mail messages back and forth and talked over the phone a couple of times. I learned a few months after she left that Lucy's mother and her husband had separated. Lucy wondered in the course of our telephone conversation whether she had been the cause—whether the strain of her presence in the household had led her mother's husband to move out. I knew from my meeting with Lucy's mother that the marital problems predated Lucy's arrival, so I felt comfortable assuring her that I was confident it was not her fault.

Lucy sent me a text message recently. She was briefly back in my geographic area visiting extended family. Her message indicated that her relatives were getting on her nerves. She asked whether we could check in. I texted back, offering to meet in person if she could get to my office or to talk on the telephone if she could not. Not unlike other teenagers who reach out in a moment of need and then drop out of sight once the moment has passed, Lucy never actually took me up on either offer. However, she did text me back: "omg . . . u r the best."

Over the course of my year long relationship with Lucy, I witnessed her wholly unconscious re-creation of crucial elements of her original family trauma within her foster family. Recognizing the powerful forces that can propel traumatized children not only to take on the roles of perpetrator and victim (sometimes simultaneously), but to draw the adults within their social system into this drama, I was able to use my internal experience as participant-observer in Lucy's complex network of adult figures to understand some of her behavior. I routinely drew upon the strength and wisdom of my consultation group to remain focused and committed to the task at hand—supporting Lucy as well as the various players in her system, while allowing her to grieve her tremendous losses and accept opportunities to move forward. I learned that when I felt overwhelmed, helpless, or emotionally disconnected, I was feeling and expressing a small reflection of what Lucy must be feeling. I utilized the interpretation of Lucy's unconscious motives with her (psychologically minded and well-trained) foster parents, as well with her social worker, attorney, and the broader child protection system. In response, the various players, most dramatically and crucially the foster parents, were able to move away from reaction and toward reflection and containment. I believe that the foster parents' immediate response to psychological interpretation was what ultimately preserved Lucy's foster placement.

In addition to sharing Lucy's story, I intended this chapter to underscore two major issues: (1) the role of unconscious forces, and the power of repetition, among traumatized children; and, (2) the clinical significance of my alliance with Lucy's foster parents—as well as with social service, legal professionals, and Lucy's biological mother—during the course of therapy. I believe the therapist's role within complex foster care systems is a unique one—not just as an individual mental health provider for the child, but also as an essential player. In particular, the psychotherapist who appreciates how traumatized children tend to play out their internalized role as bad or unwanted in their *new* families or environments—even those that are most benign—can become the interpreter/translator of the meaning behind the child's negative, rejecting, or destructive behavior. In this way, the therapist can help prevent re-traumatization through the child's destruction of otherwise "good" foster placements—an all too common occurrence in foster care (Heineman, 2007). In this way, the therapist contributes to and contains the child's support network based on her unique and intimate knowledge of the child's mind.

NOTE

1. Lucy's foster parents had received specialized training that designated their home an appropriate placement for children with identified mental health needs. They had previously cared for several other foster children, though there were no other children in their home during Lucy's stay with them.

REFERENCES

Heineman, T. V. (2007). Weaving without a Loom: Creating a self in foster care. *Fort Da, 13*(1), 55–68.

Huber, P. T., & Whiting, J. B. (2007). Supporting the work of foster parents. In R. E. Lee & J. B. Whiting (Eds.), *Foster care therapist handbook* (pp. 293–306). Arlington, VA: Child Welfare League of America.

Kishimoto, M. (1999). *Naruto*. Atlanta: Cartoon Network.

Chapter Six

Michael

In this chapter I would like to consider two particular features inherent to many therapies and yet distinctly unique in my work with a foster-adopt child. One feature is that of the therapist learning from and growing with the patient. Not often talked about, I find this is true of almost all therapeutic relationships; if I am not learning from my patient the chances are good that therapy is stalled, we are at an impasse and good therapy is not happening. Just knowing this gives me an important insight with which to reinvigorate the work: I can be curious about what I have yet to learn from my patient. While the introspective capacity of the therapist, along with empathy, are always key components to an effective therapeutic stance, this is especially true when working with children.

The second aspect I would like to address is one fundamental to working with victims of trauma; that is, the therapeutic value of learning from the relationship with the therapist what healthy relationships can bear that previous ones have not. Nowhere is this more true than in doing therapy with children from the foster care system. When bad things—abuse, loss, neglect—happen to children, they learn that they are essentially bad. Believing they are bad, worthless and chronically in danger, they develop coping strategies—defenses—that, while adaptive to their dysfunctional environment, are not useful once the children are removed from their unhealthy circumstances. Yet these defenses persist. Traumatized children may respond in ways that are contrary, provocative, and sometimes incomprehensible to those around them who are trying to help. A relationship that does not replicate the earlier, soul-damaging experiences of their childhood can be a revelation, one with a healing potential that is realized in small increments over time (Shengold, 1999). The therapeutic relationship must be one that allows for testing, for mistakes on both sides. In my work with a young boy from the foster care system our relationship has grown from the early testing, show-me phase to one where we are just now reaching deeper into his core beliefs about himself and the internal world that developed out of his early traumatic memories.

BEGINNING THE THIRD YEAR

On Tuesday afternoons at four, my office is brightened by the presence of an energetic nine-year-old. He always comes running up the stairs, often with something in hand—a drawing, some homework, a book, or the imaginary leash to an imaginary dog. What follows is a special time for us both: for that hour of the week we engage in play therapy. There are toys, art materials, music, games. Sometimes we make tea together, water the plants, build spaces with my couch cushions. We talk and we listen. As all my other patients are adult individuals or couples, having a child enter my fairly traditional practice transforms the space with a certain liveliness and energy, even on his most somber days.

The youngest of five children by four different fathers, Michael had already experienced severe neglect and exposure to dangerous and age-inappropriate situations when he was removed, at age three, from his grandmother's "care." His mother was an addict; the identity of his father was unknown. He and his birth siblings were all serially removed from the mother at birth and placed with the grandmother and her fourth husband. The grandmother herself was ill-equipped to be a parent. The house was filthy, the children were unsupervised, and reports indicated that they suffered "severe neglect." In addition to being the youngest, Michael had physical limitations (leg braces and glasses) which left him vulnerable to a troubled and abusive older brother. At the beginning of therapy, Michael was very articulate in telling me who he was and where he came from, which is a familiar part of the testing, can-you-deal-with-this phase. One of many stories he told me was of being squashed under a huge dresser that his older brothers had pushed over on him, resulting in him having to go to the hospital. There was a history of similar hurts and because some of the children still remained with the grandmother, contact with much of his biological family was limited to once or twice a year.

Michael's "forever family" is a loving two-parent family that includes his two older siblings closest to him in age, to whom he clung for safety during the ordeal of his earliest years. Although he has been with his adoptive family for nearly six years, settling into a safe, loving, and predictable household was, according to his parents, a challenge. During his first year in treatment with me, when he was seven, I was easily charmed by the uncomplicated enthusiasm that Michael showed for the activities, games and rituals we performed during the hour. These activities formed—and continue to form—the structure for our interaction in the therapy. The honest disappointment he sometimes expressed at the limitations of our play felt so normal. He was very accepting of my role in his life and his vulnerability in sharing his experiences with me was quite moving. However, I also realized that the behavior he displayed, both in the hour and outside the hour, was far more complex. It was a communication about his experience in and of the world that needed to be deconstructed to be fully understood and appreciated by his adult caregivers. The appropriateness of Michael's play in the hour belied the frequent oppositional and aggressive behavior expressed at school that sometimes resulted in his being sent home for the day. While that behavior wasn't evident in my consulting room—at least at first glance—there were subtler clues to his inner experience, some of them discovered in my own self-reflection.

As a therapist new to working with children, the concept of the family romance (Frosch, 1959) has been an integral part of my learning experience with Michael. I have struggled to resist being seduced by it—the fantasized ideal in which the child is transformed by the new, healthy family, by therapy and by time and no longer suffers from the traumas of his early experience. Heineman (1999) writes about the tension between the conscious notions of the possibility of change and the unconscious fantasies of transformation. The real limitations to a child's ability to transcend horrific abuse, for example, are painful to confront, especially for hopeful parents and therapists. So the idealization of the child serves to minimize their problem behavior and restore hope in the caregivers. Furthermore, the romanticization of the wounded or orphaned child provides plenty of fuel for such fantasies.

Because Michael has been with his adoptive family for a number of years and is no longer experiencing the instability common to many children in foster care, it is sometimes tempting simply to see him as mostly recovered from the traumatic first three years of his life. However, I have noticed that his efforts to contain his "bad" behavior (self) have been most pronounced and successful at home or in relation to important adult caregiver figures, of which I was perhaps one. When he is out in the world, with peers or adults with whom he is not as close, including school authority figures, he has been more likely to give free rein to these "bad" impulses. Relating this to my experience with my own children, who were generally well-behaved in public and saved their acting out for home where they felt unconditionally safe to do so, I wondered whether Michael's need to secure his relationship with his new, better parents (and other significant adults connected to them) far outweighed his need to cultivate other relationships, peers or adults, outside the home environment. In contrast to less traumatized children, the venue for Michael's struggle between the freedom to "be bad" and the need to "be good" lay outside the home. One reason his parents bring him faithfully to weekly therapy is their hope and belief that therapy may prevent or mitigate future psychological symptoms related to his early traumatic history. The ability to hold both possibilities—of strength and vulnerability, successful transcendence of a traumatic early childhood and avoidance of potential lifelong wounds—is a challenge for both of us.

While I am often tempted by Michael's happy countenance in the therapy hour to believe that he is more healed from the early childhood trauma than he probably is, it is important that I, and all his adults, remember that this play is his work and that what we do in the hour has a very serious dimension to it. At times, this entails differentiating between developmentally "normal" child behavior and the dysfunctional behavior that we know to be rooted in trauma.

SPOT JOINS THE FAMILY

About a year into our therapy, Michael's parents decided to try getting a dog again. An earlier pet was returned when it became clear the children were not ready to take care of it, but now they had earned the chance to try again. Shortly after a little dog joined the family, the parents contacted me, concerned that Michael was treating the dog in ways that disturbed them, but were only able to describe it as "too rough" or "too controlling" and sometimes it "felt sneaky." It was impossible for me to tell what was actually happening between Michael and the dog so I didn't know whether the parents' anxiety was warranted or whether their expectations of how an eight-year-old might treat a pet were too high. Michael was thrilled with Spot and wanted to show him to me, so I invited him to bring the dog with him to a session. Even as Michael told me, as he had been told, what the right way to treat the dog was, I saw him twisting Spot's legs into uncomfortable positions, pulling his fur and ears back tightly from his face and sitting almost on top of him. The small dog, though remarkably patient, was frantic to escape Michael and, of course, the more he tried to do so, the more Michael latched onto him. It was clear to me that Michael's behavior with the dog was not appropriate; in fact, he had no empathy for the animal, despite many demonstrations and directions by his parents, and his treatment of Spot was cruel. I was relieved that the session ended before anyone was bitten. There was clearly more work to be done here—without the dog; Michael's treatment of Spot was more than just child's play.

Raising children who may be seen as "damaged goods" brings its own stress and toll to the parent/child relationship, therefore adjunctive sessions with the parents of foster-adopt children can often be helpful to the family (Miall, 1996; Wegar, 2000). Periodically I have met with Michael's parents or consulted with them by phone. They have actively shared their problems, concerns, and successes with me and working collaboratively with them has been invaluable to me in helping to uncover the unconscious messages in Michael's play. His parents report that his behavior is mostly developmentally appropriate and they seem to manage his "misbehavior" with gentle but firm guidance toward a more socially appropriate response to a given situation. By being an educative resource to Michael's parents and providing periodic reality checks for their parental concerns, I have encouraged that cooperative relationship.

However, because Michael's world outside his home and therapy is often focused on whether his behavior is good or bad, appropriate or inappropriate to a given environment, it is important that there be a place where the unique meaning in his behavior is understood. Without understanding caregivers and/or the safety of the therapy room, it is too easy for these children, who are striving mightily to learn new coping skills for their changing environments, to interpret all the efforts to help them as further evidence of their inherent "badness."

During our earliest sessions, Michael would frequently interrupt our play and conversations, by going to the windows and looking out, raising and lowering the blinds, and even attempting to open the windows and call to people on the street until, being on the upper floor of a building, I put a stop to it. As innocuous as the behavior seems now, at the time I had a strong reaction to it. At times it felt provocative or evasive or even rejecting of me and of the therapy. But rather than thinking with Michael about the meaning of his behavior, which is what I would normally do, I found myself doubting my ability to work with him, perhaps with children in general. I thought coming to therapy must be "boring" for him or, in fact, there was nothing here to explore. Given his history, though, that did not seem possible. Instead I opted to feel something lacking in my skill and abilities. He understood and abided by the limits set on the basis of safety, but the windows and blinds still held a fascination for him. As with his treatment of Spot, this behavior seemed to be telling us something, perhaps about early experiences or feelings engendered by them. At the same time, his behavior was really not outside the range of what would be considered normal for a seven-year-old—except that it made *me* feel anxious and distressed. It was a challenge to think about what this might mean!

Similar feelings, sometimes referred to as countertransference feelings, were also evoked in me by other ways that Michael often controlled the hour. He comes to see me right after school, a time when anxiety and distress would normally be at their highest, so over time we developed a soothing ritual of going to the kitchen to make tea or get water and an apple and taking it back to my office. There he often set up a little table with a lapboard and footstool. Sometimes he had a snack that his mother had sent with him. I have a basket of toys and stack of games in a closet outside my door and a box of art supplies in my office. In our first session he came with his own bag of show-and-tell items (a broken doll, a boom box, a dollhouse and furniture) that, except for the doll, which was his, went back home with him as it turns out they belonged to his sister. Beyond showing me who he was, bringing his own toys might have said something about his lack of expectation of them being provided for him. I imagined in his earliest experience in a chaotic household with many siblings that, like people, material things were transient objects in his life and what he didn't hold onto was often lost. He also asked me a question that I imagine many children, but perhaps especially these children, ask, "Do other children play with these, too?" In fact, Michael and his siblings, who each had therapists of their own, were quite curious about each other's therapists and therapy offices. His sisters made excuses to come upstairs and peek into my office when they came to get Michael at the end of his session. Possessions, like people, could come and go, and when you found a good one you had to hang on tight! Eventually he went through all my toys and board games, finding little there that held his interest.

In the second year of therapy, as we came to the end of the board games, Michael dispensed with the rules, telling me what to do with my pieces and when the game would be over. Reading books, he would direct me to read only certain portions. Playing with the blinds, he would keep one eye on me to see just how much I would allow. His favorite way to take charge or redirect our play was to turn on a little portable radio just loud enough that we couldn't continue talking. At one point, as I played the obedient pupil to his exacting master, he said to me "Am I being too hard on you?" This uncharacteristically empathic response reminded me of a child reaching up to pat a tired mommy's face. This led to my thinking about all the pressures (not necessarily unique to him or to foster children in general) he adapts to in order to win the acceptance and approval of the adults in his world. Of course, this led me back to thinking about the way the world had been so arbitrarily hard on him! And he, in turn, on Spot.

One thing that consistently held (and continues to hold) Michael's interest is my portable radio, on which he finds the latest in pop music to which he begins dancing and lip-syncing. When he does this, as if he's been holding back (being good?) for a while, I am relegated to simply watching his performance. In these sessions, being assigned the role of the audience was another instance that evoked strong feelings in me of being manipulated or constrained by him. From what I heard from his parents and his school, many of the conflicts Michael had with siblings or peers had to do with his efforts to force others to do what he wanted them to do. Once he was sad and puzzled to learn that the parents of a younger best friend were removing him from the school, primarily because of Michael's attempts to physically control him. It sounded very much like his sitting on the dog! It seemed likely that Michael's friends felt just as I did when his need to control the play space left little room for real relatedness. What a dilemma for him! When he turns on the radio and begins dancing, often at the end of the hour, I am overwhelmed by his need for me to just watch him and I have had to consider what this feeling of impotence says about Michael and his growing awareness of himself in a world of others.

PLAY DEVELOPS INTO MEANINGFUL WORK

Entering our third year of therapy, Michael is now a smart, curious, and outgoing nine-year-old boy. He has demonstrated a strong leadership capacity with his peers, but this can sometimes border on bullying behavior, often of younger, smaller children. Michael has a flare for the dramatic and theatrical, creating plays and directing (sometimes seen as bossing) the actors he recruits to be in them. In an attempt to channel this talent into a positive experience, Michael's parents arranged for him to audition for a summer stock theater production of Medea, a serious Greek tragedy. Michael won the part of one of the two sons who are murdered by their mother, Medea, in revenge for their father's unfaithfulness and betrayal of her. Michael was delighted and rose to the challenge, studiously learning his lines and attending numerous rehearsals and, for the most part, following the rules of the adult theater world.

The story of Medea, an ancient Greek myth, as retold in the play by Euripides, is a powerful drama with adult themes—betrayal in many forms, revenge and murder. Medea was the sorceress daughter of the King of Colchis, home of the Golden Fleece. When Jason and the Argonauts came looking for the magic fleece, Medea, seduced by Jason, betrayed her family and country by giving Jason the charms and spells that would enable him to steal the fleece. Returning with Jason to Greece as an exile, she bore Jason twin sons, but Jason, seeking to further enlarge his kingdom, fell in love with and decided to marry the daughter of the king of another kingdom. In the final terrifying scene of the play, when Medea learns of Jason's plan, realizing she can't go back to her country, she kills her rival by sending her a poisoned gift and then she kills her—and Jason's—two sons. Although the parents and the director took steps to shield the children from the true, adult meaning of the play, I wondered how Michael, sitting back stage night after night, could fail to grasp at least something of the cruelty and selfishness of the father and the psychotic rage and destructiveness of the mother, who loves her children but hates their father more. While the killing of the two boys is done off-stage, Michael gleefully pointed out to me that it was his recorded scream that the audience hears at the end. Being acquainted with the powerfulness of this play, I had thoughts that if I were Michael's parent I might not have encouraged his involvement in this particular production. This led me to think of other reasons why acting might be a problematic activity for many children, perhaps to some degree all children. The deliberate blurring of the boundaries between reality and fantasy, while stimulating and affecting to adults, could have unintended consequences for children. They are at a stage in their lives where they are disentangling the two, reality and fantasy, particularly with regard to the formation of a sense of self, as well as the concepts of good and evil.

As opening night of the play approached, Michael's parents called me in distress, reporting that he was acting out at rehearsals and not following the director's instructions, specifically by stepping out of character and playing to the audience, drawing attention to himself and away from the main adult actors. Of course the director would not let him jeopardize the performance and gave him one chance to follow directions or be dismissed from his role. His parents did not want him to fail, but they could not seem to help him or figure out why he found it difficult to just follow the rules. At this point they had no leverage with him—it was between Michael and the director whether he remained in the play or was replaced. In my conversations with his parents, I found my task was that of trying to alleviate their anxiety about whether he would be able to make the right choices (follow the rules, take direction) and helping them accept that Michael might already know what the "right" choice would be for him. I was keenly aware that many things could be going on here—Michael's emotional need to "steal the scene" might overwhelm his desire to be a good (obedient) actor, acting might or might not be what he was most passionate about after all, and finally, I wondered how much of the symbolic action of this particularly horrific play was seeping into Michael's young consciousness.

Right before the play opened I received a call from Michael's mom saying that he'd had a "breakthrough." She asked whether she should tell me what it was and I said we could wait and see if he brought it up in our next session, and if not I would get back to her. This certainly sounded significant and as such I really wanted to hear it directly from Michael himself. His parents have been very respectful of the therapy relationship and have wanted to foster the notion that Michael can tell me, as well as them, anything, so as much as possible they—and I—avoid being the go-between. I was of course eager to hear what the breakthrough might be but Michael's mom and I wondered if he would remember or even think to tell me about it. The next few sessions Michael was tired, not talking about the play—he was going to summer school during the day and performing at night. Sometimes he even had to take naps! When I asked him how he felt about acting, he said he liked it, but not as much as he used to. "It's hard work!," he said. He didn't reveal what his "breakthrough" was and I began to wonder whether that might just have been his mother's characterization of it, his behavior having finally made sense to her.

But the play opened without further incident and it—and Michael's performance in it—was a success. Michael was able to sublimate his desire to be front and center and play the part he had been given. He was part of the theater company and had a wonderful (and wonderfully challenging) experience of being part of a team of actors that puts on the play. Michael was deservedly proud of himself and his parents were also. In addition, they were relieved to see he could control what they experienced as his willful, manipulative behavior and follow the rules. I wondered whether this could be attributed to his "breakthrough." Following up with the parents about it (for Michael moved quickly past his triumph and didn't clue me in on his epiphany), I found it to be a poignant one, one that allowed me to think of many instances where the same dynamics might be at play—in his life and in the lives of many foster and adopted children.

Michael's "breakthrough" related to a story he had told me at the beginning of therapy. This story was about a trip to a motel with all of his siblings and his grandmother and her boyfriend. As the youngest child in the family, there were a number of incidents where Michael was physically harmed, usually during unsupervised play. On this occasion at the motel all the children were allowed to play in the pool unsupervised. Michael, less than three years old and unable to swim, was left in the pool and began to sink. He was fortunately discovered and rescued without harm, but he has vivid memories of this "drowning" experience to this day and has had to work hard to overcome his fear of the water. As Michael was skating on the edge of being "fired" from the play for his scene-stealing behaviors, he reminded his mother of the near-drowning story and told her that having people see him made him feel safe.

The literal truth of Michael's observation was so obvious and one potentially shared by so many children with backgrounds of abandonment and loss. I began to look at the many ways, both in and out of sessions, that Michael had been saying just that—in order to feel safe I need to know that someone is watching me. I could see it in the "disrespect" he showed to the classroom teacher that often got him sent to the principal (someone he liked and trusted), and sometimes even sent home (where safety was a given). It was there in the leadership/bullying behavior he engaged in with his peers that cost him friendships in the long run but made him the daily center of (often-negative adult) attention on the playground. And, of course, the counterpart to my being commanded to watch him perform in our sessions was his need to be seen. There it was—having people see me makes me feel safe—his reality transformed by the creative process, in the performance of a child actor.

Michael has been in several plays and has invited me to attend each of them. I was able to attend two. Whether or not to see/observe Michael in this way, outside the consulting room and in a public place, was an issue that I thought a great deal about beforehand. I looked at his invitation to see his work as akin to his bringing in a toy or a drawing—albeit with more effort involved on my part. I was able to make arrangements with the parents to slip into and out of the productions with a minimum of identifying and socializing, to protect both the confidentiality of and intrusion on the work. Attending these performances also gave me some perspective on his parents' concerns about his behavior. In this sense it felt similar to the school team meeting I had attended, mostly as an observer, where I was able to assess the reality of a confusing school environment that Michael could not adequately explain to me. But most important, and borne out by Michael's response to me afterwards, I believe that my "watching" him perform contributed to his sense of trust that I was one of those caring sets of eyes that would hold him in safekeeping.

I think back to Michael's earlier window-checking and fiddling with the blinds and how, struggling with my own countertransference reactions, it was difficult to understand the precise meaning of his behavior. It did not seem like the anxious, fearful-of-abandonment response that insecurely attached children might display on being left in a strange new situation. And it did not seem like the willful, manipulative behavior his parents often described to me (although I could see where it felt like that). Then, after being reminded of his early near-drowning experience, I could see his strategy of maximizing the overall awareness, the number of eyes on him, some of which might actually care about his welfare. Over time Michael's window-checking has mostly diminished to a final check at the end of the hour to see if his mother is waiting for him in her car. Looking back, perhaps part of this behavior was related to anxiety about a new situation, a new relationship. He is certainly more familiar and comfortable with me now. But if my guess is correct, then it is also true that he can count on my full attention and that must alleviate his need to seek notice. Checking to see if his ride is outside at the end of the hour feels different than when it was a frequent interruption of our play.

Another challenge in working with a foster-adopt child is the transmission of such understandings of these hidden meanings in their behavior to the caregivers and others who encounter them (Lewis, 2011). It has been extremely helpful to the therapy that Michael's parents are very engaged with the social network surrounding all their children and proactively seek help for them. Working collaboratively, we are able to function as a team, learning from and responding to his special needs and creatively finding solutions for them out in the world. Ehrensaft (2006) refers to the 'parenting matrix' in her discussion of the many challenges therapists and parents face in working with youth from the foster care system. Therapists and parents can feel alternately buoyed by the sense that they may be "saving" this child and discouraged by the realization that there is no saving him from the experiences he has already suffered. Michael's parents have already let me know that they want me involved as a kind of insurance policy for the teen years (I refrained from any disclaimers!). I also know from Michael that his parents have expectations that he will make use of the therapy, presumably for his problems, and talk about his feelings. Early on, in my eagerness to help, I tried prompting him about his feelings, only to be told, "You're supposed to wait till I say I have feelings." Another teachable moment for me!

In addition to the home, there is the school environment, which presents its own set of challenges. Having attended one meeting there, I have some idea of the conflicting messages and offers of help that Michael may be getting throughout the day. At times it can feel like there are too many cooks stirring the pot, but the challenge of fostering resiliency and growth while containing the destructive elements of hopelessness and loss is one that needs all the help at hand. The fact that Michael has two adoptive parents who are receptive to obtaining all the help possible for their children and have engaged in their own therapy means that they are more able to be attuned to both the destructive and constructive elements in raising their adopted children.

In an early consultation with the parents they emphasized that for all their children (Michael and his two siblings), safety was a paramount concern. We took great care to make sure the therapy environment and transfer arrangements were safe and clear. The parents were and are actively involved in his academic and extracurricular activities, making sure that issues like playground safety are addressed, as well as being sensitive to obvious signs of emotional insecurity or distress. A reorganization of Michael's school the first year I knew him, due to political conflicts not related to the children, caused quite a bit of stress on Michael and his family, but throughout the ordeal the parents and I made sure to repeatedly remind him that the adults would work out a solution. Although these basic safeguards serve a reparative function in a foster child's development, the circumstances that activate them may actually reawaken old wounds. Measures to assure safety and rebuild trust often don't reach the depths of the scars borne by children whose early formative years were without a safe and secure home. For addressing those deeper traumas the uncovering work we do in therapy is indispensible for real and lasting healing.

MEANINGFUL WORK INFORMED BY PLAY

The growth I've experienced as a therapist in my work with Michael coincides with a developmental phase in my own life, that of mid-life reflection and re-evaluation of the priorities in life. When I first began practicing as a psychotherapist two decades ago I had very young children of my own and therefore made the decision to work only with adults. But revisiting this decision several years ago, I recalled that it was the work of Brazelton (1989), Ilg, and Ames (1955) at the Gesell Institute, Leach (2010), and others, whose sensitive portrayals of child development and healthy child/parent relationships were what drew me to the field of psychology in the first place. So deciding to see a child through A Home Within felt like a coming full circle, a return to something very basic and familiar.

The idea of "the familiar" is also one of the core concepts in my clinical work with adults and stems from the defensive dynamic described earlier (Miller, 1997). It is the idea that old-brain, automatic responses to a situation often represent a return to the familiar in the root sense of the word, "of the family." When a child learns through repeated experiences that her parents are unreliable, she may grow up to be an adult who finds it difficult to trust or rely on others. In the short term this strategy serves her in that it spares her constant disappointment and hurt, but as an adult she may have difficulty in relationships without knowing why. In the uncovering work I do with adults we often discover that what is second nature, most *familiar* (self-reliance and autonomy above all, for example) is now maladaptive behavior that doesn't serve or actively interferes with the individual's need for relatedness and connection. These familiar, automatic responses, perhaps a less clinical term than "defenses," to familiar fraught circumstances are maintained because even though they are not always successful they are at least less anxiety provoking than risking something entirely untried and new. In working with clients in my adult practice, the concept of familiarity has been a useful way of thinking and talking about what is not working and why it continues. For a child whose concept of family is an especially troubled or tenuous one, learning to trust and risk engaging fully with others is a complicated task.

A personal insight I've gained through my work with Michael has been the awareness of what has gone missing from the lives of many adults in my practice. The value of play—the medium through which children work through their trauma and conflicts—is almost a foreign concept to many adults who come to therapy in an effort to ease the pain in their everyday lives. The opportunity to engage in play therapy and thinking from a child's perspective in my work with Michael has renewed my awareness of how the basic components of play—creativity, imagination, humor—make an important contribution to the health and happiness of all individuals. While I have often used the metaphors of an adult patient's life to enhance our shared understanding of their life and its dilemmas, it has been a revelation to return to a more grounded, less intellectual approach as well. For a patient who is a sailor, sailing is not just a metaphor for getting through life smoothly, although it's interesting to think of it that way. It is also a very real passion, without which the meaning of her life is diminished. In talk therapy with adults, letting myself fall out of thinking metaphorically and into real engagement with whatever my patient brings to the work helps us enter that space of adult play together. I believe that is the place where connections are made and real transformation happens. At the same time, as efforts are made to get Michael to conform to the standards of behavior the adult world has set for him, it feels paradoxical to be dealing with the unhappiness of so many adults who have forgotten the value of play.

Many years before I joined A Home Within I had heard about the organization's work. "One child, one therapist, for as long as it takes" says it all. As a therapist with a psychodynamic background and training, the philosophy of A Home Within fit well with my theoretical knowledge and my clinical experience—even, or perhaps especially, as an adult-oriented practitioner. Attachment theory makes it only too clear how important those early relationships are—and how devastating the results of their failure. I was intrigued by the thought of being able to work with someone with whom I might have the chance to intervene earlier around such early traumas. The mission and the hope of A Home Within is that early therapeutic intervention has the potential to break the cycle of trauma and loss that these children often experience by providing at least one stable, empathic bond and thereby reduce some of the negative effects of having been shuffled through the foster care system. In working with A Home Within, I could at least make a difference with one child.

In the best volunteer organizations, the volunteer often gets as much or more out of the experience than those she or he helps; that has been my experience at A Home Within. Working with a child in therapy has deepened my work with adults by putting me in visceral touch with the childhood source of so much suffering. It has reminded me, as volunteer work often does, that what I have to offer can make a profound difference. It reminds me what parenting my own children taught me about the work involved in raising a healthy child and healing the wounds, major or minor, that inevitably occur. And it has again put me in touch with the value of knowing I have more yet to learn from even my youngest patient.

Every Tuesday, I leave my door open just before 4:00 p.m. in anticipation of something new about to enter my life—perhaps a challenging playmate problem or a school triumph or a youthful tiredness, silliness or longing. These are the easy days. His teacher is mean, Michael says. "She makes us follow the rules. (Pause.) Can I show you the hyenas again?" And he makes a pile with the couch cushions and literally throws himself into acting out a scene of roaring and rowdy animals from The Lion King. I am a welcome witness to the release of his "wild energy" as he blows off steam in an animal kingdom drama. Knowing there is such a dark history to his short life, I am relieved when his problems feel this manageable. On the days when more difficult issues arise, we both struggle with "bad" feelings and what they mean. Often these days coincide with some new conflict with his parents or sisters about the dog or homework or privileges or, less and less often, a tense and confusing visit with his birth family. When that happens he often becomes quiet and says he is sad, perhaps missing a brother or longing to see someone he knows he can't. My hope is that in knowing there are adults who understand and are there to help him bear the unbearable, that these losses and ruptures will not keep Michael from living a full and healthy life. By the following week he has often moved on and may even be able to tell me, in words supplied by his parents or that he and I have fashioned in the previous hour, how he has come to understand the dilemma.

REFERENCES

Brazelton, T. Berry (1989). *Infants and mothers: Differences in development.* New York: Dell Publishing.

Ehrensaft, D. (2006). Many parents, one child: Working with the family matrix. In T. V. Heineman & D. Ehrensaft (Eds.), *Building a home within: Meeting the emotional needs of children and youth in foster care* (pp. 175–190). Baltimore, MD: Brooks.

Frosch, J. J. (1959). Transference derivatives of the family romance. *Journal of the American Psychoanalytic Association, 7*, 503–522. DOI: 10.1177/000306515900700306.

Heineman, T. V. (1999). In search of the romantic family: Unconscious contributions to problems in foster and adoptive placement. *Journal for the Psychoanalysis of Culture & Society, 4*(2): 250–264.

Ilg, F. L., & Ames, L. B. (1955). *Child behavior.* New York: HarperCollins.

Leach, P. (2010). *Your baby and child: From birth to age five.* New York: Alfred A. Knopf.

Lewis, C. (2011). Providing therapy to children and families in foster care: A systemic-relational approach. *Family Process, 50*(4), 436–452. DOI: 10.1111/j.1545-5300.2011.01370.x.

Miall, C. E. (1996). The social construction of adoption. *Family Relations, 45*(3), 309–317.

Miller, A. (1997). *The drama of the gifted child: The search for the true self.* New York: Basic Books.

Shengold, L. (1999). *Soul murder revisited: Thoughts about therapy, hate, love, and memory.* New Haven, CT: Yale University Press.

Wegar, K. (2000). Adoption, family ideology, and social stigma: Bias in community attitudes, adoption research, and practice. *Family Relations, 49*(4), 363–370. DOI: 10.1111/j.1741-3729.2000.00363.x.

Chapter Seven

Isaiah

Isaiah found his way to A Home Within through a program that worked with foster youth at a local community college. He was self-referred, meaning that he wasn't "persuaded" to enter into treatment by his partner, friend, school, or family. Oftentimes, especially when working with youth who have experienced a multitude of disappointing or abandoning caregivers, they are justly hesitant to enter into another relationship where the possibility of abandonment exists (Bowlby, 1988; Fonagy, 2001; Putney, 2008; Unrau, Seita, & Putney, 2008). By actively seeking out a relationship with a therapist through A Home Within, Isaiah was communicating an important aspect of who he was, a survivor.

I consider Isaiah a survivor not in the traditional masculine ideal of a solitary, self-reliant man who overcomes hardships with unbreakable will. He is not the survivor who travels alone, functions independently, abhors weakness, and enters "courageously" into the unknown guided by stoicism and pride. This masculine archetype is the survivor of myths, legends, movies, and fairy tales. Rather, Isaiah is a survivor in a much more realistic sense, a survivor who has found not only the inner strength of self-determination, but also the wisdom to realize that the survivors of myths and movies are unfit to survive in the "real world." Those are idealized stories about characters that are unbreakable, invulnerable, and remarkably alone. Instead, Isaiah has found himself in the role of a survivor not only because of his self-confidence, determination, and creativity, but also because he is able to reach out to others and accept help. He does not see vulnerability or dependency as a weakness in itself, but rather he accepts these qualities as necessary in order to survive. That being said, conflicts around allowing himself to be vulnerable or dependent arose as central themes in the treatment, as he struggled with these issues in relation to his partnerships with others. Yet, simply by taking the step to enter into treatment and to remain committed to "doing the work" of psychotherapy, Isaiah displayed a willingness to be vulnerable and a desire to be connected. These themes will be discussed throughout this paper, as I believe that they remain central in describing the history of our work together, and also the work to come.

According to the intake paperwork, Isaiah's presenting problems were "depression, insomnia, difficulty with time management, and wanting to improve relationships with other people." In trying to think back to our initial meeting almost three years ago, it is difficult for me to remember if he verbalized those specific concerns to me. In a consultation group shortly after our initial meeting, I remember another group member asking about how he found A Home Within and what he was looking for in therapy. I cannot clearly remember my response to the queries, but I do remember a group member's answer, "He is looking for a relationship . . . to be connected." I believe this to be a very true statement and, again, this speaks to Isaiah's strength in his ability to reach out and be trusting even after being mistreated by those that he relied upon earlier in his life.

Isaiah also requested a therapist who was either LGBTQ identified or LGBTQ friendly. While Isaiah has strong feelings against either himself or others being "placed in categories" of any kind, he generally identifies as being a homosexual man of mixed ethnicity. Early in our meetings, my curiosity led me to inquire further into Isaiah's request. I was interested in understanding the root of Isaiah's question for two reasons. First, I wanted to hear more about what he was looking for in a therapist in order to determine if I might be a good match, and second, I had curiosity regarding a possible wish or fantasy that Isaiah might be expressing in his request. Isaiah's answer was quite straightforward and deliberate. He stated that he wanted to work with someone who was comfortable discussing gay culture openly and, through experience, he found that not everyone was comfortable discussing this central aspect of who he was. He wanted to make sure that it was safe to be himself, a very practical request. I replied that I was open to discussing anything that he wanted, including what it meant for him to be a gay man, and thus we began our work together.

A WOUNDED SELF FOUND IN ANOTHER

As our meetings began, Isaiah was in the midst of a long-term relationship with a young man who was also from foster care. This relationship was one of the main foci of our early treatment, as Isaiah was heavily invested in "rescuing" his partner. In doing so, he was experiencing a great deal of distress, anxiety, and emotional hardship. He watched powerlessly as his partner made decisions that were self-destructive. His partner, Mark, was a sinking ship, stuck in a powerful cycle of masochistic behavior that threatened to drown them both. Isaiah was bailing ocean water, tugging lines, patching holes, and sewing sails, all in efforts to save his partner. Meanwhile, his own ship was beginning to fall apart. He was missing classes, financially unstable, emotionally taxed, having difficulty sleeping, and just barely able to stay afloat in these turbulent and threatening waters.

I believe that I passed a test of sorts early in the treatment when Isaiah asked if I could begin either seeing Mark for therapy as well, or to see them as a couple. In fairness, Isaiah did request in his intake that he was interested in the possibility of couple's therapy, so his intention of having Mark in therapy was apparent before treatment even began. Though Isaiah was self-referred, it was actually the stress resulting from his relationship with Mark that pushed him to enter treatment himself. This is important in that Isaiah "needed" Mark in order to get connected with his own distress. It occurred to me that in asking for couple's therapy or to have his partner seen by me, this would be a continuation of the issue that Isaiah was entering therapy with, namely a furthering of taking care of his partner at the expense of his own well-being. Sampson and Weiss (1981) would consider this an example of early testing by clients in order to ascertain safety in the therapeutic relationship. Isaiah's request was understood as a disavowal of his own needs for the needs of his partner, a sacrifice of self for the rescuing of another.

I denied Isaiah's request, and in doing so, I was setting the stage for what would be the initial phase of our work together. At this point, Isaiah had not yet come to terms with his own needs, but was focused primarily on the needs of another, his partner. In the relationship, Isaiah was the "strong, put together" one and his partner was the "vulnerable, self-defeating person" who needed Isaiah's help to pull himself out of a mess. At the time, Isaiah's partner was in trouble with the law for compulsive theft, and was actively using drugs and alcohol, having sexual relations with multiple partners, and unnecessarily placing himself in risky situations. By proxy, Isaiah was continually placing himself in situations that were risky, or at the very least disruptive to his own goals of getting through college.

When discussing his partner in treatment, Isaiah would often make parallel statements reflecting the overlap between his own history and Mark's experiences. He would justify his actions for helping Mark by making claims that he (Isaiah) was the only person that was caring for "a person like" Mark. Isaiah often expressed his view that "nobody cared about" Mark, and that he needed someone to "accept, look after, and love" him because he had never received this from his family or from the community. Mark was the outcast, the forgotten, the street kid, the *other*. I understood Isaiah's overwhelming desire to care of Mark as a reflection of Isaiah's own unmet and deeply buried unconscious needs.

At this point in Isaiah's life, I believe that he was unable to fully consider the intensity of his own unmet needs in the areas of acceptance, nurturance, and love from caregivers. Instead of connecting with those painful feelings himself, Isaiah chose to create psychological distance from his painful experiences, and find them in another person *like* himself, but not actually *in* himself. Freud (1920) originally discussed this relational pattern, coining the term "repetition compulsion." The concept has been further developed by more contemporary authors (Bowlby, 1998; Davies, 2004; Flores, 2004; Fonagy, Gergely, Jurist, & Target, 2002; Winnicott, 1969, 1971, 1989) who discuss the idea in terms of attachment style and projection of painful affect states onto others. They place the relationship as a much more central aspect of the drive to repair prior attachment failures rather than a more universal substitute, as did Freud. This powerful dynamic between Isaiah and Mark—to seek out, witness, be near to, and eventually fix the painful early attachment wounds of the other, and thereby in themselves- was a powerful unconscious driving force in their relationship.

Seeing one's own emotional wounds in a partner serves two main purposes—first, to split off the most painful affect states of oneself in order to continue functioning and to give oneself the false impression of control over past losses, traumas or experiences of abandonment and rejection (Casement, 1991; Davies, 2004; Klein, 1946; Ogden, 1982). It captures the unconscious wish to be both a savior of others and to save oneself. Second, splitting off painful affective states and locating them in another also allows for the denial of one's own needs, dependencies, and vulnerabilities. If you are focused on helping another in need, someone who is "truly" suffering and in despair, it logically follows that you are not struggling so desperately after all. For Isaiah, and for so many others who get stuck in this pattern, the construct fell apart when Mark made it clear through his actions and words that he would not accept the help being offered. Isaiah's efforts were rejected, as Mark avoided contact, withdrew, and drilled more holes in the bottom of his ship as Isaiah was exhausting himself by frantically bailing emotional water.

Over time, and a great deal of discussion and exploration in therapy, Isaiah began to realize just what was happening. Slowly, he was able to gain some distance from the relationship with Mark, and recognize that "you can't help someone who doesn't want your help." It was a combination of this revelation along with a major argument between the two of them that allowed Isaiah to separate and disengage from the dangerous dance that had been created between them. In order to do that, Isaiah was forced to look at his own painful experiences of being "rejected, left out, abandoned, and mistreated," as these were the primary reasons that he felt an obligation to stay with Mark. I repeatedly introduced my observation that Isaiah's relationship with Mark was not that of two equal partners, but was much more representative of a parent and child. Isaiah was very much in a parental role, as he was providing, teaching, worrying, nurturing, disciplining, and holding Mark. Isaiah wanted to give Mark what he himself had lacked in his childhood—a present and loving caregiver who was able to see him, appreciate him, and to show him the world.

It should be noted that, I too felt strong pulls in this portion of the treatment. It was difficult for me to witness Isaiah getting pulled into a relationship with Mark that did not appear to be to his benefit. Isaiah missed classes, appointments, and work in order to care for Mark. In some regards, my response was similar to that of Isaiah's towards Mark; I wanted to rush in and "save" him from making decisions that would be to his further detriment. A number of authors (Greenberg & Mitchell, 1983; Mitchell, 1988; Stolorow, 1992) discuss how role enactments in the therapeutic process often mirror relational dynamics in client's lives, and there was no exception in my work with Isaiah. In this instance, the role enactment showed itself in my taking on a parental role that ran parallel to Isaiah's playing a parental role in relation to Mark. I felt myself pulled to say something along the lines of "can't you see what's happening here?" or "You need to get yourself out of this relationship! Look at the effect it's having on your life, your schooling, your therapy!" Fortunately, through the use of consultation and a perspective of knowing that such a stance is not therapeutic, but rather an enactment, I was generally able to withstand this internal pressure to intercede in Isaiah's decision-making process. Rather, I managed to focus on being curious about his decisions regarding his partnership with Mark, and how this intersected with his ability to take care of himself, including his ability to attend therapy regularly. This curiosity eventually led to a further exploration of Isaiah's familial attachment roots, which would allow both of us to understand more fully the dynamics being played out in his current relationships. In order to comprehend the origin of these unconscious feelings regarding himself and his attachment patterns, it was important to understand Isaiah's family history of abandonment, love, abuse, attachment, neglect, despair, resiliency, and hope.

THE DEPARTURE AND THE RETURN

Isaiah is an only child, born to an emotionally and financially unstable mother, and an absent father. Isaiah has no recollection of having any contact with his father, though he believes that he was "around" for his birth and early years of life. It is unclear when his father left the family, but there has been no contact between them to date; his father is absent in a fundamental and permanent manner. Isaiah was in his mother's care until he was of age to go to school. At that time, his maternal grandparents decided that Isaiah's mother was unfit to care for him. Being so young, Isaiah was not able to bring to mind specifics of this phase of his life, but he did remember moving around a great deal, and can recall a general atmosphere of stress. He had a single mother caring for him; she had little support from friends or family, and she was having difficulty holding jobs. One can imagine that with an overwhelmed and unstable mother, Isaiah's basic infantile need to be held, handled, and attended to was most likely not fully met. In his famous paper "Mirror-Role of Mother and Family," Winnicott (1971) states that when a "good enough" mother is looking at the baby, what she looks like to the infant is related to what she sees. In other words, the mother needs to be present enough to reflect the infant's affect rather than being overwhelmed or pre-occupied with her own in order to provide a basic holding capacity. The extent to which Isaiah's mother was able to provide this basic need during these early years is unknown. However, Isaiah was given over to the care of his paternal aunt and uncle who lived in South America when he was four or five years old, which suggests that his mother was unable to meet some of these basic needs. He was told that he would be going on vacation with his uncle and aunt, and that he would be back with his mother again soon.

His vacation lasted eight years, a period when he began learning how to survive in a world with stark resources and only the most basic forms of relational provisions. Culture, language, creativity, and tasks related to mastery and "doing" appropriately became a part of everyday life in order to survive in a foreign environment that was at times harsh and unforgiving. Both his mother and father were gone from his life, and he was not sure where he would land.

Isaiah described his time with his aunt and uncle as stable, but relatively isolated and economically poor. He remembers spending a great deal of time by himself, walking to the docks and helping fisherman with their catches for pocket change. It was here that he found his love for the ocean, and also for language. He also described this as a confusing and lonely time, as his aunt and uncle were rigid in their views concerning race and ethnicity, remained largely emotionally distant, and harsh in their application of physical discipline. Discussion of Isaiah's racial background was commonplace in the household. Isaiah was born to a mother with Afro-Caribbean roots, and a father of mixed ethnicity, having Chinese, Native American, European, and South American origins. Isaiah's aunt and uncle would often make derogatory statements towards individuals of African descent, and would deny Isaiah's connection as an African American. Statements such as "you are not like them," when referencing other "black" kids in the neighborhood, would be confusing as Isaiah looked at his mocha colored skin and wondered what they meant. Regardless, the message was clear, being black was not acceptable (Quintana et al., 2006).

Along with Isaiah's confusion around his ethnic identity and his attempts to reconcile his aunt and uncle's confusing messages about his place in this world, he was also living separated from his birth parents with little knowledge about where they were, what role they were to play in his life, and if he would ever see them again. Isaiah had a sense that he would see and live with his mother again, but there was never such discussion about his father. Isaiah said that he remembers a certain anxiety that would weave itself throughout any conversation about the possible whereabouts of his father. His aunt and uncle had heard whisperings of Isaiah's father finding them, appearing suddenly, and taking Isaiah off with him. Isaiah stated that his only memories of conversations about his father held this type of tone . . . mysterious, dangerous, unknown. He was described as a "radical and unpredictable" man who did not abide by common dictates of society. Isaiah described an underlying fear of his father that emanated from his aunt and uncle, and was thereby transferred to Isaiah. I often wondered how Isaiah's fantasy of his father's re-emergence intersected with equal parts fear and excitement, as it presented both the possibility of an element of danger, but also one of reconnection and escape from the stark and sometimes bleak reality he faced.

Within a short period of time, Isaiah's uncle passed away and his aunt fell to ill health. At the age of eleven, Isaiah was suddenly shipped back to the United States and reunited with his mother. Needless to say, the transition from living a relatively consistent and predictable life with his aunt and uncle in South America to living with his mother in the United States was not an easy one. Isaiah did not have much memory of being with his mother, and therefore did not have a strong attachment bond with her. She was also emotionally volatile, and while never formally diagnosed with a mental health condition, it appears that she had significant issues with mood lability and unpredictable behavior, and was often prone to rage-full outbursts and violence.

Isaiah experienced his mother as "scary and intimidating." He once described her as a "crazy, militant, black panther, communist, Muslim" who was able to make temporary connections with people, which would always end in turbulence and conflict followed by an isolative withdrawal. Isaiah's mother was constantly moving between jobs and between homes because of her inability to commune with others. Instability marked this period of his life, and would carry on for at least one decade. Isaiah reported living in shelters, low income housing, with friends, and even in his mother's car with her for a period of time.

All the while, his emerging sense of self was developing as he entered his teenage years. Part of this emerging self was his budding sexuality. Isaiah found himself attracted to boys and men, which was an unacceptable to his mother. Needless to say, Isaiah's coming out was an incredibly painful experience, furnished by rejection, hostility, and the threat of violence from his mother. Isaiah, having learned how to protect himself in his early years, stood firm in his understanding of his own sexuality in the face of his mother's disapproval. The conflicts between Isaiah and his mother grew in intensity and frequency during this period, and he recalls his adolescence as a troubling and overwhelming time in his life. He felt trapped, having very few outlets to escape his mother's unpredictable wrath. In our work together, he occasionally recalls the intensity of her violent fury. As is often found in recalling traumatic experiences, the memories were disturbing, painful, and immediate, as though little time had passed since his experiences of them (Lindsay & Read, 1997).

Not only was there constant conflict between Isaiah and his mother, but she was also often in conflict with her immediate community. Friends, neighbors, teachers, and community organizers would switch from "good to bad" at a moment's notice. Isaiah witnessed his mother become increasingly isolated and aggravated as she severed ties between herself and others. Isaiah often had to stay connected to friends or teachers in secrecy, as she would prohibit him from remaining in contact with those that had fallen from grace. Fortunately, Isaiah had a mind of his own and a desire to stay connected to others. He also knew that he needed help, and he was not afraid of reaching out to others for assistance.

Things came to a head when Isaiah was in his mid-teens and he knew that he had to leave his home. He and his mother were constantly getting into verbal and physical disputes, and her behavior and responses were becoming increasingly erratic. On more than one occasion, Isaiah found himself locked out of his house at night in dangerous areas of the city. He was fortunate enough to have friends to take him in, but the situation was becoming untenable. With help from friends and a trusted teacher, Isaiah eventually was placed in foster care and stayed with family friends for the remainder of his high school career. He still lived with fear of his mother's involvement in his life, as she would threaten him or those that helped him during this time. Isaiah essentially hid from his mother and to the best extent he could, managed to avoid contact with her from that point forward.

While Isaiah's foster living environment was not ideal, it was stable, and it provided enough consistency for him to be able to graduate high school. At the time, Isaiah said that he was not particularly interested in academics and described himself as a mediocre student. He lived in a state of perpetual anxiety, as he had to constantly avoid contact with his mother while also dealing with living in a new home and managing the complications of being an openly gay African American adolescent in a public, urban high school. Additionally, he knew that his welcome in his foster home was limited and conditional. This was yet another rejection, another message that others were not to be trusted, and that he had to care for himself. At eighteen, Isaiah left his foster home, and did not return.

Isaiah linked up with a volunteer program with which he traveled the country, lived communally, and received very little financial compensation.

This was mainly a decision based out of wanting to escape. He soon found his way out of that program and settled in a city a few hours away from where he spent his middle and high school years. He enrolled in a local community college, found a place to live, entered into a relationship with Mark, and worked in order to meet his basic needs. While it felt far from adequate, he had found a place to call home.

SELF AND OTHER EXPLORED

Isaiah and my work together has spanned a period just shy of three years. As previously mentioned, our initial work together was largely focused on his relationship with Mark and the impact that this was having on his life. After listening for some time, I shared with Isaiah my impressions regarding his relationship with Mark. I explained that he was getting certain needs met in the relationship, but that these needs centered on his desire to fix something that was broken from his own past. Isaiah was replicating the role of the good enough mother (Winnicott, 1971, 1989), a deeply rooted unmet need of his own, in his relationship with Mark. He was taking on the role of a protective and dedicated caregiver to a helpless and vulnerable child. In doing so, he was acting out a fantasy of what "could have been" for himself. In a manner of speaking, he was getting certain needs met, those of his need for good enough parenting. However, he was not in a position to be able to receive reciprocal care and bonding, which he was also desperately seeking. When Isaiah described his role in the relationship, to take care of, to provide for, to shelter, to teach, he was describing the role of a parent, not a partner. I did my best to make this explicit in our meetings.

This early phase of our work together was marked by significant periods of disruption in the treatment as well as unpredictability in scheduling. Isaiah would attend a few sessions, and then miss a few sessions without prior notice. In this way, he made himself available and simultaneously unavailable, present and absent, engaged in and removed from the treatment. It was my understanding that this also represented unconscious testing from Isaiah to determine if I was going to be an abandoning caregiver, a figure that he expected from past experience. This would be what Sampson and Weiss (1986) consider a transference test. In this type of dynamic, the patient replicates a role similar to one he had in relation to an early primary caregiver. In doing so, the client unconsciously places the therapist in the role of the caregiver. In essence, this is replicating an earlier childhood experience in the present relationship with the therapist with hopes of a different outcome. The "test" then becomes whether the therapist acts in a similar fashion to that of the primary caregiver, in Isaiah's case an abusive and rejecting figure. Isaiah's lack of consistency and "irresponsibility" were met with rage and hostility by his mother. The test was to determine if I would respond similarly or differently. Considering this dynamic, I chose to respond in a firm but non-punitive manner to these early challenges. In doing so, I was able to set reasonable boundaries and expectations (i.e., when we have an appointment, it is important to me that he attends), while also maintaining and empathic position (i.e., his life is chaotic, he feels ambivalent about starting treatment, and he needs help in structuring and organizing). This position allowed for movement towards safety within the therapeutic relationship, though other challenges arose.

In addition to testing safety in the relationship by presenting disruptions to the frame, Isaiah tested safety through his manner of communication. There were countless times, especially in the early phases of our treatment, in which Isaiah would use the session as a sort of psychic dumping ground (Bion, 1959). This particular style of engagement, or rather disengagement, took the form of his lengthy monologues during which I felt very much absent from the relationship. I felt much more that I was being spoken to rather than spoken with, a dynamic that often left me feeling useless, powerless, exhausted, and frustrated. Rather than feel trapped in this feeling state, I aimed to have my own feelings guide my understanding of Isaiah's interpersonal experience. My goal was to understand my own emotional response to Isaiah as an important communication of the relational issues with which he struggled, those of connection and trust.

At times, it was difficult to stay psychically and emotionally present in the room, as I felt a wave of information and affect rolling over me. There were no pauses, no time for breath, for reflection, no time to stop and think. I believe that this style of communication served a purpose, mainly that of keeping me at a distance. On the surface, we were discussing issues that were central in Isaiah's life: relationships, school, financial concerns, roommate issues, sexual orientation. At the same time, I often felt a void of emotional experience, other than anger and frustration, coming from Isaiah regarding the inequities in his life. Sadness and loss were not in the room, nor was an ability to consider the relational dynamics between us. Any attempts on my part to bring up Isaiah's feelings regarding his relationship with me were met with a matter-of-fact dismissal of the importance of such a discussion.

These therapeutic experiences reminded me of what Betty Joseph (1975) discussed in her paper describing "difficult to reach" patients. In this writing, Joseph describes patients who are "seemingly co-operative," but that this "pseudo-cooperation" is "aimed at keeping the analyst away from the really unknown and more needy parts of the infantile self." She also describes how in this state, therapeutic work appears to be taking place, but instead of the patient having "the experience of being understood," instead he is "getting understanding." My interpretation of this position is that Joseph is speaking to a more controlling position of the client. Namely, the client controls what "goes in" and what "stays out." For Isaiah, I understood this to be a self-protective element of his personality construct surrounding dependency, and what Winnicott (1968) speaks of in the "use of an object." He did not run the risk of becoming dependent on me if I was not really being "used" in the room. At times I found this difficult to tolerate, as though I myself were being tricked into a type of pseudo-treatment where it looked like real connection, but was actually just words. I often felt that I was interchangeable, that I could be replaced with just about anyone, as my voice was barely heard and my presence scarcely felt. I felt torn between knowing when to intercede, and how much to remain in an "active listening" position. In my work with Isaiah, the pseudo-treatment took the form of his words filling the space of the therapeutic hour, but the feeling that nothing was "happening." From my perspective, it felt more akin to listening to a lecture rather than having a dialogue. In both cases, there are two (or more) participants, but only in the latter is their active participation and equal involvement from both parties.

I struggled with these feelings for some time before beginning to take a more active stance in our work. I decided that I would no longer wait to share my thoughts and reflections, but that I had to "force" them in. Initially, I held some anxiety about this approach, unsure of the outcome, as if I was trying to force-feed a child who was a fussy eater. However, my fears were largely unfounded, and I experienced Isaiah not so much as a fussy eater, but more so as a boy with his guard up. We were sparring and, up until that time, Isaiah had been in the ring by himself, keeping me at bay and working out on his own. I decided to enter the ring, put my gloves on, and playfully spar with him. He was coaching me in an unorthodox manner, meaning that he was not going to *tell me* when to jab or parry. I had to get in there and mix it up with him. I had to speak what was on my mind, share my thoughts, cut him off, and keep him on his feet. Isaiah was pushing, and he needed to have someone push back.

Sparring requires contact, a degree of competitive aggression, and a level of faith that each partner will challenge the other, and both will grow stronger. If one of the sparring partners is not working his hardest, questioning the other's intentions, or if he is overly cautious in the ring, the level of growth is inhibited for both. Over the course of some time, and a number of rounds, I believe that we found an appropriate way to be each other's sparring partners. I wasn't going anywhere. We were staying in the ring together; there were many more practice rounds to come.

RACE FOR COVER

After the varying "crises" surrounding Isaiah's relationship with Mark were resolved by Isaiah's ending that partnership, our discussions shifted focus.

We began inching toward discussions that were relevant to Isaiah's sense of who he was, his identity. A remarkable degree of the issues that Isaiah brought into therapy concerned feelings of rejection, discrimination, or hostility either received or demonstrated towards others, largely based on race. Race, language, class, and culture became central organizing principles upon which Isaiah categorically placed himself and others.

The lines were clear, and they marked where people belonged. Organizing the world based on racial differences is certainly not a new social phenomenon, and Isaiah used it as others had before him, as a tool to externalize affect and make the world more understandable (Straker, 2004). More often than not, Isaiah would find himself in a position of isolation from others in this regard, feeling that he "just didn't belong" anywhere. This experience of not belonging cut to the core of who he was, and was an incredibly painful place to access emotionally. Because of this, Isaiah would often deflect such painful emotional states by engaging in dialogue (or monologue, depending on the session) on an intellectualized and cerebral level. We were discussing race, culture, persecution, and marginalized communities, but we were doing so in a distanced way. Isaiah would perhaps begin with a statement about feeling marginalized, but within a few minutes, he would shift the conversation to something obscure such as a discussion about the marginalization of a specific group of Chinese farmers in the tenth century. I often found myself wondering, "Why are we talking about this, what relevance does this have for Isaiah?"

Eventually I began stating these thoughts aloud, trying to make connections between Isaiah's passionate speeches and his actual emotional experiences. I also tried to make comments and connections about racial and cultural differences in the room as many of his communications were clinically relevant based on our own cultural differences. Sue & Sue (2003), prominent writers in multi-cultural psychology, suggest that cultural differences should be openly addressed when working with clients of a different cultural background. Following suit, I felt that our differences in culture as well as differences in class, which came up in the context of discussing the neighborhood that my office was in compared to the neighborhood Isaiah lived in, should be openly discussed. More often than not, these differences were minimalized and I was "let of the hook" for any differences or slights that I may have enacted in the course of our work together. Isaiah detested the lack of diversity in my neighborhood, but he did not associate me as a person contributing to the overall sense of "whiteness" in the area. He recognized the privilege that those who lived and worked in this neighborhood had, but he did not believe that I was "one of those people." Isaiah pointed out that in my neighborhood people ate their dinners in open-air café's on the sidewalk. In comparison he stated, "If a restaurant tried to do that where I live, the patrons would get held up and people would steal their food!"

Isaiah was angry at the class inequities, and I could not help but feel closely linked to these attacks, as we sat in my office where people were eating on the sidewalk within earshot. However, when I introduced the idea that he might also be feeling anger towards me for inequities that exist in our relationship, he denied this. While he did not say so outright, my belief was that he chose to see me more like "him" than like "them." Introducing myself in the room as a separate, distinct person was met with resistance in numerous ways. The discussion about class differences, racial differences, and cultural differences were real and apparent in the room, yet each time I attempted to bring these differences to light, they were met with a lack of curiosity. Rather, Isaiah chose to excuse me from the groups that he was often disparaging as "elitist whites," "discriminatory Asians and Latinos," or "ignorant Americans." In this way I was protected from his anger towards these groups of people who often treated him with disrespect or contempt.

After several attempts to "bring myself into the room," so to speak, I decided to back down from such deliberate, forward, and perhaps untimely remarks about my own subjectivity. I was trying to engage Isaiah in an exploration of his range of feelings towards me in a direct manner, as is often the goal in relational psychodynamic work. However, Slochower (1991, 1996) warns against the analyst moving prematurely into such a position, instead acknowledging that such work is a "hard won therapeutic achievement that often does not emerge until well into the treatment process." She suggests that before an adequate holding environment is established, "patients simply cannot tolerate the intrusion or impingement of the analyst's separate subjective presence." At this phase of the treatment, my separateness was troubling rather than enriching, and therefore was held at a distance until greater safety was established. I understood Isaiah's reluctance to explore and be curious about certain aspects of our relationship as a communication regarding safety. At this point in our treatment, it was important for him to not "know" or be curious about "knowing" who or what I was. Isaiah was coaching me (Bugas & Silberschatz, 2000; Casement, 1991) with regard to what he needed in order to feel safe. Isaiah's "coaching" allowed me to recognize my mistake of moving too hastily into a relational space. In doing so, I failed to provide containment and safety in the therapy.

Casement (1991) tells us to listen to clients' statements both objectively and also as a transference statement (i.e., what are they also saying about how they might feel about the therapist). I continue to believe that Isaiah had feelings about the differences that existed between us, but I also think that he was protecting us. To continue with the sparring metaphor, he was pulling his punches. In order to stay in the ring with him, I had to alter my rhythm and follow Isaiah's lead. Doing so meant slowing down, providing more containment, and listening and interpreting in the derivative (Casement). Casement describes this style of engagement (i.e., working in the derivative) as a way to indirectly discuss transferential aspects of the therapeutic relationship by using the client's language. In my work with Isaiah, that often meant talking about other people's attitudes, behaviors and perceptions rather than his own. It also meant tolerating a feeling of uncertainty regarding the nature of our explorations, and struggles with feeling present in the room with Isaiah in a subjective manner. I understood these to be *the tasks* to struggle with in the early and middle phases of our treatment.

Sometime in the "middle phase" of our work together, an example of uncertainty in exploration of Isaiah's discriminatory experiences arose as a therapeutic dilemma. As Isaiah began to shift from discussing the discrimination of "distant" others to more self-revealing experiences of being personally discriminated against, I felt pulled in two separate directions. On the one hand, I wanted to openly acknowledge Isaiah's experiences as valid and disturbing. Isaiah spoke of being "stared" at on the bus or treated differently at work, and he believed that these experiences were discriminatory in nature. To say that people do not discriminate based on race or sexual orientation would be ignorance and denial in its peak form. However, I also felt pulled to comment on another pattern that I witnessed reoccurring in Isaiah's stories. Race and sexual identity seemed to color the vast majority of his interactions. Countless stories centered around Isaiah being treated differently because of who he was ethnically and in terms of partner choice.

In my mind, I began to consider an alternative hypothesis for Isaiah's seemingly unending stream of discriminatory or persecutory figures in his life. I began to understand Isaiah's experience of persecution from others as a way to keep people at bay. Isaiah could not experience connections with others if they were racist or objectifying towards him. In the stories, Isaiah tried to make connections, sometimes with men in the gay community, sometimes with relative strangers, but he was constantly met with objectifying or discriminatory experiences. Was Isaiah being discriminated against, or was he engaging in the world in a suspicious manner? As his clinician, it was important for me to shift out of the binary position in order to open room for exploration of the phenomenon. Isaiah experienced real discrimination and rejection from others and he used the tendency for others to discriminate against him as a reason to "not connect."

My hesitancy to bring up this as a potential factor led to a delay in Isaiah owning this part of the equation. Part of my hesitancy, I believe, stemmed from a position of not knowing what it was like "to be in his shoes" as a gay black man. Making assumptions about his experience in the world therefore seemed presumptuous and potentially minimizing of his real life struggles. I brought this issue into the consultation group, and was then able to separate out my own anxieties about being un-empathetic from a strong feeling that race was being used as a way to distance himself. This allowed me more distance from the clinical dilemma, thereby allowing for more clarity of thought regarding the issue. When I did bring this concept up, Isaiah was able to consider it as a real possibility in his relating to others.

SOMETHING FAMILIAR, SOMETHING DIFFERENT

Shortly after ending his relationship with Mark, Isaiah became involved in another serious relationship, which became a focal point in our sessions for some time. While Isaiah found comfort in the physical companionship of his new partner, John, he often felt isolated and alone emotionally. He frequently reported a sense of distance from his partner, sharing his frustration about his partner being "snappy" or "cold." Their relationship developed at a hurried pace, and within a few months of meeting each other, Isaiah's new partner moved into his place. In therapy, Isaiah would speak openly about his challenges with physical as well as emotional intimacy with his partner.

Initially, there was a fair amount of blaming and externalizing of responsibility onto John in terms of dissatisfaction in the relationship. My focus was twofold in the sessions: holding and containing Isaiah's frustrations, disappointments, and anxieties, and challenging Isaiah's tendency to deflect and deny his own emotional experiences, instead placing them in his partner. This was a pervasive theme in his relationship with Mark, and it continued to show itself in his partnership with John. Themes around Isaiah taking on the role of the parent to his partner, the child who needed to be saved, had loosened to some degree, yet there remained a distance in the partnership. The initial period was marked by intimate physical and emotional connection, but this was short lived. Passion turned to conflict as they started to realize the stark differences they had in their approach to the world. Isaiah struggled with reconciling his own approach to living life with that of his partner's, and the effect was distancing. Isaiah often found himself frustrated by his partner's lack of exploration and rigidity in routine mannerisms. John would become distanced from Isaiah when he felt criticized or when his needs or wants were overlooked. Their relationship was beginning to dissolve, and Isaiah was devastated by another potential loss. John had become a central attachment figure in Isaiah's life. He was someone with whom to share experiences, struggle through hardships, sleep next to, and be connected to.

Not only was Isaiah attached to John, but John also had something that Isaiah desperately wanted connection to a family. Isaiah was torn—he was dissatisfied in the relationship as there appeared to be fundamental and irresolvable differences, but his relationship with John was one of the very few emotional attachments he felt he could hold onto. If he were to end his relationship with John, he would lose a pillar of stability with regard to his emotional life. Without him, he would be alone. By and large, and not without conflict, John's parents had begun to accept Isaiah into their family. He had a place to go for the holidays, a home where he could belong. In ending his relationship with John, Isaiah stood to lose not only his closest emotional attachment in terms of a partnership, but also a family. The possibility of losing both was untenable, and led to a continued unresolved conflict.

In therapy, we spent many sessions exploring these differences, and the conflicts that arose in their partnership. Isaiah was coming to terms with the reality that he and John were very different people, and that a great number of their differences were irreconcilable. Isaiah began to ask himself insightful questions and explore his emotional experiences within the relationship. How much difference could Isaiah tolerate in their partnership? Could he remain in the relationship without trying to 'fix' John to be a more ideal partner? Did he have to give up everything in order to move on? Could he be in an equal partnership with John rather than in a parental role?

Not all of the questions were answered, but the awareness of the dilemma led to a resolution of sorts. Isaiah and John remain in contact to this day, though their relationship has taken on a different flavor. They no longer consider themselves in an exclusive intimate relationship, but they continue to contact and support one another. It also appears that Isaiah has resolved the need to rescue or fix John, and thereby is more able to attain support from him and accept him despite their differences. In my opinion, an achievement was made in that Isaiah did not have to end the relationship completely because of differences between them. They were able to be flexible, shifting the manner in which they interact with one another in order to remain connected, but in a different way. This is no small undertaking, as it requires flexibility, and ability to tolerate frustration and ambiguity in the relationship.

BASIC NEED AND FAMILY AS PRIVILEGE

Another prevalent theme in our work together surrounded the litany of stressors that Isaiah was constantly facing. One of his primary and very reality-based anxieties was around being able to support his basic needs for shelter and food. Oftentimes, Isaiah used the therapy hour to share his current life experiences, complete with his struggles to support himself. He has been and continues to be a college student, and he also has worked in a number of different capacities. There have been periods where he was totally out of money, late on his payments for rent or bills, and the anxiety that this causes him is fully palpable in the room. Isaiah's situation highlights the containing function of a family "safety net," something that Isaiah does not readily have. Aside from John and his family, and a few distant relatives that might help if Isaiah was in dire need, Isaiah is completely on his own. Either he makes it, or he doesn't. Not having money for a decent meal, having the anxiety of not paying rent and having to leave his home were very real possibilities. Again, this made me consider the privileged position of having a family. While I never overtly stated the difference between us, I did hold it in my mind during and between our sessions. I chose not to raise it directly, perhaps somewhat out of my own discomfort with the inequality, and also because I had learned that Isaiah did not want to think about my world outside of the treatment hour.

One central component of what it means to be privileged, or to be identified as a member of a majority culture, revolves around the ability not to have to consider one's privileged position (Sue & Sue, 2003; Straker, 2004). As therapists, if we are open to learning from our clients, then ignorance regarding our own privilege is constantly challenged. We are confronted with our own privilege when clients share experiences that delineate where power lies and where it does not. With privilege also comes assumption. A central assumption that I made, and that my work with Isaiah highlighted, was that everyone had a family or community. While even writing the statement sounds naive, and I myself don't want to believe that I made that assumption, I accept that it was an underlying unconscious belief. When I rationally think about the question, of course I know that not everyone has a family. However, my privilege led me not to have to think about how much comfort I attain from having a family to rely upon. When Isaiah would express his financial anxieties, I would find myself trying to place myself in his shoes. Namely, no family would encompass having no safety net, no back up if everything fell through. While I don't rely on family for current financial support, the stark difference in knowing that if I needed them, I would have somewhere and someone to turn to allows me not to be a state of constant hypervigilance. Isaiah did not have that privilege, and again the difference in the room forced me to consider my privilege in a way that was profoundly moving to me.

While financial concerns are real, concrete, and can be an enormous stressor, it is also something that can be resolved. As a close friend of mine once said, "Money only solves money problems." Beyond the financial privilege that was apparent in the context of our relationship, there was a more deeply rooted privilege that I was becoming more aware of. For lack of a better term, this centered around an emotional or relational privilege I had by being connected with family. For every holiday, I knew that I had a place at the table, at my home. Again, this type of 'taking things for granted' attitude is very much connected to the position of privilege in the relational arena. This position of privilege was brought to my attention in a very real way when Isaiah would describe his experience of 'not knowing where to go' for the holidays. For me, what was once considered a given became a privilege. While these types of personal observations can be difficult to face up to, I also find them to be humbling. To be a decent therapist, I believe that one needs to tolerate the humility of one's own shortcomings and blind spots. One learns these lessons from working with clients. Isaiah has been a good teacher in that regard, and I have learned a great deal.

Feelings of sadness, disappointment, and loss around not belonging to a family ran as an undercurrent in the therapy, but they were difficult to speak to directly. In many ways these were the times that I felt starkly separated from and also were most closely related to Isaiah's experience of loss of belonging to a family. The separation took form in the contrast we had in family experiences, and arose most acutely into awareness around the holidays when I would take time off from work to return home for family visits. My usual excitement around returning home was complicated by feelings of guilt around leaving Isaiah when he most needed contact. It was yet another way that our differences arose—I had a place to go; he did not. Again, Isaiah would not openly discuss his feelings around my unavailability during this time. If I brought up the topic, he would respond in a very matter of fact fashion. Again, a protective element around the relationship arose. It was my impression that thinking about who I was outside of the therapeutic context threatened the safety of the relationship that we had established. Thinking about this, let alone discussing it with me, was not an option at the present time. I waited, Isaiah waited. We continued to spar lightly.

By contrast, the element of connection during these periods also illuminates an important element of our developing relationship. Isaiah was allowing himself to reveal real vulnerabilities during our work together. In the times that he discussed his sense of sadness and loss around having "nowhere to go" for the holidays, it is my belief that we joined in an authentic empathic connection. Isaiah connected with feelings of sadness and loss, and expressed them to me in our meetings. By turn, his feelings resonated with me in an important way, as I too felt moved by his sadness and thereby connected to him in an authentic way. This was a new development in our work, and painful as it was, I believe important in the process of tolerating loss rather than warding off painful feelings.

GOOD ENOUGH FOR WHOM

I believe that Isaiah and I have become good sparring partners. We have coached each other, observed each other's moves, and figured out a way to work collaboratively to make us both better "boxers." As our work has continued to develop, Isaiah has taken more risks in the ring. Instead of sticking to our usual routine week after week, as we did in our early work, we began moving in a different direction. With this increased comfort in our ability to spar safely came new material in the work. Instead of intellectualized debate on culture and history, a way in which Isaiah distanced himself from his core vulnerabilities, Isaiah began discussing revealing experiences regarding rejection, disappointment, self-worth, and abandonment. These themes only emerged after over two years of work together, which I believe speaks to the need for safety in discussing these matters, and the necessity for open-ended work with clients. Essentially, these were core issues, driving much of Isaiah's anxieties, but they were not fully accessible until well after two years into the treatment. This is a concern that arises with the push for short-term models of mental health care, especially as it relates to populations that have dealt with trauma, abandonment, abuse, or neglect.

People want to protect themselves from painful experiences, and Isaiah was no exception. Themes around rejection, not being "good enough," and feeling objectified arose in the context of relatedness to others. Speaking openly about his experiences of rejection left Isaiah feeling exposed and raw. In addition to Mark, Isaiah would use his time in therapy to discuss relationships with other men. Isaiah made it explicitly known that he often felt diminished, sexualized, and degraded from those within the gay community. Rejection would present itself in various forms, ranging from an offhanded comment from a man at a bar to blatantly racist remarks that were spoken from the side of a "friend's" mouth. Trust in people's motives and intentions came constantly into question, and Isaiah found himself feeling particularly alone even when he was in the physical company of other men.

Perhaps even more disturbing was Isaiah's fear that he was "becoming his mother." Isaiah described his mother as a bitter, angry, and cynical woman, whose viewpoint on the intentions of others often strayed into suspicion and perhaps, at times, paranoia. He recalled her endless array of lectures on the evils of one race or another; the antagonist would shift, but the message was quite clear, "Be suspicious, and don't trust anyone." In her relational worldview, people betrayed, disappointed, manipulated, took advantage of, and eventually abandoned her. One can consider the remarkable anxiety that Isaiah felt when his experience of relating to others ran parallel to many of his mother's "warnings" about people when growing up. In essence, his experience of the world began to parallel that of his mother's. His response was also similar to that of his mother's, as he too began to retreat into an isolative and polarized world. Men who were attracted to him were only interested in him as an exotic sexual partner, not as a "real person" to become emotionally attached to. Friends he thought that he could trust made hateful comments regarding Isaiah's racial background behind his back. Family members wouldn't respond to attempts to connect. Managers at work were not giving him rightfully deserved shifts. Co-workers were excluding him from groupings, teachers did not understand his academic struggles, and friends were more interested in using drugs or alcohol than having a conversation over dinner.

Following these series of rejections, emotional abandonments, and relational betrayals, Isaiah, too, became suspect of others. This was what he meant when he stated that he had concerns about "becoming his mother." Isaiah's mother was not able to overcome her painful experiences of rejection and disappointment in others, and as a result she became an island. Isaiah witnessed this, saw the devastation that followed, and wanted something different. However, Isaiah's mother's words rang in his ears each time he was disappointed, disavowed, or disregarded by another. He began to wonder if she was actually correct in her worldview, and perhaps that he had been a fool, naively believing that people could be kind, generous, and trustworthy.

Isaiah's reconciliation of this dilemma is a work in progress. One key aspect that has become a central theme in our work has been that of partner choice. Through exploration in therapy, Isaiah began to become more conscious of the ways that he was contributing to the self-fulfilling prophecy that began with his mother's teaching. Many of the people that Isaiah chose to surround himself with were more likely to confirm his mother's cynical worldviews rather than to dismiss them. Namely, Isaiah often, though not exclusively, would engage with people who were unavailable in some way. Their unavailability took a number of different forms, physical, emotional, relational, but the commonalities began to become more transparent. We began discussing this dynamic in his early relationships with Mark and John, though the theme remains present in our current work.

The first step in trying to make a change in a pattern is recognizing that a pattern exists. I believe that Isaiah is now at the point where he can recognize a pattern. He has recognized that he often finds himself in the company of people who are both "like" and "unlike" him. The "likeness" to himself frequently has to do with their background, often times coming from dissolved families, the experience of abuse and neglect in childhood, time spent in the foster care community, or having some identity with a marginalized population. The way that this same group of people is "unlike" Isaiah relates to the nature of trauma that they experienced, their manner of coping with trauma, their intellectual abilities, and their ability to relate emotionally to others.

Isaiah seems to gravitate towards individuals who often had severe trauma and neglect in their personal and family history. Because of this, their ability to trust, to form lasting and meaningful relationships, to maintain emotional stability and sustained personal relatedness are impaired in one way or another. As a result, Isaiah often finds himself in the company of others, yet remarkably alone. The desire to "fix" has faded into the background and has been replaced with a desire to belong, for likeness, for a common thread. If we were able to peek inside Isaiah's mind, an internal thought process might appear as follows: "Because of my history, sexual orientation, and ethnic background, I have been marginalized in the community. Therefore, I belong with other marginalized groups. At the same time, I also recognize strengths and resiliencies that I carry that many others from these communities do not. My desire for relatedness, conflicted though it may be, is real and available. While I feel like others from marginalized groups in some ways, I feel quite distinct from them, and my attempts to relate to them often leave me feeling deeply unsatisfied. Do I belong with other marginalized people? Do I belong with those that are my intellectual and relational match? Do I have a responsibility to help out others who are marginalized and don't have the internal resources that I have? If so, how much should I do? How much can I do? When do I give up? If I don't feel fully comfortable with either group, then where do I belong?"

These are the questions that Isaiah is exploring in psychotherapy at this time. Not only is he considering the extent to which other people are able to relate to him, but he is also challenging his own ability to relate to others. In session recently, he quoted a high school mentor's remark, "If you are finding problems with everyone around you, take a look at yourself." This captures a monumental shift from the desire to split off and externalize affective struggles to a rich exploration of Isaiah's internal emotional experiences. In moments of crisis or emotional overwhelm, Isaiah may return to a more distanced, intellectualized and externalized position. Clinically, I then have to make the decision of when to "contain" and when to challenge Isaiah's defensive pattern. One way that I subjectively measure treatment progress is by witnessing clients' response to such challenges. While in the past, Isaiah may have felt defensive or protective of his need to externalize, he now is able to be curious about this tendency, and notice how it gets in the way of, or at times is informative of, his internal experiences. In a recent session, Isaiah stated, "I have been feeling a lot more introspective lately, but I've also been feeling really sad." I believe that this marks significant progress in Isaiah's ability to tolerate uncomfortable and painful feelings that arise with an increased ability to consider his internal states.

THE FISHERMAN RETURNS: BLENDING FANTASY, HOPEFULNESS, AND REALITY

I began this paper by sharing my experience of Isaiah as a "real world" survivor. In contrast to fantasy-based survivors, who often are represented as lone heroes, invulnerable, omnipotent, and all giving, Isaiah's survival required reliance on others, self-determination, an acceptance of limitations and vulnerability in the face of hardship. The fantasy-based survivor and the real world survivor share commonalities; both require courage and an ability to tolerate anxiety, overcome hardships, take risks, and be creative. Isaiah is a survivor for whom I have the deepest respect, and from whom I have learned a great deal about the values of connection and the importance of family.

Isaiah entered treatment with many of the qualities that made him a survivor. In fact, his desire to enter into treatment was an aspect of this same spirit. He knew that he needed help, and had enough of a foundation of trust in others to allow himself to connect. This connection did not come easily or without tests in the relationships. Could I be relied upon? Could he take actual emotional risks with me? Could he become attached in a meaningful way? Would I abandon him, objectify him, dismiss him? These were core anxieties that many clients bring into treatment, but they were particularly highlighted by Isaiah's relational and familial history. And, they were questions that could not be answered with verbal reassurance, but through the long-term process of building a trusting relationship. Trust was built from our experience working together, by my being available and providing containment, safety, and consistency. None of these crucial therapeutic aspects would be possible in a short-term treatment, as this form of work is removed from the essential elements of what Isaiah sought from the beginning. As my consultation group colleague said simply and elegantly, "He is looking for a relationship."

Isaiah is an avid fisherman, a childhood passion that he discovered when he was living with his aunt and uncle in South America. He frequently speaks about his fishing adventures, the people he meets, the challenges along the way, the feeling of freedom and stillness while out on the open water. He often fishes alone, as he has yet to find a companion that shares his passion for the sport and love for the ocean. Though he is often alone when fishing, Isaiah does not express feelings of loneliness in these moments. Rather, he describes these moments as peaceful, tranquil, and disconnected from the frenetic pace that he often has to keep. It is a time for him to slow down, to retreat, to settle into the rhythms of the water and enjoy the quiet beauty of his natural surroundings. One of my favorite mental images and hopeful wishes is of Isaiah the fisherman, peacefully sitting on a dock or gently bobbing in a canoe, fishing pole in hand, breathing in the briny ocean air, feeling rested and at ease, taking a much needed break. In my mind, he is content, relaxed, half focused on catching a fish, half day dreaming of something pleasant and non-purposeful. He is alone, but not isolated, by himself but at ease and secure. As he returns to the dock, there seems to be someone there to greet him. He holds up his catch, puts down his fishing pole, docks his canoe, and returns with a beaming smile, ready to share his hard earned prize with someone who values the bounty of the ocean, the importance of companionship, and the deliciousness of freshly cooked fish.

REFERENCES

Bion, W. R. (1959). Attacks on linking. *International Journal of Psychoanalysis, 40*, 308–315.

Bowlby, J. (1988). *A secure base, parent-child attachment and healthy human development.* New York: Basic Books.

Bugas, J., & Silberschatz, G. (2000). How patients coach their therapists in psychotherapy. *Psychotherapy: Theory, Research, Practice, Training, 37*(1), 64–70. DOI: 10.1037/h00-87676.

Casement, P. (1991). *Learning from the patient.* New York: Guilford.

Davies, J. M. (2004). Whose bad objects are we anyway: Repetition and our elusive love affair with evil. *Psychoanalytic Dialogues, 14*(6), 711–732.

Flores, P. (2004). *Addiction as an attachment disorder.* Northvale, NJ: Aronson.

Fonagy, P. (2001). *Attachment theory and pyschoanalysis.* New York: Other Press.

Fonagy, P., Gergely, G., Jurist, E. L., & Target, M. (2002). *Affect regulation, mentalization, and the development of the self.* New York: Other Press.

Freud, S. (1920). *Beyond the pleasure principle.* New York: Bantam Books

Greenberg, J., & Mitchell, S. A. (1983). *Object relations in psychoanalytic theory.* Cambridge, MA: Harvard University Press.

Joseph, B. (1975). The patient who is difficult to reach. In P. L. Giovacchini (Ed.), *Tactics and techniques in psychoanalytic therapy* (vol. 2). New York: Jason Aronson.

Klein, M. (1946). Notes on some schizoid mechanisms. In M. Klein, *Developments in psychoanalysis.* London, England: Hogarth Press.

Lindsay, D., & Read, J. (1997). *Recollections of trauma: Scientific evidence and clinical practice.* New York: Plenum Press.

Mitchell, S. A. (1988). *Relational concepts in psychoanalysis.* Cambridge, MA: Harvard University Press.

Ogden, T. (1982). *Projective identification and psychotherapeutic techniques.* New York: Jason Aronson.

Quintana, S. M., Aboud, F. E., Chao, R. K., Contreras-Grau, J., Cross, W. E., Hudley, C., & Vietze, D. L. (2006). Race, ethnicity, and culture in child development: Contemporary research and future directions. *Child Development, 77*(5), 1129–1141. DOI: 10.2307/3878421.

Sampson, H., & Weiss, J. (1986). *The psychoanalytic process: Theory, clinical observations, and empirical research.* New York: Guilford Press.

Slochower, J. (1991). Variations in the analytic holding environment. *International Journal of Psychoanalysis, 72*(4), 709–718.

Slochower, J. (1996). *Holding and psychoanalysis.* Hillsdale, NJ: The Analytic Press.

Stolorow, R. (1992). Subjectivity and self psychology: A personal odyssey. In A. Goldberg (Ed.), *New therapeutic visions: Progress in self psychology* (vol. 8, pp. 241–250). Hillsdale, NJ: The Analytic Press.

Straker, G. (2004). Race for cover: Castrated whiteness, perverse consequences. *Psychodynamic Dialogues, 14*(4), 405–422.

Sue, D., & Sue, D. W. (2003). *Counseling the culturally diverse: Theory and practice* (4th ed.). New York: John Wiley & Sons.

Unrau, Y. A., Seita, J. R., & Putney, K. S. (2008). Former foster youth remember multiple placement moves: A journey of loss and hope. *Children and Youth Services Review, 30*, 1256–1266. DOI: 10.1016/j.childyouth.2008.03.010.

Winnicott, D. (1968). Playing: Its theoretical status in the clinical situation. *The International Journal of Psychoanalysis, 49*(4), 591–599.

Winnicott, D. (1969). The use of an object. *International Journal of Psychoanalysis, 50*(4), 711–716.

Winnicott, D. W. (1971). *Playing and reality.* New York: Routledge.

Winnicott, D. W. (1989). *The infant-mother experience of mutuality: Psychoanalytic explorations.* Cambridge, MA: Harvard Press.

Chapter Eight

An Experience in a Long-Term Consultation Group

WEDNESDAY NOON

On this particular Wednesday, I was tired. I hadn't slept well the night before, and I was not feeling at my best as a therapist. I finished my eleven am session and walked up to the office of our consultation group leader. I was running a bit late, as I had had trouble ending the previous session, and was feeling a bit guilty about both. I was also feeling lonely at the time. Lonely, as therapists tend to get, tempered to some extent by that degree to which we allow ourselves to be in the room with our clients. I was not at my best.

As I entered I saw the familiar sight of my leader sitting in her chair, and the other three members seated in their usual arrangement. As always, there were snacks generously laid out on the table, and my loneliness and guilt quickly subsided as the faces of my group members greeted me warmly, even though I had interrupted their conversation. I also felt the familiar relief of being in the presence of a group of people who knew me on a deeper level than the people I spent most of my day with: my clients. This brings a sense of openness and playfulness that are a relief from some of the guilt and constriction that I walked in with. I have been with this consultation group for three years. They likely know my faults better than I know my own and somehow seem to like me even more because of it. This kind of safety brings about many good things.

For one, I felt that if I had something to say about my case or anyone else's, I could share it. We started our check-in, our usual ritual in which all members check in about their A Home Within case. This is normally followed by a more thorough presentation by a group member who has been assigned to present that week. When it comes time for one of our younger group members to check in, Judy, it is clear to me that she does not want to talk about her case. I know her well enough to tell. It's in her voice as she begins to describe it and the way she doesn't make eye contact with us. Judy has a painful case in which a twelve-year-old girl looks as though she might be falling into psychosis, and Judy can do little to stop it. I feel compassion for her and want to help her.

Judy and I have had many discussions together, inside and out of the consulting room, about our cases, our lives as therapists, as well as our lives outside of the work. We have never gotten together socially, but I think we both have wondered what that would be like. I believe that if we are doing the work, which in this case consists of putting both feet into our consultation groups, we sometimes wonder these things. We need to let the other to group members in, which means into our hearts and sometimes even into our fantasy lives if we want to get the most out of our group. The times when I am reassured and feel most connected with the group are the times when I have allowed myself to be most vulnerable in talking about my feelings about the cases that we discuss. This is how our group gives to us and moves forward, by providing a home for us to visit every week to let down our guard and soak up what the group has to offer.

At the risk of sounding trite or simplistic, I think the work we do is primarily about love. So please excuse what might seem to be a digression, but I can't, with any integrity, talk about the work we do in our consultation group, and what I enjoy about it, without talking about what motivates us and sustains us in it. In my group I feel loved, and I would venture to say that the others feel this way to one extent or another as well. I don't know how much I would be able to get out of the group, or how I would continue to do the work, if we didn't feel that way. These relationships, and the emotional space they create, the strength they give us, are an important part of what we bring back to our work with our clients. The struggles we go through in our pursuit of such connection speaks not only to our own desire for such connection, which is in its strictest sense, selfish, but also to how strongly we feel about its value in the world and in our clients' lives. However, there are certain criteria that are necessary for this particular kind love to thrive and having a group to help you with that is one of the keys to allowing that love to be expressed in a way that is helpful to our clients—clients that need it more than most.

If I am right, that this work is about love, then how am I not to "fall in love" sometimes with my group members, who in turn, love their clients, and how are they supposed to help me without feeling something for me? How are we supposed to be fully in the room with our clients and help them feel loved if we hold back with our closest colleagues? I think that most of us get a little uncomfortable around conversations about love. I think this fear stems from many sources, amongst which is the fear that it will lead to potentially harmful places. There is a basis in reality for these concerns, since boundary violations do occur. Because of this, however, there is a temptation to avoid the idea of love completely, so as not to SEEM inappropriate. I believe that there are big risks to leaving love, and conversations about love, out of the work altogether. Perhaps the biggest is that by keeping such powerful feelings in the closet we deaden the work and ourselves in it, as well as provide shadows in which such feelings can more easily be acted on in destructive ways. What I have learned over time is that the power of these loving connections, when appropriately channeled, is not only the most beautiful part of our work, but also the most helpful.

Ideally, we get to enjoy feelings of love in their safest form: simply being in the room with someone and connecting with them. I can almost hear (Bion, 1974) insisting that love is one of the most oversaturated words in the English language, that we only use one word to describe so many different ideas. Eskimos have many different terms for describing snow, but we only have one, more or less, for love. Yes, it's important that we situate such a loaded word in a larger context. We don't go around saying, "I love you" to our clients and colleagues out of nowhere, because they wouldn't be quite sure what we'd mean by it. The Oxford dictionary's definition of love that most accurately describes what I am trying to convey is the one listed first: "an intense feeling of deep affection." What I am saying is that we have strong feelings of deep affection towards everyone who is important in our lives at one time or another, and I'm saying that our clients and colleagues with whom we share our work are very important. Love is just the closest word we have to what I'm trying to describe. Our group has worked together for some time; because the work we have done has been thoughtful, respectful, and because we have attempted to put our whole selves into our work, one of the products of our work is our love for each other.

So, back to my fellow group member, Judy, who is sharing her thoughts. I think that she doesn't want to talk about her case because she doesn't want to THINK about her case. It may feel like too much to her to think about all the implications for her client's life, and Judy's relationship with her, if she plunges into psychosis. Will she be institutionalized? Will she wind up homeless? Will she be in unbearable pain for the rest of her life? Is there something I could have done to prevent it? I don't know all of what was going on for her in that moment, but I know that these are all fears that those who work with foster children commonly feel. These are depressing, but very real, potential scenarios that our clients face, and it is sometimes simply more comfortable to avoid thinking about them. We are witnessing our clients' pain for years on end. We are also often bearing witness to their families' struggles with internal and external forces, the pain of the teachers who have to contain their feelings without the resources, and the neglectful stance that society has taken towards our foster children. It is a luxury and a privilege for us to go to a place at the end of the day where we do not have to face the same harsh realities as our foster children. But in order to help our clients face their realities, both internal and external, we as therapists need some external support ourselves.

There is a great deal of research on "vicarious traumatization," which results from listening to others' stories of trauma (Canfield, 2005). This can lead to burn out, depression, poor work performance, anxiety, and difficulty in one's relationships, to name a few. Without proper supports, in the form of groups like ours as one example, such effects are much more likely to take hold. Although I haven't discussed this explicitly with the founders, I am confident that in setting up these groups, vicarious trauma is one of the problems they were attempting to alleviate.

Luckily, we are at the point as a group, having been together for many years, where we can at least make a good guess at what Judy needs from us right now. We are grateful to be able to give this to her, and I sense that she is, on balance, grateful to receive it, despite some requisite ambivalence, especially since she is struggling with how to give her client what SHE needs. We are aware of the "parallel process," in which what is happening in the group echoes what is happening in the therapy.

My guess is that, for one thing, Judy wants to be given the space to decide how much she wants to talk about her client. This is a common feeling in our group: the ambivalence that contains the desire to help our clients and the myriad of seemingly indigestible feelings that talking about our cases brings up in us. So we wait, and we empathize. We might even use humor, which I like to do. I try to speak to something through humor, but sometimes each one of us just needs some relief from the deadly seriousness of our cases. Any concerns that my often-edgy humor was not welcome were put to rest a long time ago.

"Nice job making her psychotic," I say. The group laughs. With a joke like that I was trying to speak to the guilt that I sensed she felt in having this happen to her client, and hopefully to offer a little relief. Fortunately, she gets it—she understands that I am saying that she does not have that power. I believe that humor can be useful in our work with our clients. It allows us to deal with topics that would otherwise be too anxiety provoking to talk about. If used thoughtfully, humor can allow us to speak to something directly and empathically at the same time. To use an analogy, levity can be like a little sugar that helps the medicine go down. This is true for our clients as well as group members. Care must of course be taken to make sure that the humor facilitates a sense of connection rather than alienation.

Judy begins to tell us what is going on in her case, that she is feeling frustrated, hopeless, and ineffective in the face of her client's apparent regression into a type of pathological lying; she is lying for no reason and never seems to take responsibility for it. Sometimes I don't want to hear about the pain either and find myself thinking about other things. I try to notice this and return to listening. I want to listen because I respect Judy, I care about her and her case, and I want to try to continue to give her some of what she and the group have given me: a calm, perceptive, and caring ear. The group expanded on their theories about what is going on with this client, which we sometimes call a diagnosis. They theorized that this little girl may be on the verge of a collapse into psychosis, as she seems to believe her lies, becoming increasingly divorced from reality, and is apparently exasperating everyone in her life with the unpredictability and disruptiveness of her behavior.

The entire group has listened to Judy's case go through periods of ups and downs as well as periods of stagnation and periods of movement. Most vividly, we've gotten a sense of our colleague's feelings for this girl, the depth of the attachment between the two, and the sense of responsibility Judy carries for her. Because all of us in the group have had the experience of watching one of our child client's experience pain that we could not prevent, Judy knows that she is in the company of those who understand. Anyone who works with foster children knows the sense of responsibility that comes with the work, the sense that if it weren't for us, these children might easily fall through the cracks of society and wind up institutionalized, homeless, addicted to drugs, or dead. We face the terror of these things happening and the pressure to prevent such occurrences by trying to give the children a sense of safety and containment in our relationship with them. Our group provides a place for us to share our fears, frustrations, and hopes where we know we will be heard and understood. We can then take this experience and give our clients a sense of such a space. We can pass along the safety that we feel from the group to our clients.

Ideally, the warmth we feel toward our group members doesn't interfere with our ability to give one another the clinical feedback that is also so important in this work. Fortunately, our talented group leader has been able to forge an atmosphere in our group in which we can offer feedback that is both compassionate and truthful, allowing members to present, knowing that they will be respected as well as given an honest impression of our reaction to the case.

I share my impression of Judy's case, which is inspired in part by our group's recent reading (*Live Company*, by Anne Alvarez, 1992). I talk about my impression that her client has disconnected, and taken an adversarial and somewhat hopeless stance towards others' attempts to reach out to her, and that I can relate to Judy's feelings of frustration. Given the suffering I know she is enduring around this case, I have more than my usual level of sensitivity around adding to her pain in any way by making her feel criticized or disrupted by my comments. There is always a tension between caretaking and giving helpful feedback in the group that I think comes from what we know about how these cases live in us, and *need* to live in us. Since we care about the people in our group and have a deep respect and compassion for the difficult work we do, we may have a tendency to pull punches when we have a criticism. It is important, both for the health of the group and for the sake of the case that we find a way to include reactions we have that may be critical, and helpful. The framing and delivery of these comments is an important and delicate art, but as a group grows, so do the members' comfort in delivering constructive criticism. We know where everyone else is coming from when they speak, more or less, and we know how to repair hurt feelings and misunderstandings if they arise. Group members ultimately feel much more comfortable if they believe their group will be honest with them, and they also can return to their work with more confidence, knowing that they doing their best to look at every aspect of their work, even the difficult ones.

Our clients at A Home Within are often deeply insecure, and in many ways disturbed. It follows, then, that in order to fully understand what is going on inside them and for them to feel that we really "get it," we have to allow ourselves to be disturbed by them. Without any explicit conversation around this, our group intuitively has made space for us to inhabit and express some of this disturbance. Despite all of these concerns, and because of the history we have together, I share my thoughts with the confidence that, regardless of Judy's reaction—whether it be annoyed, hopeless, defensive, or appreciative—we have built the trust in the context of the group to weather any bumps, and emerge with a sense of connection. Just like in the work with our clients, the trust that builds up over the years is what allows us to continue to take risks in opening our minds and hearts to one another, continually pushing our own and others' envelopes in the spirit of improving ourselves, helping our clients, and connecting even more deeply.

Our group intervenes in a myriad of ways with one another. Clinical work is so complex and can be looked at from so many different angles, we believe it is important to push ourselves and one another to grow in our knowledge of every aspect of treatment, which includes keeping abreast of the latest findings in neuroscience, trauma, family systems, cultural and ethnic issues, as well as the latest clinical thinking about how to work with the symptoms with which we are presented in our work. The readings we do together as a group emphasize these topics and add to our enjoyment of the group, but more importantly, they assure that we are providing the best possible treatment to our A Home Within clients.

Regardless of our level of confidence, it is always feels risky to begin to advise someone else on a client whom we have never even met, and with whom the therapist has spent countless intimate, vulnerable hours. When I take such a risk, playing with a new idea or trying to get a handle on a new feeling that I am aware of as I listen to the case, there is always at least a moment when I'm not sure how my thoughts will land. It is this moment, when I see they land safely, even if misunderstood or ultimately incorrect, that allows me to enjoy continuing to make use of the group and want to keep coming week after week, year after year. This is also the process our clients go through with us.

I need to take a moment at this point to describe my A Home Within case, as I will be referring to him in the pages that follow. My client's name is Tyree. I have seen him for individual therapy for the past five years. Tyree is a sixteen-year-old African American boy who suffers from depression, anxiety, and drug abuse and demonstrates oppositional behavior and poor school performance. When he was eleven years old, he was referred to treatment for defiance, lack of motivation, and academic performance below his potential. He lives with a foster mother in her fifties, whom I will call Sylvia, a sweet and thoughtful Caucasian woman, albeit quite anxious and insecure, who had previous battles with drug addiction. Tyree has been with her since the age of two, an unusually long period of time for the foster care system. Sylvia and her husband, Derek, split up when Tyree was six, but Derek remains a part-time caregiver in his life.

I think if we are allowing ourselves to connect with someone, we carry around a version of him or her inside us. I think I take a little version of Tyree with me into the consultation group every session, where I can play out how I can help him to make contact with others. When I describe my work with him, I express, consciously and unconsciously, how he lives in me. When we care about people, their struggles become our struggles to some extent. As I bring my case into the group, the group then struggles with me, and inevitably a group member will express feelings that I had toward the client for which I had not yet found words.

This happens with other group members and their clients as well. Whenever I feel distant or annoyed with a member or her client, I have found that it can inevitably be tied, at least in part, to a struggle that the client is having with those same feelings. For example, when I was feeling bombarded by criticism from Tyree, Derek, and the other therapists involved in the case, I was irritable, and easily felt criticized by the feedback that the group members had to offer.

As another example, a couple of our group members found themselves being annoyed with the client of another group member, a therapist I will call Meredith. Meredith's client had suddenly decided that she had ADHD, that this was the source of many of her problems, and that the solution was medication. Another therapist in our group, along with myself, found ourselves feeling the same way and felt free to express our irritation with the client, out of an understanding that this type of reaction often has clinical utility. Meredith did not become defensive of her work, but was surprised by our reaction and did not understand the source of our aggressive feelings. As

Meredith learned more about the case, she became aware of how much subtle aggression was being expressed unconsciously by her client through missing sessions, and devaluing the therapy in other subtle ways. Meredith then became aware of her own frustration with her client and, through this process, was able to engage the client in a way that brought the aggression into the therapy and felt more alive to her. Meredith was thereby able to bring a more integrated version of her experience of her client into the session. This is what I refer to as being able to be present with the client. It is crucial that we not overlook the subtle but utterly important power of these dynamics. The more we make use of this process of introspection, the more we realize that it can become one of the most important tools in our tool belt.

Further, I believe that since there was room in the group for discussion of such feelings, this opened space for those feelings to be discussed between Meredith and her client, and therefore created more space for the client to begin to heal. Peter Fonagy (1952) has described this process of thinking about the feelings that occur in the room between client and therapist as akin to the process of metabolization. That is, clients can overwhelm us with feelings that are both powerful and subtle; the degree to which we can metabolize them, that is, think about them, and offer them back to the clients with compassionate words, correlates highly with the degree to which we can help them find relief. What I am also suggesting is that when therapists have a compassionate and thoughtful group in which to discuss a case, the group can help them digest these feelings, allowing them to pass the relief onto our clients.

This experience of a holding environment, as described by Winnicott (1965) is a setting in which a subject feels as though his inner experience is seen, understood and respected. The fact that I can process my own feelings about my case gives me the freedom then, to be annoying, immature, or sometimes silly in the group, knowing that the group can help me process whatever it is that I am feeling about the case. There is an assumption that in consultation groups, the members just come in and talk about cases to come to a better understanding of their clients in some sort of intellectual way. Thank goodness this is not the whole picture, because to feel truly held, our clients need not just our intellectual selves, but also our whole selves.

On that day in consultation group when Judy discussed her case, I also suggested that it may be necessary for Judy to actively insert herself into her client's psychic world to let her know that she was still there, and that Judy would not settle for the client's state of lying to herself and others, a sort of deadened world, despite Judy's fears of being intrusive or inflaming her client's anger. It was a comment that contained some obvious directives, and in some contexts, this type of comment can be taken as arrogance or judgment, and can lead to hard feelings, which may or may not be acknowledged. To my relief, Judy responded with what I perceived to be genuine appreciation of my comments, saying that I had a "really good point." In retrospect I think I may have been doing with Judy something similar to what I was suggesting that she do with her client. That is, I was risking putting my nose in some place where I didn't know if I was welcome, in hopes that in making contact I might also enliven something important (Alvarez, 1992).

Working with these cases can feel like a battle between staying present and checking out, between fighting to help them and giving up. This is an ever-present theme in work with foster children. Beginning with the child, who is often shuttled from caregiver to caregiver, bringing about intense feelings of abandonment and hopelessness, checking out is an understandable option. This is no small feat, and one for which I believe that we need our group sometimes to rally around us, telling us stories of old battles, victories and defeats, the emotional tolls and the lessons learned, to give us a context for our own battle, and to give us enough faith in what we are doing to continue to allow ourselves fully back into the room with our clients. I know my group has done this on countless occasions for me, such as when my client went through a period of silence and falling asleep in session while his life was falling apart and I felt I could do nothing about it. I am eternally grateful to my group for providing a setting where I can share such fears, as well as my insecurities, fears, frustrations, and joys, and emerge, patched up, connected, and better at what I do.

ANOTHER WEDNESDAY

On this day it was my turn to discuss my work with the foster mother of my client. Being the only man in the group, I sometimes feel self-conscious talking about my work with this woman, with whom there are sometimes feelings of attraction in the therapy room. The women in my consultation group have been splendid at making me feel as comfortable as possible, but let's face it, talking about this work is never completely comfortable, especially when feelings of sexuality are involved, and especially when you're the only man in a room with three or four women. Yet, I keep coming back, without excruciating discomfort, to talk to the women in my group about these, and many other topics related to my case.

I describe the awkward moments that we often have in our session when Sylvia looks at me in silence. She has described her own feelings of intimacy in these moments, as well as her anxiety about them. I describe to the group the quality of the charge in the room at these moments, and how uncomfortable both Sylvia and I seem to be. I talk for a little while about my associations and experiences in this predicament, namely that I feel under tremendous pressure to produce something for her, and not to let her feel rejected. The group members, knowing a great deal about Sylvia already, and possessing a great deal of affection for her, share their thoughts about the intense needs that this mother seems to be expressing in her stare, and how difficult it must be for my client to know how to react if and when she expressed these same needs to him. We are talking about the confusion and anxiety that result when parents have difficulty shielding their own problems from their child-especially a foster child. This is unfortunately quite common in the foster care system. For reasons that are quite complex, foster parents often have their own internal struggles that interfere with their ability to effectively parent foster children, a group which is difficult to parent under perfect circumstances. We discuss the dynamics in the relationship between Tyree and Sylvia that seem apparent, that is, how Tyree's and Sylvia's issues play off of each other, sometimes creating a perfect storm of misunderstanding and misattunement. We also discuss Tyree's understandable reaction to Sylvia's tendency to burden him with her own needs, or to withdraw emotionally, or periodically explode with anger. The group's comments allowed me to feel that they understood my experience as well as Tyree's, so I could take not only the insights, but also the experience of being understood and loved, back into my work with Tyree and Sylvia.

A FEW WEDNESDAYS LATER: DEALING WITH "THE SYSTEM"

Today, I was steeped in my case. Every time I thought about it, I was anxious and angry at the same time. "How could she throw me under the bus like that?" "I hate this woman." "I have no support from the treatment team." By "she" and "woman" and "team" I am referring to a particular therapist on Tyree's treatment team by whom I was feeling very mistreated. In particular, I was furious at her because I felt that when Derek had asked her whether Tyree needed to stay in therapy, she had responded that she didn't have an opinion on the subject. I knew that she was being political, as she was the family therapist, and felt that she couldn't take sides, but she denied that this was the reason, and kept insisting that insisted that she wasn't sure that Tyree needed therapy! I felt strongly that I needed her support, and if I didn't get it, the case that I had been working on for four years, could be sunk!

To clarify, there were multiple therapists on this case at any given time—a family therapist, individual therapists for my client and his two siblings, a therapist for the mother, and a social worker. There was also turnover within this treatment team at various points due to internships ending, people quitting, or therapists being fired by the family. The treatment team had decided to meet once per month to share notes on the case, and in the spirit of Altman's (2004) thinking, help the family by sharing our perspectives on the case with one another and thinking about them as a team. Working as a team requires a great deal of communication, since without communication, there is a high likelihood that rifts will occur between treatment team members that are otherwise difficult to understand and repair. Treatment team members tend to side with their own client in a family that is rife with conflict, and then tend to blame the other members of the family, along with their therapists. This typically plays out by a child or parent being scapegoated, followed by the corresponding treatment team member being singled out as the source of the problem. Being on the bad end of a split is one of the most difficult parts of this work, since it plays into fears that nearly everyone has of being hated, blamed, ostracized, or having done something wrong or hurtful.

I knew I was taking the other therapist's treatment of me a little too personally and was being a bit petulant, but the fact remained that this treatment team member hadn't supported Tyree's treatment, and it looked like Tyree might successfully end his treatment as a result. I knew a great deal about this family's dynamics and was also angry with Derek, as I believed he was trying to sabotage Tyree's therapy due to his own insecurities about Tyree's contact with me, another male figure. Derek was a very fragile man, a former addict, who would sometimes call me before his foster son's session to cancel, saying things like "He's not coming in, because he's with me today, another kind of therapy. Ha ha." I had a very hard time getting him to come in to meet with me, which would have been the typical format for helping him work through some of his feelings about the treatment. On top of all this, there was another therapist on the case who refused to confront Derek on his use of intimidation as a disciplinary technique, and often condoned it, then wondered why Tyree would then proceed to try to intimidate his mother and brother.

I should add that my client's behavior wasn't helping to keep him in treatment either. He had been complaining about therapy to his foster parents, saying it was a waste of time and wanted to stop, making me sometimes feel useless and frustrated with him as well, though I was careful to spare him from my reactions. Tyree would not respond to me verbally or would fall asleep on my couch around half the time in sessions. Sometimes he would grunt responses to me; for only about ten percent of the time were we engaged in actual verbal conversation. I thought about this pattern a great deal over the course of my work with this client, and have sought extensive consultation about him from my A Home Within group as well as my individual consultant. I came to understand that Tyree's behavior in sessions represented multiple communications and attempts to heal. He was using the consultation room as one of the few safe spaces in his life where he could relax and sometimes fall asleep. He was also passive-aggressively expressing anger towards me that he did not feel safe to express to his foster parents, since Derek would threaten him if he sensed any anger from him, while his foster mother would crumble into the position of victim. There was a great deal of other evidence for these hypotheses that is outside the scope of this chapter.

Taking Tyree into A Home Within from the clinic where we started allowed me to deepen my work with him. My participation in the consultation group allowed me to think about my client from many angles that I had not thought of before. We devoted a good deal of time to his distancing behavior and silence. The anger and the longing that lay within it became more apparent after those conversations with my group. There were many times in which I felt utterly hopeless about my ability to reach this child—when he was smoking pot seemingly incessantly, cutting school, failing classes, physically threatening his foster mother, and getting into trouble with the law. Everyone in the family was scared of his temper, except perhaps Derek. All this was going on when he came into my office, often barely speaking to me and falling asleep.

I felt alone and frustrated because I felt that the other therapists involved in this case were complicit in its dissolution and devaluing of the work that I believed was very important. From my perspective, they were unable look at the family dynamics of splitting, coddling, and triangulation (Bowen, 1985) that the therapists were then acting out in their relationships with one another. This can often happen in clinical teams, where they find themselves at odds, deeply split, and really disliking each other. If no one was aware of the intense feelings that this case elicited in all of its therapists, no matter who happened to be on the case at the time—feelings of guilt and simultaneous blame, rescue fantasies and concomitant feelings of failure, and unacknowledged anger at one another. I was also aware that my own feelings toward the other therapists were fueled in part by the way in which the family treated, attacked, dismissed, and demonized one another, which then spilled over to the treatment team as each therapist tended to take the side of his or her own client. Despite this intellectual understanding, I remained in a very painful place with this case. Sometimes we have to live the case before we really get it, and often our emotions and intellect are distant cousins.

To summarize, I had a client who seldom spoke to me and told his foster parents that therapy was useless, a foster father who was threatened by the therapy and was actively undermining it, a foster mother who spent most of her energy being angry at the foster father or my client, a family therapist who told the family that she didn't know if my client needed therapy, and a brother's therapist who had poor boundaries and was basically encouraging the foster father to be physically aggressive towards my client. I felt alone on an island in a sea of insanity. I needed someone to talk to.

Enter my group. I spent some time updating them on some recent developments in the case, including Derek's recent attempts to get Tyree out of therapy. Even more helpful than the insights that my group provided me about the case, including the likely connections between the therapists' behavior and my client's inner world, as well as the likely involvement of the therapists' own issues, was my group's very presence. As simple as it may sound, I needed them to listen to me. I'll say it a little differently now: I needed THEM to listen to me. That is, they weren't just three people sitting in a room with me. Because they know me and I know them, because they know what it feels like to do this work, to feel alone, and to be trying to hold not just a client's pain, but the pain of a whole system trying but often failing as they try to help these children, I felt that they really heard me. Because of all of these factors and more, some conscious, some unconscious, and many beyond my ability to articulate with words, I felt I had a home into which I could bring my client and my feelings about all the characters in his world, a place where I could put the pieces together in my case, and in myself, so I could return to giving what I had to offer to my client.

With their help, I was able to move to a place internally where I did not feel like I had to defend myself or take a combative stance with anyone in the case, and could move forward with a sense of purpose for what I was supposed to do: think. I was freed up to think about the case, think about how I wanted to intervene with both my client and team members, and relinquish control over its outcome. That is, I could not control whether the case imploded, or how the other team members saw me, or even whether my client got better or worse. This is something that all therapists learn at some point-that try as we might to help our clients, and though sometimes we do, there are often forces more powerful than we at work, both inside out outside our clients. I was able to remind myself of limits of my powers without dissolving into a sense of futility. My group had bolstered me so that I was able to bring myself back into the room with everything I had. They did not do this through false encouragement or empty compliments, but through listening with their wise clinical ears, sharing their thoughts and experiences with me, and letting me know when I messed up.

Altman (*Analyst in the City*, 1994) elucidates the powerful forces at work in families that can lead to dysfunctional dynamics in the organizations that attempt to be useful to them. There are identifications, allegiances, resentments, and fantasies within foster families and foster children that are then absorbed by the therapists, who have the choice of acting them out in not-so-helpful ways, or thinking about them to better understand their client's experiences. Every version of acting out by the professionals in my case could be traced to their identification with, and reenacting of, a "crazy" or disturbed part of a client or family member.

As an example of this, in my case there were times when a clinician would walk into a treatment team meeting and basically be blamed or verbally attacked for a perceived mistake, neglected intervention, or often, perceived bias toward or unfair treatment of a family member. It is a horrible experience to be on the receiving end of such an attack, and usually stems from some level of "splitting" in the family, that is, the need of one or more family members to locate all of the bad qualities in another in an effort to avoid having to consider those qualities in themselves. When a family member shares this perspective with a therapist, who is trying hard to stand in the shoes of the client, it takes a great deal of work not to accept the client's perspective as the whole truth. When this happens, the therapist of the "bad" client sometimes gets identified with the client.

Since Tyree often played this part in the family, intimidating other family members, getting into trouble, and defying their wishes, I would often pick up on other therapist's resentment towards him as well as their doubts about whether I was doing my job well enough. I could then become self-conscious, defending my client or myself, which worsened the problem, since it would make them feel I wasn't taking the problem seriously enough. Before we knew it, we were acting out the very patterns that occurred in the family-my client being blamed for the problems in the family, becoming defensive and acting out angrily, thereby perpetuating their perception of him as bad. This is one of many examples how family dynamics would play out in the treatment team. It is the job of the therapists, as Altman (1994) emphasizes, to observe and give voice to these parallels as they happen, thereby deepening the therapists' understanding of the family's experience.

This is not to say that these dynamics are the sole cause of these professionals' behavior. Therapists have issues too, of course, but it has struck me over and over again how often treatment team dynamics reflect the dynamics of the family. These cases seem to have the power to channel whatever existing issues there are in the therapists and between the therapists into a configuration that reflects the client's inner life and dynamics within their family.

Altman's research into these dynamics, as well as my own experience, suggests that if the feelings, experiences, and dynamics surrounding a case and within the agency that treats them are discussed on a regular basis in an attempt to make meaning of them, the case has a better outcome (Altman, 1994). I believe this is one of the important reasons why these consultation groups are so valuable for clinicians who treat foster children. In other words, if our clients are talked about thoughtfully and lovingly, even though they are not present, they do better. This is my belief. This chapter could be seen simply my attempt to elucidate some of the ways that this might happen.

I don't know how I wound up with such great group members. Sometimes I think that I am just plain lucky. But I also believe there are a number of factors that contributed to my experience that are common to nearly all A Home Within groups. The organization, being one that is voluntary in nature, tends to attract interesting, generous people. It also tends to draw people who are interested in open-ended work, in other words, committed, dedicated, and thoughtful people. In addition, consultation groups self-select for people who are interested in connecting with others around their work. This wonderful set of qualities, among others, I am sure, seems to be a necessity for being a member of A Home Within, and luckily for me, my group is full of them.

I don't mean to paint a picture of a group that is all rosy, either. There are difficult feelings towards other members of the group that often represent a facet of the case that is under our care. There are hurt feelings, along with jealousy, anger, annoyance, and anxiety, right alongside the comfort, containment, affection, laughter, and caring attention. I have had moments when I was worried that I was doing something wrong in therapy, being too active, too passive, or that I was not engaged enough in the work or feeling self-conscious about my anger towards him. In these moments I would sometimes feel quite vulnerable in the group, not wanting to talk about the case, and feeling very self-conscious if I did, afraid that the group would see and criticize what I had already beat myself up for. Invariably, the group would respond with compassion, even if confirming a mistake of some sort, but ultimately tying it back to the case in some way that moved the work forward. Anger and self-consciousness were both things that Tyree felt powerfully, and was communicating to me on a subtle, sometimes unconscious level. With the group's help, I was able to digest these feelings, and put them into words for Tyree, helping him to feel understood and experience compassionate witness to his experience.

Working through, acknowledging, and repairing the hurt feelings, either in the consultation group or in our personal therapy, is indeed what allows the group to move forward and connect on a deeper level. We progress as a group, a lot like in the clinical work, not despite the tough feelings, but because we allow room for thinking about them. Home is not always pretty, and is by necessity filled with all of the emotions that go along with living, I would much rather have a home for such experiences than not, and I think offering it to clinicians is one of the most important ways we are then able to offer something like it to the foster children we treat.

I want to end this chapter with a recent anecdote from my A Home Within experience. For a few weeks in a row, now, I have been leaving my jacket in my group leader's office. She has had to call me and let me know that she has it and that she will leave it on a table in her waiting room for me to pick up. There is an old axiom that therapists hold that if a person leaves something behind in your office, it means that a part of them wanted to stay there. I have been doing this so often lately that my group leader's most recent e-mail to me was simply, "Your jacket is in its usual home."

REFERENCES

Altman, N. (2004). *The analyst in the inner city: Race, class and culture through a psychoanalytic lens.* New York: The Analytic Press.

Alvarez, A. (1992). *Live company: Psychoanalytic psychotherapy with autistic, borderline, deprived and abused children.* New York: Tavistock/Routledge.
Bion, W. R. (1974). *Experiences in groups—and other paper.* Oxford, England: Ballantine.
Bowen, M. (1985). Family therapy and family group therapy. In H. I. Kaplan & B. J. Sadock (Eds.), *Group treatment of mental illness.* New York: E. P. Dutton.
Canfield, J. (2005). Secondary traumatization, burnout, and vicarious traumatization: A review of the literature as it relates to therapists who treat trauma. *Smith College Studies in Social Work, 75*(2), 81–101. DOI: 10.1300/J497v75n02_06.
Fonagy, P. (2001). *Attachment theory and psychoanalysis.* New York: Other Press.
Winnicott, D. W. (1965). *The family and individual development.* Oxford, England: Basic Books.

III

Shared Memories

It is not unusual for therapists who have been in practice for many years to have clients reappear after an extended absence. The child who initially came to treatment because her anxiety interfered with her forming friendships asks if she can come for a few sessions at the age of sixteen following the breakup with a boyfriend. The forty-year-old who saw you when she was just getting her sea-legs as a young adult calls because her marriage of over ten years feels stale and she's worried that she can't make it better. The middle-aged man who consulted with you during a painful divorce when his children were young calls when he is feeling overwhelmed by the needs of teenaged son who is struggling with depression and an aging father whose health is declining.

When clients initiate contact with a therapist they have not seen for a matter of years, it is usually with a sense of relief that someone who knows them is just a phone call away. In a time of stress, they don't have to tell their whole story. They reconnect, comforted by the knowledge that the therapist will remember the important people and events of their lives. Whether meeting for just a few sessions or over a longer time, what is important in the context of this volume is first, the expectation that the therapist will be available and second, that the therapist will remember. These calls don't begin with "I don't know if you will remember me." The appointment begins with some basic information to bring the therapist up-to-date, not with questions about what the therapist remembers from their earlier work together.

When we have enjoyed stable and sustaining relationships we take for granted that we continue to exist in the mind of the other—as they do in our mind. Even if the memories have become a little fuzzy or some of the details have faded over time, the essence of what was important often re-emerges relatively quickly when our memory is jogged by a name or the sound of a familiar voice. While the cases presented in this section are somewhat different, in that the therapists were present and active participants in the clients' lives over an extended period, the unifying and crucial factor is the spoken or unspoken expectation that the therapist knows what is important and holds the memories, even when the clients cannot.

In each of the cases presented in this section, the therapists saw their clients over the course of different developmental stages. For Clemee, her therapist was the only person with a distinct memory of her life as a young child in foster care. Zina's therapist knew first-hand the history of her desperate attempts to ward off the unbearable knowledge of the trauma she suffered throughout childhood. Ben and his therapist grieved together through more losses than any child should have to endure. Because of their shared memories, the therapists could offer a richness of historical and contextual understanding that simply would not have been possible for new clinicians coming into their lives at any point along the way. Had any of the three stopped therapy and resumed with someone new, none of them would have been able to convey the story of their lives that lived in the minds of their therapists. This is not to suggest that new or different therapists could not have been helpful, it is to remind us that shared experiences bind people in important ways and that new relationships do not easily substitute for those that are built over months and years.

Because of their history together these therapists were able to make emotional and cognitive connections for their clients that helped them make sense of, and ultimately change, their behavior. Children and adolescents who have suffered multiple and complex traumatic experiences cannot keep their stories in mind. Trauma is not stored as verbal memory that can be retrieved and reported coherently; rather, traumatic events reappear in flashbacks as jumbled fragments of sensation or in actions that seemingly have little relationship to current events. Traumatized children and youth must rely on others to hold and tell their stories, just as children, too young to have the emotional or cognitive capacity to narrate the story of their lives, must depend on parents to tell them who they are.

Sometimes, sadly, the therapist, as in these three cases, is the most dependable person in a foster child's life. When we worry that an extended relationship with a therapist raises the danger of the child becoming too dependent on therapy, it is important to remember that dependency is the normal, expectable precursor to independence. Infants and young children must depend on adults for their very survival. Children and adolescents only gradually learn self-reliance, which, importantly, also means knowing when to turn to others for help.

When we are learning something new, we often depend on those with more expertise to help us navigate unfamiliar territory. And, when we have lost our bearings in the face of an upsetting event, we may turn to others for help in reconstructing the story of the upsetting incident. For these two reasons alone, we should not be concerned about foster children developing lasting relationships with a competent therapist. They are learning something new—what it means to have a healthy relationship with someone upon whom they can depend. And when they have lost their emotional bearings in the face of trauma—they need to have someone explain what happened until they can know it for themselves.

When working with victims of trauma we often must rely on others to help us reclaim our emotional bearings. The feelings we sit with as we hear about unthinkable horrors that are inflicted on children can and do leave us shaken, making it hard for us to know for sure that we have heard correctly or remember that we have the tools and skills to help in such dire circumstances. The final chapter in this section captures the power of the collective memory of a consultation group that has worked together over time.

Just as the clients rely on their therapists to know and remember, the therapists depend on their colleagues to hold what they cannot know by themselves. These concentric circles of emotional protection are at the heart of the work of A Home Within. In the therapist's work with John and with Mark, members of the consultation group helped to verbalize the therapist's thoughts and clarify the ways in which the therapist was unknowingly contributing to both progress and resistance. Without the presence of the consultation group, each of these cases would likely have ended differently, likely much sooner and with much less healthy development for the client.

Chapter Nine

Clemee

It is 3 p.m. on a bleak November afternoon. I am on the sidewalk of a busy street. Edgy, I look across the street and up and down. Is that it?! Nothing. I run to one corner, nothing, then to another, nothing. I can't remember the color or even the name. I repeat this scenario over and over again. Still nothing. It is now ten minutes after the hour. Edgier and edgier, thoughts racing through my mind—there won't be enough time, why did I agree to do this? Why didn't I bring my cell phone? It's like this every time. I need to call someone. What if they come and I am not here? Upstairs, I listen to a message. "Where are you? They are out there! Waiting for you!" Like a child who has done something wrong, I race downstairs. Through the busy traffic I see it now—"People Porter." Yes that is it. I traverse the dangerous street and lift a human form, more wooden soldier than little girl, out of the van. Together now, anxious and relieved, carefully, without acknowledgment, we navigate the middle of the street to the other side. Even before she arrives, before we have a chance to say hello, I have entered, both physically and psychologically, the fragmented world of nine-year-old Clemee.

When we work with individuals who have experienced complex trauma, we, as therapists, are required to "walk through the valley of the shadow" of that trauma whether we wish to or not (Pearlman & Saak Vitne, 1995). As we walk through that shadow, these powerful subjective experiences become the basis for significant communication. It is through these subjective experiences, felt in the context of trauma, that we relive the patient's own history.

In order to manage overwhelming emotional experiences, traumatized patients disconnect from disturbing feelings and memories through dissociation. Because of the neurobiological changes that severe stress creates, the emotional experiences remain unformulated and cannot be expressed with ordinary language (van der Kolk, 1988). These unspeakable memories and emotions are expressed and received by the environment as enactments or felt experiences (Black, 2003). For the therapist, these felt experiences are an essential tool for understanding and empathic connection. When the therapist is able to hold these subjective experiences, to process them, make empathic connections and transform this understanding into something meaningful for the patient, the treatment becomes generative and moves forward. However, too often, as therapists participate in the patient's relational world through the felt experiences, they, like the patient, become overwhelmed by the disturbing feelings that are evoked. They may respond with emotional withdrawal, anger, or retaliation in order to extricate themselves from feelings they would rather not experience. When this occurs it produces a rupture in the treatment, breaking the attachment to the therapist and creating a reenactment of trauma for the patient.

This paper follows a five-year treatment of a little girl in foster care from latency to early adolescence. It is full of enactments, demonstrating the pervasive nature of unprocessed trauma where felt experiences of the child's history reverberate in unremembered form throughout the system. It focuses on the way children with multiple placements in long-term foster care repeatedly reenact their traumatic, dissociated experiences of early and recurring loss. The recurring reenactments take different forms as the child develops chronologically, but the undergirding themes of abandonment, destruction, and loss of self pervade. When these unformulated affective memories are triggered by the environment, the child often reenacts in destructive and aggressive ways that neither they nor important others can understand.

For many children in foster care the ever-changing environment is without continuity or memory. This absence of memory mirrors the child's loss and represents one more traumatic enactment. Because the environment cannot remember, its punitive and chaotic response to the child's destructive behavior often serves to stimulate further trauma. When the therapist works with the child over time she is able to carry the memory that the trauma and inconsistency threaten to erode.

A PLACE FOR EVERYONE

Clemee and I are seated on the floor, Calico Critters, little toy creatures, spread about waiting their turn to be placed within their home. Nearby is Turtle. Everything is about the home. We have to make sure that everything that is needed is here and if not, we must make it. Over time the house has expanded with the addition of small cardboard boxes. All the calico critters are named for the people in the family except for Jenny, who also lives there. Most of the focus is on Miss Marcia, the mother. She is the first to be placed in her bed. The bed is made and the room arranged over and over again.

Everything must be perfect for Miss Marcia as she lies in her beautiful bed. Then we must see that everyone else has their place, their room, their bed. But it is so difficult to get things right and things have to be done over and over again. Nothing is settled. There never seems to be a place for everyone and often it is Clemee who is left out.

I am instructed that baby Jeremiah is crying and that I must bring this new addition to the family downstairs to give him his bottle. My chubby fingers pick up my Calico Critter and I place baby Jeremiah between my two tiny paws. As I bring the baby down the stairs, to my horror he slips out of the tiny paws and drops to the floor. Spontaneously and in complete dismay I exclaim "Oh My God! I have dropped the baby." Clemee looks at me, eyes wide and startled, and then suddenly she exclaims, "Oh my God, Jenny, you dropped the baby!" She starts laughing hilariously and I join in and we laugh and laugh as we pick the baby up and say "poor baby" and drop him again and again. At last we place baby Jeremiah lovingly in his bed. Now Clemee moves to the sofa and lies down, the baby bottle in her hand as she sucks her thumb and desperately holds onto Turtle. "Poor baby" I say and pat her back. "It's all too much." She takes her thumb out of her mouth, looks up at me, and smiles.

DISPLACEMENT

At this writing Clemee is thirteen years old. The session above occurred when she was nine. She has been in the foster care system since birth. She in now in her seventeenth placement. In the case of Clemee, "placement" is a misnomer. Her world is more about displacement than placement, always struggling, rarely finding a place where she can believe she truly resides. It is a theme that will be reenacted over and over.

For her first two years Clemee was placed in foster care with grandparents until the police conducted a raid on the home and found drugs and arms. Since that time one placement has followed another—some very brief and temporary, others thought to be more permanent, but like the rooms that never get settled, always changing. There have been placements for evaluations, placements for treatment—placements, placements, placements. For Clemee, however, each new physical place is a further loss, abandonment, displacement, a further retreat into her wooden world.

At the time of the above session Clemee had been with her foster care family for a year and a half; her foster mother was six months pregnant. There were many concerns that motivated foster mother's request for treatment. Clemee was chronically enuretic. Frequently soiling herself, Clemee would then attempt to hide the evidence of the enuresis. She "lied" about insignificant as well as important things. She also exhibited highly suggestive sexualized behavior and "strange" disconnected states. She had difficulties at school in spite of her intellectual ability. The foster mother also had many questions about childhood sexual abuse and was concerned that Clemee had claimed that she had been sexually abused in her previous foster home.

Clemee was eight years old when we began our work together. She was initially brought to her sessions by her foster mother and asserted herself as friendly and attractive but understandably shy. She made a quick, superficial attachment to me. Her good intellectual functioning was immediately apparent. She was quite proud of it and clearly it served as a source of compensation. Her affective development was more problematic. It was restricted with little spontaneity. Her response to everything was "good" and "fine" and for a while we just colored pretty flowers and rainbows. Her response to my dropping the baby, in a session nearly one year after treatment began, was one of the first spontaneous gestures to occur between us.

Clemee, like many traumatized children in long-term foster care, has developed what is clinically referred to as an adaptive false self (Winnicott, 1960a). Everything is fine and good; there are no complaints. These children have little connection to their real emotional sense of self and therefore have no meaningful way to express the feelings that undergird the self. There have been no consistently available adults to make deep connections to their emotional life. Without empathic adults to facilitate, interpret and give words to the child's emotional experiences, memories and feelings cannot be symbolized and only serve as disruptive events in the child's experience. These children believe that if they please and adapt to the expectations of the external world they will not be abandoned or abused. This attempt to preclude abandonment is at a great cost to the sense of self. Powerful feelings and spontaneous gestures have to be tamped down or disavowed. There can be little room for expressions that give vitality to the self and enrich experience. The self remains brittle, depleted, underdeveloped, and disconnected. If the external world responds to the child in a positive way, for the most part the false adaptive self feels relatively safe but without real joy. If it responds negatively, the depleted self has no way to process the overwhelming stimuli of terrifying abandonment. The only way that many of these children have to manage the overwhelming stimulation is by physical discharge often in the form of destructive and aggressive behavior or through dissociation. Both of these solutions create further isolation and displacement for the child (Applegate & Bonovitz, 1995; Borden, 2009).

When Clemee entered treatment with me the foster home consisted of the foster mother, Miss Marcia, and her two biological children, thirteen-year-old Liberty and fifteen-year-old Christina. The foster mother was also six months pregnant. Two months before the new baby was born she was hospitalized and placed on bed rest, which meant Clemee had to be brought to therapy by transportation provided by social services. Clemee's anxiety about her foster mother's safety and her own was brought into the play and even weeks prior to the actual delivery of Baby Jeremiah, Clemee introduced him into her play but always in a very protective way.

The session above occurred in November, several weeks after the birth of Baby Jeremiah. It reveals Clemee's struggles to maintain the integrity of the family—trying to find a place for everyone and her need to destroy the interloper who threatened her safety. At this time there was a significant increase in the enuresis, "lying," and hiding activities as well as difficulties at school. Clemee's legacy of trauma rendered her greatly limited in her ability to have access to or understand her own emotions. It was very difficult for her to use relationships for comfort. Although she longed for relationship and closeness, meaningful attachments to others presented the greatest danger of abandonment, hurt, and betrayal. Emotions were expressed in disconnected, incoherent behavior that left everyone confused, helpless and frustrated. Everyone in the system experiences the fallout of living and working with a child who has been traumatized.

The pregnancy, the hospitalization of her caregiver, and the demands of the new baby created an all too familiar, crushing danger and loss for Clemee. Again there was no one and no place for her. In the session above we see her attempts to express and master her feelings of anger and anxiety about displacement and abandonment as well as her own great longing to be the baby and have a special place in the family.

For Clemee the chronic enuresis was the primary vehicle through which she somatically expressed her overwhelmed and out-of-control feelings. Yet, it also carried with it an intense feeling of shame and only served to further isolate her from relationships at home and at school. Enuresis is a significant obstacle for any latency age child but for a child whose home and school are repeatedly changing, there is little chance of developing friendships that can carry one through such difficult times. When things go wrong there seems to be no one and no place to belong.

Clemee was racked by intense feelings of shame related to the enuresis. Underneath the shame lay a deeply internalized sense of "badness." She believed the "badness" of herself and her family had to be the reason that no one wanted her and she had no home. The denying and hiding activities were attempts to protect herself from the shame and other feelings generated by her loss of control and fears of abandonment. For Clemee there is no place for her aggressive feelings. They represent a further expression of the "badness" that resides within. Any aggressive feelings, any true feelings of hostility about her situation threaten further abandonment. These feeling must be denied and split off from the experience of her self and projected onto the outside world. Yet, the previous "good" adaptive behavior that helped her receive positive reinforcement from home and school are no longer possible in this overwhelmed and depleted state.

CRISIS

In mid-December there was a two-week hiatus from therapy and from school because of the Christmas break. With little structure, no place to express her feelings, and everyone focused on baby Jeremiah, Clemee lit fire to her foster mother's bedroom carpet. She had no memory of doing so. Her foster mother also found a hidden cache of soft drink bottles filled with baby powder.

The system, now overwhelmed, experienced the panic and rage that had previously subsumed Clemee. We immediately held a conference in my office with Miss Marcia, her boyfriend, and other important people in this system—impressively, her caseworker and supervisor, the case manager, guardian ad litem, teacher, and pediatrician were all there. Everyone was trying to hold things together but the confusion and helplessness was intense and palpable. Did Clemee need to be hospitalized? Did she need to be on medication? Was she psychotic? Just as Clemee had experienced an increased sense of fragmentation without the supportive function of school and therapy, the system as a whole was experiencing that same sense of fragmentation. Everyone was looking to me to do something and my first task was to create a holding environment not only for Clemee, but for the system as well. If I could not hold the system through this traumatic experience it would also mean another placement, another confirmation of "badness" and further trauma for Clemee.

Winnicott (1960b) described the creation of the holding environment as an essential function for emotional development and regulation as the caretaker soothes, organizes and calms the infant during periods of distress. In other words, the caretaker holds the infant through this difficult period providing regulating functions that the infant cannot yet provide itself. Over time the infant internalizes these functions and increasingly is able to provide self-regulating functions. Winnicott used this metaphor of the holding environment to describe an important function of the therapist, especially when working with individuals who have experienced trauma.

Just as important as providing the holding function for the child is the need to provide the holding function for the entire system as the system enacts the unprocessed terror and rage of the child (Scholtes & Kennell, 1998). This is a monumental task for the therapist and she, too, is vulnerable to non-therapeutic and defensive enactments. In order to manage secondary traumatization, the therapist must extend the system to contain crucial resources for herself. These include consultation for herself, the therapist's own therapy, and a driving interest in understanding clinical theories and research related to trauma. We as therapists must make certain that these professional holdings are there for us and take advantage of them so that we, too, are not alone (Ammerman, 1996).

In order to provide the holding function for the other members of the system, I listened carefully and respectfully as each member of the system spoke. I was empathic and supportive as I addressed each of their concerns. They then turned to me to provide a coherent narrative of what had occurred and to explain the dynamics that had precipitated the fire setting. I reiterated Clemee's ongoing history of displacement and abandonment as well as the possibility of earlier sexual trauma. I explained the way in which the repeated changes in placement precluded the consistent availability of a deeply connected human being who could transform and calm Clemee's feelings of terror and helplessness, someone who could understand how she felt, give words to those feelings, and let her know she was not alone. Without words to understand and communicate her feeling states, her only recourse at times of great distress was to retreat into her numbing wooden states. These wooden-like, dissociated states are very common for children who have experienced complex trauma (Van der Kolk, 1988). Yet, even these dissociated states cannot contain the overwhelming terror of a world out of control. For Clemee this feeling was so terrifying that it could only be communicated through actions not words, through actions like loosing control of her bladder and lighting fires as a way of saying "I am disintegrating" and screaming "help." I then addressed the particular events that led to this present crisis.

It is not unusual for latency age children who have been in foster care since birth to hold onto the fantasy that this time is for real. This time they will be adopted and have a real home and real parents. However, there is a tension between the fantasy of adoption and the terror of displacement and abandonment. There is much vacillation between these two poles. There is, however, a third pole—the fantasy they will return to their families of origin. All three poles are defensively intensified with each additional placement. This was no different for Clemee. When she was placed in Miss Marcia's home, she was greatly invested in the fantasy that she would be adopted and truly belong. But as Miss Marcia became more debilitated by the pregnancy and less available to Clemee, Clemee began to panic and to feel increasingly that her world was unsafe and out of control. The birth of the baby was the final declaration of her displacement. Lighting the fire was the self out-of-control screaming for help. I went on to explain the loss of Miss Marcia and the loss of her teacher and her therapist over the break left her cut off from feeling connected and protected. She had no means to adequately hold or process her terror.

Miss Marcia wanted to know about the hidden cache of bottles filled with baby powder. I explained that these were Clemee's own baby bottles for herself. They represented her desire to be a baby, to receive the most fundamental forms of loving care, and to have a future that would be very different from her own. This regression carried with it the hope of going back. As Winnicott (1953) described it, regression is the hope for a new opportunity, an unfreezing of a failure situation, a return to point at which growth was impinged upon and suspended. In therapy, the patient's ability to move back and forth between what is most terrible and what is reliable and each time gathering up bits and pieces of self and other makes it possible to move forward to a sense of a consolidated self, rather than a self that is fragmented and feels cut off from itself (Ammerman, 1996; Winnicott, 1956).

LIFE GOES ON

Everyone left the conference feeling that we were all on the same track and hopeful for this little girl. In retrospect, I have a better sense of how I participated in the traumatic enactment as it reverberated through the system. It was easy for me to avoid involving Miss Marcia in the difficulties Clemee was having. Although I reported my concern that Miss Marcia was not present in the way that Clemee needed her to be to the caseworker, I failed to make direct efforts to involve Miss Marcia in the treatment. She no longer brought Clemee to her sessions, was on bed rest, or at times in the hospital. Her situation over-shadowed Clemee's needs. Miss Marcia was not available and Clemee was just expected to cope. Once again the adults abandoned her. But for the moment, everyone was reengaged in the system.

Foster parents need and deserve ongoing psychologically informed support. Most foster parents are not adequately prepared and do not understand the dynamics at play with children who have histories of complex trauma (Jill, Sonya, Errick, & Lorri, 2011; Pasztor, Hollinger, Inkelas, & Halfon, 2006). They, and the entire extended system, are vulnerable to responding to upsetting behavior with enactments that only perpetuate the experience of trauma and create reverberations that resonate from child, to home, to institutions. Not only foster parents but also foster care workers and clinicians are hungry to understand the echoing dynamics that affect all of them. Throughout the system there needs to be a greater awareness of the real impact, both psychologically and neurologically, of trauma and the repeatedly ruptured attachments that ensue.

Five days after the conference, I received a phone call from Megan, the caseworker, informing me that she had accepted a new job and in two weeks would be leaving the agency. She had been involved with Clemee's case since Clemee was two years old. She represented the most consistent continuous relationship in Clemee's life to date. My heart sank. The voice inside of me was screaming, "Do you know what you are doing?!" as I, too, was forced to inhabit Clemee's world. Instead, my professional self spoke as I tried to assuage the worker's own feeling of guilt. We discussed specifics as well as a transition plan. On Tuesday evening, she would tell Clemee that she was leaving, I would see Clemee on Wednesday at her usual appointment and, on the following Tuesday, they would say their final goodbyes, followed by Clemee's session with me on Wednesday. We all knew that this was a potentially dissembling situation and that this plan had little chance of sustaining Clemee.

When I arrived at my office Wednesday morning, there was a message left by the caseworker the previous evening. After she explained to Clemee that she would be leaving the agency, Clemee immediately responded that the foster mother had whipped her on the legs when she had started the fire. The caseworker was mandated to report the incident to child protective services. Within hours, Clemee had been removed to a temporary home some distance away. Much later, the report of the whippings would be declared as unfounded by the agency, but by then the foster mother, reeling in her own traumatic experience of the fire and accusations, refused to take Clemee back. The caseworker said it would be unlikely that Clemee would be able to get to our session that day. Within a few hours, Clemee lost the person who had known her since she was a baby, lost the home that she rebuilt over and over again, and was about to lose the promise of her therapy and the access it gave her to her internal world. I protested loudly.

An issue that had concerned me when I first began my work with Clemee was the way in which treatment itself has the potential to become a traumatic repetition in working with children within the foster care system. The therapeutic process gets subsumed by the chaos of the system and eventually becomes one more experience that intensifies the attachment to loss. I had been insistent upon taking the case that the agency make a commitment to get this child to treatment and they had put that commitment in writing. Later that afternoon I got a call that, in fact, someone from the agency would be bringing her to her session that day.

When I saw Clemee that day, the wooden soldier from the early days of our treatment once again occupied the space. Without affect, she told me in her usual way that "everything is fine," that she likes her new home better than the one before. We talk about Megan, who has known her since she was two years old. Clemee wears the jewelry that Megan has given her. As we sit there, many questions arise in my mind regarding Clemee's fantasies stimulated by the news that the caseworker was leaving. In her panic of abandonment, did Clemee hope that the caseworker would rescue her and take Clemee with her? Perhaps there was the fantasy that with the loss of Megan and destruction of Miss Marcia she would be returned to her grandparents? Were there thoughts that the caseworker's leaving was her punishment for "being bad" and starting the fire? Was this a projective process in which Clemee was trying to assuage her own sense of "badness" by exposing the "badness" of the foster mother? Perhaps it was all or some or none of the above. Regardless, the set of circumstances and Clemee's inability to symbolically represent and reflect on these experiences created a sense of destructiveness too overwhelming for a nine-year-old child to endure.

FINDING NEW PLACES FOR EVERYONE

The session continues and, with bravado, Clemee tells me all the great things about her new home, yet somehow she could not remember her new foster mother's name. We talked more about her goodbye to Megan and I asked if she had had a chance to say goodbye to Miss Marcia and the family. She said "no." Then I said that I could see what a brave little girl she was and how hard she tried to be so good and to do everything just right. Without a sound, huge tears began to roll down her checks. She lay down on the sofa clutching Turtle and sucking her thumb as I patted her back. Calmer now, she looks up at me and says, "Can we play?"

Once again we are fixing the house, and again it is all about Miss Marcia. But this time the play shifts. The shoebox room gets detached from the house. Fifteen-year-old Christina is moving into her own apartment and Clemee tells me that the whole family is coming to visit her in her new place. I say that it is good to get to visit when you move away and I wonder how everyone feels with Christina moving away. She does not respond. We end the session but Clemee is not ready to go. She is worried about her clothes. Can she go back and get her clothes? She implores the new caseworker who has brought her—how will she get her clothes? Can she go back? Clemee is asking how she can survive, how she can get the things she needs, or has everything already been destroyed?

When I see Clemee the next Wednesday, she has been moved again. I only know this because I have called the supervisor for an update and to make sure there will be no glitches in getting her here. When she arrives, I see a depleted little girl. This time neither she nor I can remember the new foster mother's name.

Two weeks later Clemee has been moved again, this time to her next new "permanent" home. This also meant she had been moved from her previous school where the teacher in consultation with me had been very involved in setting up structures that helped Clemee feel safe and enabled her to function better in school. I, too, am exhausted and numbed by the thought that we were starting all over again. New home, new family, new school, new teacher, new caseworker, a whole world of important relationships just vanished.

Although this new family seemed loving, they were quite chaotic. There were also sexual tensions for Clemee in this male-headed household. Clemee was not able to settle down in her new school. She demonstrated the typical hyper-aroused state of distress. She was yelling out in class and was involved in verbal arguments with both adults and students. And, she would occasionally shift into a dissociated state of psychic numbing (van der Kolk & Greenberg, 1987). The enuresis continued. At the end of the school year, Clemee had failed third grade and was required to go to summer school.

In our sessions, the smell of urine permeated the room. Clemee seemed oblivious. She could not settle into play and regularly requested that we "go to the store." Confused and unable to soothe herself through our regular relationship, the activity of going to the store provided physical discharge for her agitated state, buying things for her was the only way that she felt she could use the relationship. Instead, I moved the sessions into the garden and Clemee began digging up and transplanting plants. Thus the garden took on a parallel function to the playhouse where Clemee could rework all the things that were not right. The plants were perennials that would be there for the years to come. The work in the garden, the idea that the plants would return from year to year, and the experience that she was the facilitator of this endeavor created a calming effect and a sense of control, competency, and purpose.

As summer progressed, a curious dynamic occurred in the sessions. Clemee began bringing her things from home and asking to keep them in the therapy room. This was her way of asking me to keep her safe. She would ask, "Who pays you?" or make a statement that someone "ain't going to therapy anymore cause they ain't gonna pay for it." I understood that this represented her worry as to whether I would continue to be here for her. Things did not improve and Clemee failed summer school. Her sessions in the garden provided a great sense of comfort to her and as we planted together she would speak of her difficulties at school. In the midst of our gardening activities, each of us involved in parallel activities, Clemee began to struggle to use words to communicate her distress.

FINDING YET MORE NEW PLACES FOR EVERYONE

Toward the end of the summer it was revealed that the foster father had lost his job. Soon after the foster family announced that in three weeks they would be moving out of state. Clemee would not be able to go with them but there were many promises of visits. These never materialized. On some level Clemee was aware of the undercurrent of chaos that pervaded this family, yet all of these anxieties remained on a preverbal level and made it difficult for her to process. Thus, she acted them out in her own chaotically, destructive states. Where would she go, what would the new people be like, what school would she go to, and what grade would she be in? Lost and confused, she had no way to deal with the overwhelming uncertainty except through dissociation.

The week that school was to start Clemee was moved once again to her new "permanent" foster home—nine years old and her seventeenth displacement, this time in a different community and a different school with endless vestiges of self-left-behind, remembered or recognized by whom? The current foster mother's home is an all female household headed by an experienced foster care mother with two other foster care children and no biological children in the home. Clemee is the youngest in the home. This foster parent is not easily ruffled. In our sessions, Clemee again seemed disorganized and confused but there was now a level of hostility that she had not exhibited before. When Clemee began to exhibit similar behavior in her new school as she had previously, the foster mother, with coaching, was encouraged to quickly engage the school, helping them to understand Clemee's difficulties and needs. With the foster mother's intervention, the teacher established a structure that supported and affirmed Clemee's higher level of functioning and things began to improve in school. In our sessions she began to fantasize about having a birthday party and inviting friends from school. She also revealed that she had told a child at school that she was in foster care. This was a significant achievement for Clemee, to acknowledge her desire to have friends and to feel that it might be possible in spite of her circumstances. At the end of the first semester, Clemee's teacher referred to her as a model for other students. The next triumph occurred over the Christmas break when Clemee achieved bladder control. In January she returned to school for the first time without wearing pull-ups!

Over the next year and a half things were more or less quiescent. Her foster mother reported few difficulties at home. Clemee's functioning had only occasional, manageable problems. I maintained close contact with her foster mother and encouraged immediate interaction with school when difficulties occurred. She became a real advocate for Clemee, who ended the school year with honor roll grades and positive relationships with teachers and schoolmates. The ongoing stability continued through the summer.

A TRAUMA REVISITED

In November, Clemee's foster mother began to report difficulties both at school and at home. Clemee was in a contentious relationship with a male teacher with whom she had several classes. She was doing very poorly in all of her course work and having difficulties with several other teachers as well. She also reported some sexual acting out issues among the girls at home and Clemee told one of the girls that she had been sexually active. This, like the earlier whipping revelation, turned out to be unfounded.

During this time, Clemee's sessions began with an adolescent version of familiar play, even though it was not spoken of as such. She would begin by complaining of being tired and needing to sleep. I would mirror how exhausted she was, that she needed a nap, hand her Turtle and put the cashmere blanket over her. She would look up at me and smile. After a few minutes rest on the sofa she would suddenly come to life and say "can we play?" This activity and play has represented a piece of continuity in our relationship which harkens back to our first year of working together when Clemee was having great difficulty with the recent birth of a biological child by her then foster mother. In those sessions she would often play being the baby, needing to be put to sleep and given a bottle. This, like now, has always represented a period of anxiety, disorganization, and fragmentation for Clemee when the vulnerability of important attachments felt threatened. It is a manifestation of the impact of early traumatic loss together with the subsequent sixteen displacements this thirteen-year-old has experienced. Our little ritual represents a calming piece of memory and continuity that pervades the years and stress.

In one session, in a most matter of fact way, Clemee told me that she was going to be moved to another foster home. Shocked, I asked, "Why?" She responded that she had been at this foster home for two years. It was true. Two years was the longest she had ever been in a single home.

Clemee's difficulties at school with suspensions continued. Like the report of her sexual activity, during the Christmas break Clemee reported to one of the other foster children that she wanted to kill herself. The agency immediately had an emergency psychiatric evaluation. The hospital did not feel that Clemee was a danger to herself. As soon as everyone gathered around her, the distress seemed to subside. Once again the extended system gathered for a conference in my office. We asked the same questions that had been asked four years ago. Did she need hospitalization? Was she psychotic? Did she need medication? What had been going on since November to trigger these months of concerning behavior? Everything was the same except that most of the people gathered had changed. The experience was an uncanny déjà vu. Even more uncanny was that the only significant change in the environment was that a fourth foster child, younger than Clemee, with many special cognitive and emotional needs, had been added to the family. This child, much like baby Jeremiah, required almost total focus on the part of the foster mother. This was an adolescent mirror version, even to the month and number of children, of the events that had occurred four years ago. When we *remembered*, we understood. Clemee's behavior was an enactment, an overwhelming experience of abandonment and loss of self that could not yet be fully processed. There were three of us from the original group that had gathered in my office four years ago. The sense of vitality and energy in the room was palpable as we regarded each other with mutual recognition as well as a calming presence for the other members as a sense of coherence pervaded the room.

In therapy, Clemee responded well to the explorations and connections that provided a new sense of understanding and meaning for her. Everyone in the system rallied around her to give her the care and support that she needed. The quick turn around surprised us all. By the next grading period Clemee was back on the honor roll and one could feel the real sense of pleasure she and foster mother shared when we all spent time together in our sessions. In the spring, as we worked on the garden together I asked her what she thought had made the difference. She told me she had made a best friend at school, a girl new to the school who was very smart and did not get in trouble. Her friend had told Clemee that Clemee was too smart and did not need to act like a baby anymore.

NO MORE THE WOODEN SOLDIER

It is 3 p.m. on a bleak November afternoon. I am on the sidewalk of a busy street. I look across the street and up and down. Yes, I see her. No more a wooden soldier but a lovely, smiling teenage girl is coming toward me and once again we embrace each others' world.

We are seated on my sofa, Calico Critters snuggly in their home. Turtle is nearby resting on the ottoman where he has been for the past five years. This is our little shrine, hardly acknowledged now but holding the symbols and the memories of so many moments that have brought us to this moment. Clemee is giving me a manicure. She tells me all my nail polishes are for old ladies. She has brought her own and now is painting my nails peacock blue.

Deeply involved in my personal transformation she casually asks me about the Christmas break. What are the dates that I will be gone? I tell her, give her the details of where I will be. I remind her that she can e-mail me now and we discuss the plans for our annual Christmas tea for two. My nails are gleaming, perfect without a smudge. I am truly impressed by this feat.

The transformation almost complete, she asks if she can leave the polish for next time and screws on the top with a new sense of intensity. I understand that once again she is asking me to keep a part of herself safe. With the same intensity she looks up from her polish and says to me, "You know, Jenny, Christmas is always terrible for me. It is the time of the year when so many bad things have happened. I don't understand why I can't be with my family like everyone else. This will be the first time I have ever spent Christmas three years in a row in the same place. Every Christmas something bad always happen. This Christmas I just want it to be different."

I look around the room and see this little home that we have built and rebuilt together over all these years. I remember the sadness that it contains and the triumphs, too. And I remember that this is the same Clemee who struggles to find herself and the place where she belongs. Over and over again. And yet, no more the wooden soldier but a lovely young girl who at last can speak and tell in words who she is, how she feels and what she desires. Her words echo "this Christmas I want it to be different" but I know that in so many ways it already is.

CONCLUDING THOUGHTS

In our continued efforts to preclude trauma and restore stability, it is essential for the therapist to provide a holding environment. One important function of the holding environment is memory. The therapist holds the patient by helping the patient make connections through bits and pieces of self-experience that are known to the patient but not remembered. Without memory, the self remains fragmented and there is no continuity of being for the child. The therapist, walking in the shadow of the child's trauma, uses her memory and understanding of felt self-experiences to gather up the bits and pieces of shattered child and hold them through unbearable anxieties. This holding function must extend beyond the child and also include the foster parents and child welfare agencies and others who make up the extended system of care. The members of this extended system are all vulnerable to participating in enactments that recreate the child's unformulated experience of trauma. Equally important are the crucial holding resources available to the therapist as she too inhabits the child's history through felt experiences. The first person who must be held in the holding environment is the therapist herself (Cohn and Sherwood, 1991). Her strength and resources become a holding frame that can tolerate attack but cannot be destroyed. With her supportive resources holding up the frame there is not a need for withdrawal or retaliation. This case affirms the importance of the holding environment for the extended system and its essential function of holding memory in order to create a sense of vitality, cohesion, and coherence in self-experience for the traumatized child.

REFERENCES

Ammerman, P. (1996). *Functions of countertransference in psychotherapy in borderline disorder.* Unpublished Dissertation. Institute for Clinical Social Work, Chicago, IL.

Applegate, J., & Bonovitz, J. (1995). *The facilitating partnership: A Winnicottian approach for social workers and other helping professionals.* Northvale, NJ: Jason Aronson.

Black, M. (2003). Enactment: Analytic musings on energy, language, and personal growth. *Psychoanalytic Dialogues, 13*(5), 633–655.

Borden, W. (2009). *Contemporary psychodynamic theory and practice.* Chicago, IL: Lyceum Books.

Cohn, C., & Sherwood, V. (1991). *Becoming a constant object.* Northvale, NJ: Jason Aronson.

Jill E. S., Sonya J. L., Errick, C., & Lorri S. M. (2011). Parent management training, relationships with agency staff, and child mental health: Urban foster parents' perspectives. *Children and Youth Services Review*, *33*(11), 2366–2374. DOI: 10.1016/j.childyouth.2011.08.008.

Pasztor, E., Hollinger, D., Inkelas, M., & Halfon, N. (2006). Health and mental health services for children in foster care: The central role of foster parents. *Child Welfare*, *85*(1), 33–57.

Pearlman, A., & Saak Vitnee, K. (1995). *Trauma and the therapist.* New York: Norton.

Scholtes, R., & Kennell, S. (1998). *Personal communication.*

Van der Kolk, B. A. (1988). The trauma spectrum: The interaction of biological and social events in the genesis of the trauma response. *Journal of Traumatic Stress*, *1*(3), 273–290.

Van der Kolk, B. A., & Greenberg, M. S. (1987). Psychobiology of the trauma response: Hyperarousal, constriction, and addiction to trauma reexposure. In B. A. Van der Kolk (Ed.), *Psychological trauma* (pp. 63–88). Washington, DC: American Psychiatric Press.

Winnicott, D. W. (1953). Transitional objects and transitional phenomena: A study of the first not-me possession. *International Journal of Psychoanalysis, 34*, 89–97.

Winnicott, D. W. (1956). The antisocial tendency. In D. W. Winnicott, *Through pediatrics to psycho-analysis* (pp. 306–315). New York: Basic Books, 1975.

Winnicott, D. W. (1960a). Ego distortion in terms of true and false self. In D. W. Winnicott, *The maturational processes and the facilitating environment* (pp. 140–152). Madison, CT: International Universities Press, 1965.

Winnicott, D. W. (1960b). The theory of the parent-infant relationship. In D. W. Winnicott, *The maturational processes and the facilitating environment* (pp. 37–55). Madison, CT: International Universities Press, 1965.

Chapter Ten

Zina

INTRODUCTION

In this chapter I will describe the unfolding of a still ongoing work, with Zina, a twenty-two-year-old young woman whom I began seeing when she was twelve. At first sight, the turn of events I will describe might seem like a "treatment failure," a perception I held at times during our work, especially when measured by the manifestation of her symptoms. But, with a deeper look into the development of Zina's narrative, a more organic and genuine self emerges and a new direction for hope is set in motion.

I will describe the hard transition for patient and therapist as a result of Zina's psychotic break and the long period of false manic presentation that led to it. The perception of Zina's psychotic break changed for both of us as an outcome of our recent journey. We both came to realize that the breaks, as discouraging as they are, create a crack that allows access to more real and genuine aspects of self that Zina had been warding off for years. By relating our story, I will illustrate what I learned to be the most important aspect of my work with Zina and what I believe is the most valuable gift we can give to foster youth—specifically, we give them a stable, lasting, and open-ended relationship. We create a space where the child can express feelings, weave narratives, be seen, feel understood, and most of all have a safe and honest home within—a home where the child can be his/her true self.

THE FIRST SESSION

Zina, a twelve-year-old adolescent of black, Latina, and Jewish descent, arrived right on time for our first appointment. She entered with a big triumphant smile, catching her breath, and started in on a complex story about how she had managed to make it on time to the session. She told me about the foster mom who thought the appointment was on a different day, the difficulties in finding the office, and the last minute negotiation with a teacher so that she could leave school early. All were presented as challenges overcome on an ultimately successful journey. This motif of presenting a complex story with an eventual happy ending became the pattern of many of our hours together. I was immersed in Zina's story, as I would be with many future stories. I felt absorbed with admiration for the bubbly, skilled twelve-year-old who smiled at the world with an infectious optimism. Zina appeared very different from the girl described in the report I received from the adolescent unit where she had been hospitalized. The notes described an intelligent young girl who had a depressive episode after she disclosed a ten-year history of abuse by her father from age two to twelve. Days after her disclosure, Zina and her siblings were removed from their home and put into different foster homes. Her father was arrested and soon after Zina began to experience intense guilt followed by a deep depression, which ended in her hospitalization. Yet, I saw no traces of depression in Zina's behavior, but rather a hypomanic affect that seemed to bypass pain and difficulties and turn them into triumph.

That first session was ten years ago. Zina is now a young adult. She fights hallucinations and delusions with a substantial mix of medications and at times struggles with basic functioning. She currently lives with her mother and often feels compromised and sad.

BACKGROUND

Zina was placed in a foster home at age twelve after she told a friend in school that her father had raped her on a regular basis after forcing her to drink alcohol. The ongoing penetration caused her constant back pain and the alcohol created a syndrome of severe migraines. When Zina disclosed the secret of the abuse to her friend, she added that her mother forbade her from telling anyone about it, and that she feared for her and her mother's life if the secret was ever revealed.

Zina was sent to a hospital for evaluation after she exhibited symptoms of severe depression stemming from feeling responsible for her father's arrest and the placement of herself and her siblings in different foster homes. During her evaluation Zina revealed that her father, who had contracted HIV from an extramarital affair, had attempted to infect the whole family with the virus. Zina was checked immediately after her disclosure and found to be HIV negative. However, a clean bill of health could be issued only if she tested negative again in six months. Thus, our work began with my anxious anticipation of the upcoming results, exacerbated by the news that her mother was found to be HIV positive. Zina's optimism, on the other hand, was non-negotiable. It felt to me partially like a dangerous denial waiting to be burst and partially like a resourceful defense in the face of uncertainty. Fortunately, six months later Zina was found to be HIV negative. Zina was indifferent to the good news and my celebratory reaction seemed inflated in comparison.

ATTACHMENT STYLE

From the first session Zina seemed to feel almost overly comfortable with the idea of talking about her life. Although I felt very close to Zina, and was taken by her vivacious and clever engagement, I found myself wondering how this alliance became established so quickly. Over the years, I observed her immediate and complete attachments to others as well. This behavior might be diagnosed as Reactive Attachment Disorder, Disinhibited Type, in which a child exhibits indiscriminate sociability or a lack of selectivity in choices of attachment figures. The willingness to seek and accept comfort from almost anyone, including strangers, is discussed at length in the adoption literature (Zeanah, 2000).

Zina's relationship with her mother shifted significantly once her father left. For the first twelve years of her life, Zina felt distant and distrusting of her mother. However, from our first session, she argued that her mother was doing the best she could under the worst of circumstances. Zina refused to explore her feelings further, seemingly intent on creating a narrative that would protect the image of her mother as a functioning parent who was able to care for her and her siblings. That fantasy, I believe, helped reduce her guilt for breaking up the family and brought hope for the family to reunite after returning from their foster homes.

At first, Zina did not wish to discuss her father's actions in detail but spoke freely about his personality. She described him as extremely intelligent, interesting, fun, and playful when sober, but controlling, menacing, cruel, abusive, and violent when under the influence of alcohol. Zina could not decide whether his removal from the family was something she really wanted and she felt conflicted about the totality and finality of the consequences. She was never able to miss him or talk about him with her mother. The very few times she did let herself talk about missing her father in therapy, she felt very anxious and in later sessions denied her disclosures.

Zina seemed to trust and admire all the health professionals involved in the case including medical doctors, social workers, psychologists and psychiatrists. She did not like or connect with those in administrative roles like foster parents, attorneys, Child Protective Services (CPS) workers and investigators. Things, people, and events were organized as good or bad by Zina and any complexity or ambivalence was eliminated so that they could be categorized as one or the other (Klein, 1946).

EARLY TREATMENT

In our early sessions, it was apparent that Zina had no interest in the toys, books or art supplies in my office—she was not interested in the "baby stuff" but in mature talk. In one of the sessions, however, she asked me whether I would like to watch her draw. She drew a perfect face of a girl—like a Japanese-style Anime—paying extra attention to the over-sized eyes and the intricate straight hair. She struggled with the nose, erasing and commenting all the while about her lack of mastery. When I said that I often find that imperfection makes things interesting, she giggled and said, "That's silly." The face she drew—ideally proportioned—floated on the paper without a neck but with a mane of hair around it. As she handed me the drawing Zina said, "it's not perfect, but you can keep it." It became a habit for her to leave artwork, poems, and stories for me to keep.

The desperation of Zina to present perfectly, to be the best at everything, became clear when things actually did not turn out the way she expected. It was the struggle over drawing the nose that showed her intolerance for any flaw in appearance or in her technical ability. She wanted to erase the imperfection and then to erase her wish to be rid of the imperfection. I was able to connect to her as long as I joined with her successes. When I tried to tend to the frightened, wounded, or incapable aspects of her, she rejected me in the same way she rejected these parts in her own self. When I expressed pain or worry, Zina's affect would turn distant, detached and sometimes bemused as if saying, "Let's not make a big drama out of this." It is clear that this uncompromising drive for upbeat, positive perfection created a lot of her astonishing successes and admiration. However, her achievements came with an enormous price of intolerance for pain which prevented her from having genuine connections.

Zina loved coming to our sessions, talked without hesitation, and went out of her way to avoid canceling. She had difficulty ending the sessions. No matter what the quality of the hour had been, I felt her disappointment at the end. She often offered her poems to me after I told her that we needed to stop, extending the hour a bit longer with a mix of charm and desperation. Looking back, it seems that Zina's main effort in our first few years was to weave a positive and coherent narrative of her life. As she told her stories, Zina would watch my reactions carefully to see how they registered on my face, as if watching the story displayed on a screen. Zina's need to watch the impact of her success, or heart wrenching stories, on my face was a recurring theme throughout our work. She needed and used my reactions to actually know what she felt, or would have felt, had she had a safe space to process her feelings. This was a theme in many of our hours over the first few years (Bion, 1956; Klein, 1946).

At the time, I felt that calling attention to this process by commenting or making an interpretation would detract from what she needed. My feeling was that this process needed to happen without making Zina self-conscious about it, and that only after her thirst was quenched would we be able to discuss and understand it together (Bion, 1956; Brown, 2010).

I often felt as if Zina assigned us specific roles. She was the artist/creator/performer and I the audience, the receiver and the keeper of her creation, be it the art, the poems or the oral narrative. However, these assigned roles often felt rigid and prevented true intimacy and freedom between us.

In one of these sessions, I commented on one of her poems, describing its impact on me. Zina reacted strongly to my attempt to expand the space between us. She told me in a cold, bewildered, and somewhat disappointed tone that my comments were not helpful or relevant since the poem was already finished. I spoke about the value of dialogue and exchange of connections and relationship, but Zina met me in this hour and in the following few sessions in silence, strikingly withholding her creative gifts from our interaction. My attempt to explore the connection between the insertion of my feelings and her withholding the "goods" was minimized and brushed off with repeated comments such as "I just don't feel like making anything lately."

THE RETURN FROM FOSTER HOME TO ORIGINAL FAMILY

A year and a half after Zina spoke out about her abuse, her father was given a life sentence in a maximum-security prison. She was then able to move back home and reunite with her mother and siblings, a prospect that excited her greatly. From that point on, Zina excelled in school, continued to write poems, and practiced several musical instruments, but also stopped mentioning her father altogether. Zina felt like she could have her mother's love only if she succeeded. It was, and in some way still is, a frail relationship conditioned on Zina's triumphs.

Zina's mother struggles with accepting the consequences of her past actions. Her guilt led her to enter into an unconscious agreement with Zina to erase the past by not mentioning the abuse and not manifesting any distress symptoms. As long as Zina was successful and acted happy, she had a mother.

It is important to note that the split between good and bad, success and failure, was also strongly reinforced by Zina's mother. For example, scheduling a meeting with her is hard in general in part because she struggles with her health and has a demanding job. However, throughout the years, I could also see a pattern in the times she was willing to make an effort to come to my office. When we met to discuss Zina's achievements and possible choices, her mother showed up and felt part of, if not the reason for, Zina's success. When the meeting was to discuss crises and emergencies it was hard, if not impossible, to get her in the office and when on the phone she tended to minimize and discount the problems, similar to the way Zina did.

Almost fourteen years old when the transition to high school was in motion, things started to get harder socially for Zina, in contrast to her smooth academic successes. She fell in love with boys and girls, changing her love object frequently without being able to articulate why a particular person caught her interest. The moment she noticed that someone was interested in her, she felt compelled to desire him or her. In an atypically vulnerable session around that time, Zina intimated that she often felt proud of being wanted by her father. Being wanted by people always made her feel special. This genuine openness in Zina's discourse made me feel that it would be good time to discuss more openly our relationship and perhaps help expand the emotional arena of our interactions. However, Zina made it clear that she was not interested in discussing our relationship or curious to look into other ways of possible relating. She wanted me to be there beyond words or thoughts and she came to see me just because she came to see me—no explanations were needed or wanted—just like a child does not need to explain her relationship with her mother (Winnicott, 1953).

HIGH SCHOOL: HIGHS AND LOWS

At age fourteen, upon graduating from middle school, Zina was accepted with a full scholarship to a prestigious private school. She felt proud and excited. Attending the new school changed Zina's social milieu dramatically. For the first time she interacted with kids from a different social strata and a different racial mix. Her initial feelings of insecurity oscillated between blame and judgment and an overwhelming wish to please and be like them. For the kids in her school, Zina became an "exotic phenomenon." They were pulled into and curious about her life story. She, in return, disclosed the most intimate details of her experience to them. She would tell whoever wanted to hear about—the occasional shooting in her neighborhood, her relationship with gang members, the full story of her abuse, an account of her financial situation, the struggles of her HIV positive mother, the despair of her siblings, and her therapy process. As in our sessions, Zina wanted to be seen for the pain, the injustice, and the unimaginable experiences she had gone through as well as her ingenuity in surviving them. She needed her astonishing stories to be mirrored in order to be able to relate to them herself (Kohut, 1971).

I expressed my worry about her intimate life becoming selectively public. I discussed with her the difference between disclosing in a safe place with an established relationship versus emptying her stories out to random people. Zina seemed to agree and intellectually understand the importance of safety and trust, but the behavior of leaking out indiscriminately remained. Her need to live vicariously through her projected feeling onto others was unassailable. When she asked me to write letters for scholarships, if I attempted to protect her privacy, she would tell me I was "doing the white thing" by being too careful and too protective.

At age sixteen, Zina had her first emotional breakdown while at school. It followed a sexual encounter with her boyfriend. Zina had sexually experimented with boys and girls previous to that incident. However, during this encounter, she later told me, the boy's sweat smelled just like her father's. She became overwhelmed with panic and forgot where and who she was. Soon after, she was diagnosed as bipolar and was medicated with Lithium, which stabilized, but also significantly dulled, her affect. This was one of the first times Zina was unable to push the darkness aside. Although as soon as she could, she patched the crack that revealed the terrifying shadows she had been holding inside. In the following session, Zina explored the bright future she imagined after college as if there was never a dark cloud in the horizon. She debated whether she wanted to be a judge, a writer, a vet or start a non-for-profit for low-income kids, nourishing them with sustainable food.

A ONE-YEAR BREAK IN OUR TREATMENT

A few months after her breakdown at school, I told Zina I was planning to take a sabbatical in Europe. A few weeks thereafter, Zina told me that she was planning to join a summer program for teens in Europe learning about different cultures through their foods. With her extraordinary resourcefulness she was able to raise money for the summer program and told me that all I would have to do is write a letter about her bipolar condition and send it to her coordinator. I was left to carry the anxiety about her emotional stability and the prospect of her managing her medication during her travels while she focused on excitement and hope. In spite of my attempts, Zina was not interested in discussing the "coincidence" of her decision to go to Europe at the same time that I would be there.

Once again, Zina needed to be in the spotlight, to be the one who leaves. It is interesting to note that throughout our work together Zina never asked about my private life. She was never interested in whether I have kids and never inquired about my accent. When I told her about my sabbatical she never asked for any specifics about where I was going or why. To me, once again this seemed to be a manifestation of her desire to be the observed and not the observer.

For the time I was away, we were able to find another therapist through A Home Within, Dr. B, who was willing to treat Zina in my absence. The relationship with Dr. B was very successful and, although we work quite differently, Zina seemed to find no problem in shifting from me to her and back again. In our recap of the time with Dr. B, Zina told me how different therapy felt. Dr. B worked from her home, spoke fluent Spanish, and most importantly, brought food for Zina in the sessions. Although Zina described it as nourishing and fun, she did not express any feelings of loss or longing for Dr. B. When I asked her if she missed Dr. B and encouraged her to talk about their relationship, Zina insisted that since we had followed a known plan there was no reason for her to feel an absence or loss of any kind. At the same time, she made a few jokes about missing the smell of home-cooked food during therapy.

COLLEGE AND EMOTIONAL BREAKS

In spite of Zina's struggle with her bipolar symptoms and a host of physical ailments such as acute migraines, joint pain, back pain, and the side effects of lithium, she was able to graduate from high school with a high grade point average and, at the age of eighteen, was accepted to a good college on the East Coast. At that point, our work shifted from talking therapy to hunting for resources such as books, clothes, grants, and loans. I found myself in a difficult position of having to feed Zina concretely rather than symbolically. Our hours were taken up with logistical planning, and the attempts to reflect faded away.

To celebrate the end of nearly seven years of work and her acceptance to college, we met for a long lunch in a restaurant of her choice. She talked extensively about her expectations and plans for the future. We both felt that this would be the end of our intensive work together, though we clarified the ways we would keep in touch. At the end of our meal I handed her a gift, a warm coat for the east coast winter, which she decided to open later. She, in return, handed me a poem and asked me to read it right away, all the while watching my expression closely. The poem spoke about love and its bitter taste. Below are a few lines from the middle of her poem:

> remembering how love is in the beginning
> its all sugar coated
> its only love notes
> its only sweet odes of everlasting something
> and I whimper softly
> its being the only thing

I know
it is so much more than
simple I love you
there are these who are jealous
there are rocky roads
and I see teary eyes.

The poem is long and twisty, honest and at times coarse. Yet, its directness and rawness evoked strong feelings in me. Once again, Zina was not open to hear me telling her how touched I was by her poem. Yet she closely watched my eyes tearing up as if examining the veracity of a phenomenon.

The next time I saw Zina was when she came home for winter vacation after experiencing a psychotic break triggered by lack of sleep, anxiety about grades, and the darkness of the winter season. Zina seemed upset but not discouraged. She had energy and hope for the future, and asked me to create a plan that would help her if and when another attack occurred. She returned to college and a month later had another break, induced this time by alcohol consumption, something Zina had avoided throughout her teenage years. She was then diagnosed with schizoaffective disorder at a local psychiatric hospital, for which she was treated with antipsychotic medication. Shortly thereafter, Zina decided to leave college. We had numerous phone calls about the possibility of finishing out the year, but the hope she expressed only a few weeks before had turned into despair. She returned home and we resumed our work together.

OUR CURRENT WORK

Some of the reasons for Zina's psychotic break(s) may have been physiological, such as the expression of a genetic predisposition and the effect of the dark cold winter. However, the physical distance from her mother lowered the constant pressure to excel and the daily remainder that she will have a mother only if she is successful began to fade away. This helped, I believe, the rigid, artificial, false self to melt away, allowing her imperfect self to crack open. The loss of her audience (i.e., teachers, mother, siblings, old friends, and therapist) played a role in the emptiness, loneliness, and lack of motivation she experienced. It seems to me that the voices she started to hear were a substitute audience for the actual ones she had just lost. However, the new audience—the voices—encouraged her to look into the darkness that she had kept at bay for years.

Depending on her mix of medications, Zina would arrive to our sessions, which at this point were two to three times a week, either very early or significantly late. She spoke in a flat affect and in rambling and tangential patterns. She mostly talked about her lost interest in everyday activities, such as bathing and grooming, as well as her attempts at fighting hallucinations.

This was the saddest time in my work with Zina. I felt lost, desperate, and, more importantly, that I had failed Zina and didn't have much more to give her. When I began to realize that my hopelessness was an amalgam of projected feelings from Zina onto me, that realization became my main tool in treatment (Bion, 1959). This visceral window into Zina's experience deepened my understanding of her pain—it was the first time we were together in the same dark place without assigned roles and without her insistence that I join in her denial. The quality of the sessions changed into a space infused with the sense of being together in a shared reality, a reality that was perhaps grim but not lonely.

In a recent session, Zina shared some painful memories. This time, she spoke of her abuse, her identification with her father, and her recent difficult time in college from a more vulnerable place. There now seems to be a renewed sense of hope—different than before—a hope that is more authentic, less grandiose and, most importantly, is a shared hope for her and me.

Meanwhile, since Zina's ability to think clearly and articulate her feelings has been severely compromised, I encouraged her to reevaluate her prescribed medications with her psychiatrist. Soon after her medications were adjusted, there was a flare of hallucinations; however, at the same time, a spark of curiosity and interest for exploration surfaced. It was as if a part of the old inquisitive Zina reemerged. A few exchanges from a recent session illustrate this new phase. From the very beginning, this session started with a change in our roles. I was coughing as I greeted her in the room and was surprised when Zina asked me whether I was getting sick—she acknowledged my presence in a way she hadn't done before. Later in the hour:

> Zina: Yesterday there were demons in the room. They were wearing black robes saying to me: you worth nothing—they say it in unison—they like to sing. I thought they were gone. They are so mean. You can't see their faces—they all wear black robes and sharp hoodies.
>
> Me: Just before you are about to sign up for a class in the new school the demons show up.
>
> Zina: Yes, they are mean that way, but sometimes they are cute. I don't want them to know, but they don't freak me out, like they used to. I wish I knew when they are coming—so I can be prepared.
>
> Me: They often appear right before you are about to take a challenging step, and then they often say discouraging things to you.
>
> Zina: The last class I took, it was an evil imp that nagged me, remember?—It had a red hat. It kept saying that I'm ugly. They are all so nasty. They want me not to succeed, but I am smarter than them. . . . I also know

that they don't really exist. . . . because my mom tells me. . . . I decided to ignore them completely. . . . Just not to pay attention to anything they say. . . . What do you think?

Me: When I think about the imps and the demons I think about them as parts of you, not as real creatures. I don't really think about them as things outside of you so I prefer not to ignore them. It's more like your imagination takes your own fears and puts them into images—like demons with hoodies and imps with hats.

Zina: (smiling)

Me: What?

Zina: The red imp looks like a tooth—has two hands and a tail—I don't know. . . . It's crazy to think it's real. . . . The problem is that sometimes they are right there . . . especially in the morning.

(Long silence)

I had an idea for an art project. I am going to write a quote on my wall—in big letters—all made from pieces of magazines—really colorful—a collage from all the ads.

Every time I wake up I will see the quote the first thing when I open my eyes—and it will be an uplifting quote like "today is the best day of your life" or something like this: I will make it rhyme or look for a good quote from a Martin Luther King speech.

I believe that this new ability to talk about her experience as evidenced above is due to in part to the modification in the dosage of Zina's medication, but the main cause of the shift is the fact that we both now view her psychotic break in a different light.

CLOSING THOUGHTS

As I write this, there are still difficult weeks, when Zina experiences anxiety, depression, somatic delusions and hallucinations, but now there are also times of courageous attempts to touch real pain—old and new—and to connect, mostly to me at this point, in a real and open way. Zina has been "on stage" for most of her life. She played the role of a successful, bright, talented, cheerful, and resourceful girl who grew up to be a promising young woman. This was the image she presented to herself, to me, to her family, and to society. Zina's break was a way to reclaim the disowned parts of her—

the unattractive, dependent, fearful, angry, sad and confused Zina. All of these "intolerable" aspects of herself were repressed in order to avoid rejection and abandonment. The breakdown brought forth the hidden parts—in full force.

In looking back over my years of work with Zina, I wonder how she managed to maintain a polished façade for so long. What factors brought on the psychotic episodes? And why did it all fall apart when it did? Did Zina finally reach a point of exhaustion in having to pretend that all was well? Was the break at school triggered by not having me in her admiring audience? Was it the emergence of a genetic predisposition triggered by alcohol consumption? Was it an outpouring of rage for all she had endured as a child? Was it all of that and more that we don't yet understand? It's hard to know. However, I believe that one of the main dynamics was an unconscious wish finally to bring the dark and repressed feelings and fears into the open. In this regard, I believe that the last break offers some hope for Zina to be able to integrate these aspects of her psyche into a fuller, richer identity. I feel that our present work is about linking Zina's fragmented psychic parts into a more coherent and authentic narrative. As Leonard Cohen (1992) says in his poem "Anthem," "It's through the cracks that the light comes in."

I think that in working with Zina, and perhaps in working with any of the children who come to A Home Within, we are sometimes trying to fill an impossible hole—to serve a maternal function, which was lost and can never be replaced. And yet, I believe that the relationship Zina and I have is a crucial and vital component in her development and psychic health. For my part, I have been touched deeply by my relationship with her. Watching Zina survive horrific trauma with ingenuity of stunning creativity, sharp intelligence, and relentless hunger for life brings into focus the essence of life in its fullest. In closing, a few sentences from Zina's recent poem:

yes dignity takes up no space
even in the flash drive,
when you decide to eject
and load your problems elsewhere.
I have choked up enough anti-bodys;
now white blood cells are on the move—
blood does not understand love
yet, we are related, right?
We are all god's children.
And where the lights bends
god lives—I tell you.

REFERENCES

Bion, W. (1956). Development of schizophrenic thought. *The International Journal of Psychoanalysis*, *37*(4–5), 344–346.

Bion, W. R. (1959). Attacks on linking. *International Journal of Psychoanalysis, 40*, 308–315.
Brown, L. J. (2010). Klein, Bion, and intersubjectivity: Becoming, transforming, and dreaming. *Psychoanalytic Dialogues, 20*(6), 669–682. DOI: 10.1080/10481885.2010.532392.
Cohen, L. (1992). Anthem. *The future*. New York: Columbia.
Klein, M. (1946). Notes on some schizoid mechanisms. *The International Journal of Psychoanalysis, 27*(3–4), 99–110.
Kohut, H. (1971) *The analysis of the self: A systematic approach to the psychoanalytic treatment of narcissistic personality disorders*. New York: International Universities Press.
Winnicott., D. W. (1953). Transitional objects and transitional phenomena. *International Journal of Psychoanalysis, 34*(2), 89–97.
Zeanah, C. H. (2000). Disturbances of attachment in young children adopted from institutions. *Journal of Developmental and Behavioral Pediatrics, 21*(3), 230–236.

Chapter Eleven

Ben

In many respects Ben's story is typical of children and young adults who have the misfortune of being born to people who are profoundly impaired and unprepared for the task of parenting. This is a story of grief, unbearable loss, and a family riddled with tragedy, in which repeated trauma became a familiar part of the landscape. This is also the story of a boy desperately struggling to stay afloat, a seventeen-year therapeutic relationship, and the support and community of A Home Within, which allowed for sustainable, creative, and thoughtful work.

Those of us who treat foster children have no idea whether we'll see a child once or dozens of times. We don't know if the interested adult who referred the child for therapy is going to stay interested, remain involved with the case, or continue to be a presence in the child's life. We don't know whether the child we're treating might, in the next week, be relocated to a different county, or whether transportation to therapy might fall through. And we almost always have to disavow our awareness of all the uncertainties in order to open our minds and hearts to the child sitting across from us.

One of the sad facts that those of us who work with foster children learn early on—sometimes before we even meet these patients—is how fragmented and fractured their stories are. All too often, no one exists who knows the child's history over time, or the child's likes and dislikes, or the multitude of losses the child has experienced, or the qualities and meanings of those lost relationships. We are frequently left to piece together hastily written chart notes, or rely on the factual data given to us by the child's attorney as we try to understand the child's inner world. Not only do foster children come to us laden with trauma and without a coherent history, they often come to us with unacknowledged injuries, or if recognized, not sufficiently healed before the next blow falls. And, unlike children from intact families, who are confident that they are loved, foster children appear in our offices either hungry for relationships or so damaged from repeated loss that they have no hope that relationships can, and do, last.

There is, all too often, no witness to their trauma. We are confronted with the cruelties of suffering alone and are painfully aware that the gaps in memory and mourning can never be filled by the child alone. These traumas require the presence of others for both their registration and their reworking. Therapists working with foster children, by definition, function as witnesses to this trauma, an other who can bear knowing that which can not yet be represented in words—an accompanying other with the memories to fill in the gaps and the resilience to withstand the mourning.

Foster children in the care of A Home Within therapists may be aware that there is an organization called A Home Within. They also may be vaguely aware that A Home Within therapists are usually the only adults in their lives who are not being paid to care for them. It is doubtful, though, that they are conscious of the presence, let alone the significance and consequence of their therapist's Home Within consultation group. As a whole and individually, the members of each therapist's consultation group knows the foster children of the group members intimately, keeps them in mind, mourns their losses, and celebrates their achievements. For both the foster child and the therapist, the consultation groups function in what Harris (2006) has described as the shared labor of relational mourning, a communal holding of the trauma.

My consultation group was essential in helping me contain and understand my feelings of impatience, boredom, judgment, and uselessness during the first months with Ben. Even more important, the members of my group provided me the support and strength over the years to return to Ben when his loss and pain seemed unbearable. Throughout my work with Ben, the combined wisdom of the members of my group allowed me to become an enduring presence, committed to remembering in the face of fear and forgetting, someone who could simply stand with him in times of despair and mind numbing aloneness.

When I began working with Ben seventeen years ago neither of us could have imagined the depth or duration of our relationship, or the unimaginable losses he would endure. Neither of us could imagine the many roles I would play in his life as he grew up, or that he, in turn, would become one of my most important teachers.

THE EARLY MONTHS

Ben and his younger brother, Joe, were referred to A Home Within by their mother's therapist as it became clear that termination of her parental rights was inevitable. Ben's mother had a number of debilitating physical conditions and struggled with an addiction to crack cocaine. She also suffered from psychotic and paranoid symptoms, and was noncompliant with her antipsychotic medications. At the time of referral, Ben and Joe were living with their mother in a small ramshackle apartment. The refrigerator and cupboards were often empty and the boys ate most of their meals at neighborhood restaurants where their maternal grandfather, Mr. Harvey, had set up accounts for them. Ben and Joe saw their father, also a crack user, only infrequently, when he would drop by without warning. His visits would end abruptly, often following a violent conflict with their mother.

Despite the difficulty of maintaining a relationship with his daughter, Mr. Harvey was a generous father and doting grandfather. He paid the rent and other bills; stocked the cupboards with groceries; set up tabs for the boys at local convenience stores and restaurants; showered them with gifts, games, and sports equipment; and made sure they had all their material needs attended to.

Eleven-year-old Ben arrived for his first appointment and plunked himself down in the chair. He was pale and chubby, with carrot-top hair, coke-bottle glasses, rumpled jeans, and wearing a wrinkled button-down shirt. In answer to my question, he replied that he had been sent to see me because he was getting in fights at home and at school with his brother and kids at school, and had behaved aggressively towards his teachers. He told me that he had no friends and that everyone hated him. To make matters worse, everyone compared him to Joe. This was articulated less as a complaint than as a statement of fact—one that caused Ben much anguish. His assertion that Joe was more loved and more loveable proved true in numerous ways. Where Ben was chubby and uncoordinated, his brother was cute and nimble; where Ben struggled intellectually, his brother excelled; where Ben was alone and lonely, angry and prone to violent outbursts, his brother took refuge in friends, sports, school, and social activities. Despite the fact that Ben was, in every respect, outmatched by Joe, he idolized and loved his brother deeply. Joe was a presence in every session and in virtually every story and event that Ben relayed to me. For Ben, Joe was the stabilizing factor in his life; he had Joe and together the two of them could weather the worst circumstances. Joe was the only one upon whom Ben could depend.

Early in our first meeting, Ben mentioned that his grandfather had taken him to see *Star Wars* the previous weekend. Again. He asked if I had seen it and I said that I had. He then began a word-for-word exposition of the beginning of the movie. By the time the session was over he had narrated the first ten minutes of the movie. Little did I know that we would spend, with few exceptions, every minute of our time together for the next three months immersed in a scene-by-scene re-telling of the saga. Each week he would plop down in the chair, remind me where we left off, and launch in. I made occasional attempts to link Dark Star, Luke Skywalker, R2-D2, Darth Vader, power, loyalty, and friendship to events in Ben's life. These were met with a frustrated sigh, an impatient scowl, a short pause, then a seamless resumption of the narration where I had so confoundedly interrupted.

Every session was the same. I began to feel as if Ben's storytelling was designed to keep me out and, more importantly, designed to exclude from our sessions both his internal and external world. Any attempt to make a link or inject meaning was, in itself, disruptive. Ben seemed to experience any contribution from me as an intrusion or assault. It occurred to me that he was experiencing not only my attempts to engage him, but even the sound of my voice, as traumas of both commission and omission—he was bombarded by responses that were not at all related to his needs, while his actual need for me to just be there was neither recognized nor met. Eventually I was able to settle in with him, and to simply listen to him tell the story. He, in turn, relaxed, and his storytelling took on a less pressured cadence. He seemed not to notice the few occasions when his storytelling nearly lulled me to sleep. I often wondered if he had ever had the experience of being gently rocked to sleep with a bedtime story.

Admittedly, I had moments of unadulterated dread during those first three months as I calculated how many years it would take us to complete the entire *Star Wars* trilogy. There were also moments when I couldn't imagine how we were going to make the transition into another way of being together. Three months later, as we reached the end, as Hans Solo returned to save the day and Luke Skywalker successfully destroyed the Death Star, I suggested we take a walk to the corner coffee shop for cupcakes—a ritual we continued for many years to celebrate transitions, triumphs, birthdays, graduations, and other important occasions. To my relief, Ben seemed amenable to pursuing new territory as we discussed what to do together now that we had finished *Star Wars*. He suggested that we play Battleship. And so we did. For months.

The early Battleship months were similar to the *Star Wars* months in that there was a single-mindedness to Ben's approach and very little room for deviation into other subjects or activities. The difference was that, for the first time, he allowed me to be an active participant. Yet there was very little sense of play as a pleasurable activity in those early games; rather, Ben brought to the activity an almost grim determination to win at all costs. He would change the rules wildly to achieve this goal, and became angry and distraught at my rare wins.

Over time, Ben relaxed and relinquished his fierce control over every moment of our time together. He slowly began to reveal his sense of humor and was occasionally able to poke fun at himself or at me, a far cry from the grimness of our initial months together. Ben and I began to talk about winning and losing. When he beat me at a game of Battleship he, for once, didn't feel like a loser. He explained that he felt stupid at school, on the playground with other kids, and always at home. He agreed to coach me on strategy—always change up the starting placement of your ships and, most importantly, learn your opponent's strategy. He began to take some pleasure in my occasional wins.

THE LOSSES BEGIN

During these first months while Ben and I were occupied with *Star Wars* and Battleship, the situation at home was deteriorating. Ben's mother was growing more psychotic and Mr. Harvey was progressively taking over more of the day-to-day care of the boys. He began to pick them up from school, help them with homework, and take them out for dinner before dropping them off at home at bedtime. They increasingly spent weekends at their grandfather's apartment.

Embedded in Ben's descriptions of his frustrations with Joe, difficulties at school and with his teachers, and longings for a friend, he revealed a chaotic and disorganized life at home. Eventually Ben began to talk more directly with me about the events taking place in his world. He was often outraged at the injustice meted out by his teachers, furious at Joe's achievements and special treatment, dismissive of his grandfather's caretaking, and protective of his mother; meanwhile he directed his anger at people and agencies who were, at best, interfering where they weren't wanted or needed and, at worst, directly responsible for his mother's unraveling.

Preserving the therapeutic relationship and protecting Ben's trust in me was complicated as plans were being formulated to remove the boys from their mother and place them with their grandfather—a change that was well overdue and inevitable, and yet one to which Ben was desperately opposed. There were numerous demands by Social Services for Joe's therapist and me to participate in dependency meetings and court proceedings. During this time we also met numerous times (both separately and together) with the boys' social workers and teachers.

Placing Ben and Joe with their grandfather was fraught for all concerned. Joe's therapist and I each began to meet weekly with Mr. Harvey. Despite his devotion to his grandsons and the countless sessions over the years in which Joe's therapist and I provided parenting advice, coached and encouraged him, and interpreted his resistances, Mr. Harvey never made the transition from generous and loving grandfather to the limit-setting parental figure the boys desperately needed.

When Ben was thirteen his mother was finally hospitalized, and the boys were permanently placed with their grandfather. Ben remained fiercely protective of his mother, often skipping school to stay with her in the hospital. He railed against both the system that failed to help his mother and the drugs that destroyed his family. Ben blamed his grandfather for his mother's illness and addiction to drugs. Yet his behavior contradicted his words. Within weeks of his removal from his mother and permanent placement with his grandfather, Ben was noticeably calmer. He could not hide the fact that he was happier and was much more relaxed. When I commented that he seemed more settled at his grandfather's, he firmly denied that this was the case and insisted that he belonged with his mother, that she needed him. He worried what would happen to her if he were not there.

Despite the fact that Ben spoke passionately about his mother, his psychic experience of her was oddly one-dimensional. She seemed to exist only as a goal for him, an absent prize. His fantasies of saving her felt much the way he approached the game of Battleship in which winning was the only thing that mattered. The prize for Ben was the hope that his mother would finally find some value in him. Ben saw himself in his broken and diseased mother, and he seemed to agree with her that there was little in him to love.

After the brothers' removal from their mother, Ben's father emerged as a subject in our sessions, with Ben alternately expressing warm early memories and anger at his abandonment. At the boys' behest, their grandfather took Ben and Joe to Colorado to visit their father and his extended family. The visit evoked Ben's fantasies that one day soon his father would send for him. Two months after the visit, Ben received a phone call informing him that his father had committed suicide by hanging himself. Ben's despair filled the room as he quietly talked about his recent hopes that his father would some day come for him. He wondered what could have been so wrong that drove his father to suicide, and hoped that he had done nothing to cause his father to make such a choice. Ben's continued hope that he and Joe would be reunified with their mother became more pressing.

Ben's mother died of pulmonary failure just three months following his father's suicide. Ben's response to his mother's death was strikingly subdued. I struggled to make sense of his lack of affect—he wasn't quite flat, he seemed distantly effected but not dissociated. Ben didn't really have much to say about his mother's death and yet he didn't seem to be avoiding the subject. He was subdued but not particularly sad. His anxiety and excitement about starting high school became the focus of his attention.

HOPEFUL BEGINNINGS AND MORE LOSS

High school was the first time Ben experienced an environment where he was not being compared to his younger brother. He soon began a concerted search for a man he could look up to, a pursuit in which he was serially successful with relatively short-term results. He started a sequence of new activities: first wrestling, followed by Junior Reserve Officers' Training

Corps (ROTC), ice hockey, and karate. He was not a natural at any of these activities and worked hard to excel.

Ben joined the wrestling team early in his freshman year. His large-for-his-age, beefy physique served him well; he won most of his matches and, more importantly, the eye of the coach. Ben would arrive at my office eager to show me how he had achieved his most recent victory. My carpet became a wrestling pad as he got down on all fours and demonstrated how he had taken his opponent down. This was serious business as he explained the rules, techniques, and penalties. As wrestling season was winding down he turned his attention toward Junior ROTC, very much aware that, unlike in wrestling, girls were actively involved in ROTC.

He arrived at my office one afternoon with his first award patch sewn crookedly onto his brand new sash. He pulled a needle and thread, scissors, and a copy of an Army placement guide out of his backpack. He said that despite one attempt by his grandfather and his own three tries, this was the best he could do and it wouldn't pass muster. He asked if I would show him how to sew it on. As I showed him how to position and sew his patch onto his sash, we talked about his sense that in Junior ROTC he had finally found something to hold onto that would break the spell of bad luck; something he could do well that carried the prospect, finally, of friends.

Ben progressed quickly up the ranks thru Cadet and Cadet Squad Leader to Cadet Platoon Sergeant, assuming more and more responsibility, including administration, budgeting, and planning for the Platoon. This was the first time that he had excelled at anything and was in a position of leadership. He was driven in large part by the relationship with the Company Commander, a retired Army officer who took Ben under his wing and encouraged him every step of the way. The two of them often met on the weekends to plan future activities for the Platoon. Ben flourished in the structured and rule-driven atmosphere of Junior ROTC, and dreamed of joining the military when he graduated.

Again, my office was his place proudly to display his accomplishments and receive praise. He would arrive outfitted in his dress uniform with a sash progressively displaying more medals and awards as he earned more responsibility and rose in rank. He proudly presented his newest medals to me and, with great precision, demonstrated drill team, color guard, rifle guard, and honor guard maneuvers as he marched from my office onto my outdoor patio and back. His dreams of joining the military after high school solidified and he could imagine no other future plans. Junior ROTC and, more significantly, his Company Commander, came to represent a father figure that could embrace Ben and provide him a sense of pride and source of identification.

Ben's budding interest in girls took off as he grew more confident at school and in his role in Junior ROTC. It was clear that he had no idea how to negotiate his way in this new realm. I found myself, from time to time, offering up motherly advice: "Pay her way into the movies and buy her a soda." We both approached each new crush with hope. He alternated between focusing on his feelings of longing and desire for a certain girl, and viciously berating her for rejecting him. The anticipated rejection was always close to the surface.

Ben fit in more or less successfully with his brother's large group of friends. He was acutely aware that he was lacking something essential—something that the other boys came by naturally, a fundamental sense of who he was and what he thought—how to relate to others, and how to get along in the world. Ben modeled his adolescent self and his thoughts about the world after this group of boys. As he did with wrestling and Junior ROTC, he brought these new ideas, new ways of dressing, and stories of new experiences for my review. He was trying on attitudes, politics, and behavior that were, at various times, dangerous, appalling, and endearing.

As his brother and his friends became increasingly involved with drugs, Ben followed. However, unlike his brother, Ben could not maintain his hard-won academic achievements, and he began to fail classes and cut school. His three years of Junior ROTC ended in missed drill classes as he avoided his Company Commander.

Ben attempted to modulate his drug use—primarily alcohol and marijuana—by enrolling in a karate school and exercising strict control over his diet and workout regimen. He worked hard at progressing through the formal grading examinations and earning his belts. During his karate period he would arrive in his karate gi and perform moves, kicks, and examination routines for me. Ice hockey season would bring him lugging an enormous duffle of equipment into my office and long play-by-play explications of his most recent game. During a rollerblading period he would arrive in his skates—up a flight of stairs, down a long carpeted hallway—and glide into my office.

Ben managed to graduate high school and enrolled in a community college with a career in the military as his ultimate goal. He started college with great enthusiasm for his classes and would arrive at my office with a backpack stuffed with textbooks. But he quickly fell behind and, after a time, quit going to classes entirely. This was a pattern he repeated for a number of years as he re-enrolled at the beginning of each semester. His hopes of becoming an officer in the military—with its required college education—faded with each failed class.

After seven years, Ben decided to take a break from therapy. He continued to call me from time to time to update me on his latest attempts at college and his progress in finding a girlfriend. In addition, I kept track of Ben through Joe's therapist in my consultation group and occasional meetings with Mr. Harvey when things at home deteriorated.

A year after Ben interrupted therapy I received a call from Mr. Harvey. He told me that Joe had died that morning. A few hours later Ben walked into my office. This was the most difficult meeting I could have imagined. Ben spent the entire hour sobbing on my couch. I sat in the chair next to the couch and stroked his back. I was filled with a deep and aching sadness for Ben, for his grandfather, and for Joe's therapist. During these early days I, like Ben, couldn't imagine how he could go on.

Filled with despair, I phoned my consultation group leader who convened a group meeting the following day. Joe's therapist and I were embraced by our colleagues who had, through the group, known both boys as long as we had and almost as intimately, and fully understood the enormity of the loss, the depth of tragedy. Joe's therapist and I had, in the members of our consultation group, a family who mourned with us.

I saw Ben almost every day for the next couple of weeks and slowly the details emerged. His brother, who had recently begun taking Prozac for depression, had also been using large quantities of prescription narcotics. The night he died he mixed various pills with alcohol and marijuana. The two teenage boys shared a bedroom and a set of bunk beds—Ben in the upper bunk and his brother in the lower. Joe arrived home after Ben had gone to bed, and although Ben heard him come in, he did not speak with him. At some point early that morning Ben heard his brother coughing and gagging, but went back to sleep when the coughing stopped. A few hours later, Ben woke to find his brother lying his own vomit and unresponsive. When emergency crews arrived they determined that Joe had been dead for several hours.

Ben blamed himself for his brother's death. He was sure that he had been awakened by Joe's struggle to breathe. If only he had checked on him. If only he had not gone back to sleep. These sessions were heartbreaking, as were meetings with his grandfather. We were all drowning in despair. I spoke very little during these sessions and Ben often fell asleep on my couch.

Ben decided to join the Marines. He and I spent session after session trying to untangle his hopes and fantasies regarding what such a decision might mean. In part, he was driven by anger and spoke passionately of his fantasies of going to war and killing people. He seemed impervious to my attempts to link his despair and anger over his brother's death and the profound unfairness of life with his desire for retribution and violence. He could not be dissuaded; three months after Joe's death, Ben left for boot camp. Despite my certainty that he was in no shape to enter the military and that this would end badly, I harbored a small fantasy that he would find containment and healing in the structured and male military environment. Three weeks after he left for boot camp he was discharged after admitting to his Sergeant that he used marijuana regularly. He returned home and to therapy—angry and depressed and contending with yet another loss.

Bad decision followed bad decision when Ben and his grandfather contacted an attorney and filed a lawsuit against the physician who prescribed Joe antidepressants. The suit was settled quickly and they were awarded about $100,000. Ben and his grandfather divided the money among the two of them and their extended family. This windfall allowed Ben to sink into nine months of daily cocaine and alcohol use, near-total social isolation, and the emergence of cocaine-related psychotic symptoms, including auditory and visual hallucinations. We kept in spotty contact during this period. Phone calls with him were troubling. He was often obviously high and his thinking was quite disorganized. His grandfather, once again, provided food and checked up on him several times a week. I finally received a call from Ben asking for help getting into a treatment program. We quickly found him a sixty-day residential program, which he completed, followed by a nine-month aftercare program.

Ben resumed weekly treatment with me during his after-care program. Clean and sober, Ben redoubled his attempts to be readmitted into the military and spent the next several years searching for a branch that would accept him. He spent his days at various centers with encouraging recruiters. Yet each time he was close to being admitted, a background check would reveal his past and he would receive a letter of denial.

As Mr. Harvey and Ben mourned the loss of Joe, and as each questioned why it was Joe, who had so much promise and potential, and not Ben, who died, their relationship with each other deteriorated. Eventually Ben left his home with his grandfather and moved in with his uncle and his uncle's family. Ben was angry and depressed, and had little patience for his uncle's three young children. After much conflict, his uncle moved him into an empty house he owned. Mr. Harvey again stepped in and paid the utility bills and delivered food weekly. When Ben wasn't at recruitment centers, he spent his time alone in the empty house playing video games—lost in a fantasy world where law and order prevailed in a world of rules and violence. He immersed himself in first-person shooter video games and haunted white supremacist and survivalist websites. He was a sponge absorbing racist and hate-filled ideology.

It would be an understatement to say that it was difficult to be with him during this time. He would borrow his uncle's car for the four-hour round trip commute to my office and spend his time instructing me about his newly acquired ideology. Reminiscent of the early *Star Wars* and Battleship days, my attempts to interpret his rage or interject a comment was met with a few seconds of silence followed by a seamless resumption—this time of hate speech. The only moments of mutual exchange came when I challenged his ideas and became argumentative myself. I dreaded our meetings and often felt assaulted by both the content and the relentlessness of his need to convince me of his worldview. Remarkably, he remained clean and sober.

His uncle's car became unavailable and, for a time, he took public transportation to his sessions—a train, a subway, and a bus. He spent entire days traveling to and from our meetings. He refused referrals to a therapist in his town and eventually decided to stop therapy for a while. We maintained fairly regular phone contact for the next several months, during which our conversations remained indistinguishable from one to the next. Over time, our scheduled phone calls dwindled to once a month, then every other month or so. Over the next couple of years I would receive a call from him "just to check in" or when he got a job or met a girl. If I hadn't heard from him in several months I would call him "just to check in."

Some months ago, as I was formulating this chapter, I received a call from Ben. He said he was depressed and didn't know if he could go on. He reassured me that he was not suicidal but felt that he couldn't continue to live such an isolated and unhappy life. He told me that he had an apartment in the city and a job as a security guard. He said that, despite his fear of antidepressants, he felt he had no choice and asked for help finding a psychiatrist. He was approaching his five-year clean-and-sober anniversary, and was fearful that unless he addressed his depression he wouldn't be able to remain drug free. I began to see him weekly while he waited for treatment with a psychiatrist and therapy at a clinic.

I referred Ben to a clinic run by Joe's therapist. This was a decision based not only on the quality of care he would receive at this clinic, but my desire to "keep him in the family" and my certainty that Joe's therapist, despite the formidable responsibilities of running a community mental health clinic, would make sure to watch over Ben. I set up an appointment for Ben and told him that Joe's therapist was peripherally involved in the clinic. As was his wont, Ben had no reaction, but chose to see a psychiatrist at another clinic where he was prescribed a different antidepressant than his brother, hopeful that it would help lift his depression.

Several weeks later I received a call from Ben letting me know that his grandfather had passed away that morning. He came in for his scheduled appointment that afternoon. The fact of Mr. Harvey's death wasn't a particular shock to either of us—he had been in very poor health for several years. Yet Ben's utter aloneness, and the number of losses that he had endured over the course of his still young life, was and still is staggering to me.

REFLECTIONS

My seventeen-year history with Ben is less the story of a long term, open-ended treatment than the story of a mutually enduring relationship that has been in and of itself therapeutic. It's also the story of the tenacity of a boy who always assumed that I would be where he left me—the next day, the next week, the next year. The first year of work with Ben was difficult as he quickly laid bare my fantasies that my thoughts, theories, and ideas—that is, my mind—could be useful to him. As I was adjusting to simply being a presence in the room with him, he was creating in me someone with the patience to wait for him to find a way to make use of me.

Over the years, he called upon me to fill a number of gaps. While I willingly stepped into these roles, he slowly and tentatively allowed the two of us to consider his life. As I was sewing his Junior ROTC badges onto his sash, or admiring his wrestling skills, or teaching him how to impress girls, we were both very much aware that I was filling in for his absent mother. For Ben, his mother was simply experienced as the absence of love. She didn't otherwise exist. Andre Green (1986) conceptualized a situation in which the mother is not actually dead, but is preoccupied to the extent that she is unavailable and is consequently experienced *as if dead* (Hart, 2012). Green went on to describe how devastating the child's subjective experience of this relationship is and how it "carries in its wake, beside the loss of love, the loss of meaning."

For all of us, and Ben is no exception, the work required in creating meaning is arduous and painful. Ben held tenaciously to the notion that nothing had meaning. As his losses mounted, this denial gave him the strength to simply put one foot in front of the other. From time to time, though, Ben would open a session with "I've been thinking. . . ." I learned to recognize these words as a sign that he was, however fleetingly, resilient enough to allow his mind to function and extending an invitation to me to think with him. These were difficult conversations as Ben struggled to make sense of a mother who couldn't love him and what that meant, or didn't mean, about him.

Joe's death was devastating for Ben, who had now finally lost the one person he loved without reservation and upon whom he felt he could rely. Ben slipped into a melancholia fueled by a refusal to care any longer, and entered a world of cynicism and indifference, itself a desperate, manic attempt to deny that any loss mattered enough to merit mourning.

The odds are so profoundly stacked against foster children that those of us who work with them must be able to recognize small victories. That Ben is still physically alive despite more tragedy than many of us could bear is not a victory, per se. After all, for many years he kept his body alive while deadening his internal world through depression, denial, and substance abuse. Relinquishing drugs and alcohol was Ben's first step from behind the defenses he had relied on for so long to protect himself from a profound sense of emptiness. He can now tolerate knowing what is absent from his life; unlike emptiness, absence holds the possibility of fulfillment. When I met Ben, he was a boy who could not dare to hope; he is now a young man ready to search for meaning.

REFERENCES

Green, A. (1986). The dead mother. In A. Green, *On private madness.* London: Hogarth Press.

Harris, M. (2006). Beyond the 50-minute hour: A continuum of care for a foster child. In T. V. Heineman & D. Ehrensaft (Eds.), *Building a home within: Meeting the emotional needs of children and youth in foster care.* Baltimore, MD: Paul H. Brookes.

Hart, C. (2012). The "Dead Mother Syndrome" and the child in care: A framework for reflecting on why some children experience multiple placement breakdowns. *Journal of Infant, Child, and Adolescent Psychotherapy, 11*(4), 342–355. DOI: 10.1080/15289168.2012.732905.

Chapter Twelve

How Consultation Groups Change Therapy (and Therapists)

I began my work with Mark after many years of experience as a child therapist but as fledgling member of a newly forming chapter of A Home Within. My commitment to working therapeutically with foster children was deep and solid. A Home Within offered an opportunity I craved—the chance to work in a close community of like-minded clinicians, something I missed in the world of private practice. I believed this could take the work further than I'd been able to take it before—believed that, more than I had a sense of how it would feel, or work.

When Mark was referred to our chapter, he was twelve and newly arrived in the area, to be in foster care with his aunt. His parents—both with long criminal and substance-abuse histories—were "in the wind." His protective services caseworker thought he needed a male therapist. I was ready. Or I thought I was. Mark was described as angry and often unresponsive to his aunt and his teachers, but I had dealt with "tough customers" before. I thought things would go well this time because Mark would be seeing me in my private office—no broken toys, no missing game pieces, decent lighting, comfortable chairs, a thermostat that worked.

I had taken in the A Home Within model, but was not sure how going over my work with Mark as part of a consultation group would feel "from the inside." My consultation group, at that time early in the development of our chapter, was our steering committee—our commitment and excitement were such that most of us were eager to see foster children. Our steering committee continues to support each other, even as several of us have gone on to lead consultation groups of our own. We were experienced therapists, used to thinking of ourselves as teachers and certainly not as neophytes. We soon learned that we had a lot to learn—that A Home Within therapies were going to be a lot more different from our past treatment experiences than we initially expected.

Mark liked coming to see me, and we formed a bond almost too quickly. Only in hindsight did it dawn on me that he was so hungry for relationships that he was willing to attach with a brittle, indiscriminate quality—that his angry strength was a very thin veneer. Mark's hungry eagerness to connect was where the problem began and centered itself. His aunt/foster mother cancelled sessions with little notice or sometimes just did not bring him. Sometimes she later explained she had to work late; she was the sole support of a large, extended family household with shifting membership and needed the extra money when she was offered overtime. Other times, family members had crises she felt needed urgent attention. Mark often arrived late. Sometimes, there was no explanation—perhaps because he was ambivalent about how close he found himself becoming to me, or wanted to test me, or because he was used to lying about things rather than struggling to express complex feelings that confused him.

I'm in many ways a fairly traditional psychotherapist. I believe that, most of the time, therapy is better served by waiting to see when and how a child brings something up than by opening up a topic before the child does—that more is often accomplished through patient exploration of byways than by taking on complex problems head-on. Mark was always polite, always friendly with me. His play was heart-felt and emotionally communicative—he had a way of playing Uno with his whole body engaged. I would tell my consultation group how things were going with Mark but, in hindsight, was more invested in reporting than exploring or questioning.

I felt Mark and I were on familiar turf. I hoped time—for Mark and his aunt to get more familiar with therapy and with me, to see that I was reliable and respectful—would help. But time wasn't helping. Mark's attendance became more sporadic and a part of me was relieved when he missed. Mark's play became less wholehearted and more like he was going through familiar motions. He said less—more worrisome, he seemed less curious. He was pulling away.

I came into a consultation group meeting with an emerging sense that we had been wrong to take on Mark as a patient—that he and his family were a "bad" case, not a "good" one—committed to therapy, able to take advantage of what we had to offer. After nine weeks, I was ready to give up. But my consultation group challenged me—with empathy; they did not let me off the hook. Was I supporting the aunt/foster mother enough? Was I trying to do too much too fast? I thought, "Playing endless Uno games is doing too much?" But I held back from saying it in the group. I did not feel confident enough, yet, to speak up more freely.

I soldiered on, but Mark seemed to notice my subtle withdrawal of the heart. He got a bit rougher around the edges, angrier, in the ten- to twenty-minute sessions we were (sort of) having. And then it came to me: We had created, in the structural frame of the therapy, the exact conditions of his foster care life: adults were not reliable, and not effective in their roles and responsibilities. Nothing was sure or predictable in his life; if he was foolish enough to develop a little hope, it would be quickly and thoughtlessly dashed. Better to withdraw, disinvest, turn hard, close down inside.

My consultation group helped me appreciate that my insight was a victory, not a defeat. Much of therapy depends on recreating in a therapeutic relationship what went wrong earlier in life—so that it could be understood and, with committed and focused effort, repaired.

But how? The consultation group and I brainstormed. "It takes a village to raise a family" was in the air around that time. By that time, Mark's sister was also in therapy through A Home Within and was missing too many sessions. We concluded that the two therapists needed to explain to the aunt how the unreliable attendance was affecting Mark and his sister. I wanted to make clearer to her why therapy was so important to him, even when he sometimes said it wasn't, and how it could help repair the damaged expectations that lay at the heart of his difficulties. I hoped that we could think together about what to do. Could it work to mobilize the extended family to support his therapy by bringing him to sessions?

We arranged a meeting with the aunt. With three busy schedules, this was no small feat—but when understanding leads to will, a way can emerge. She bought into the plan—in hindsight, paralleling Mark, maybe a bit too readily. But her tone changed. Yes, it would not be easy, but some of the extended family might be able to help. She could explain to them how important it was.

Not only did Mark start coming more regularly, and burrowing a bit deeper into his feelings and his past experiences when he did, but also an uncle started bringing him. He was a huge, shy, quiet man who seemed to fill my whole waiting room, at first uncomfortable to be there, over time less and less so. It seemed to mean a lot to Mark that his uncle was there—a man in his life, other than me, showing up, reliably, committed to him and fulfilling his role.

I learned something important about myself through this episode. I was too ready to cherry-pick my therapy cases—to do what fit comfortably with my understanding and my style. It wasn't enough to assert what I (thought I) knew. I had to start asking myself different questions, very hard ones: What else did I need to be doing? When was being with and thinking with Mark, listening with patience and empathy, insufficient or, worse, the wrong move (Alvarez, 1992; 2012)? What would happen if I started believing that giving up wasn't an option? And how had I arrived at the belief, not fully conscious, that it was? What was that all about?

The most radical change was that I began to experience the consultation group not as a developmental tool, but as an essential component of therapy. Foster care explodes the notion of privacy in a child's life, and I chafed, as did the many foster children I have treated, over that fact. I was used to therapy helping, in no small part, by restoring a sense of safe, private space. Fair enough. But, for many children—and for Mark—foster care was also a necessity, and involved coming to some kind of terms with all that that implies. So maybe that was true for me, too—that, by no longer keeping my therapeutic experience quite so private, I could bring something important about the foster care experience, for the better, into the way I thought about doing therapy.

There is a lot more I could say about Mark. We worked together for four years, before a part of him gave up on himself, perhaps in part because his aunt had given up on him and felt that she could no longer manage the effort involved in getting him to therapy. My consultation group helped me understand the layers of resignation at work in this constellation. With the group's help, I could even, though not without ambivalence, find some empathy with the aunt for her decision. Her life was overloaded with stressors, and it was not entirely unfair that she wanted more time for herself.

The group also helped me understand that, come what may, Mark was taking part of me with him. Mark and I had worked hard together and both of us had grown from our relationship. On bad days I worry that his gains will not hold in the face of fading family support; on good days, I hope that they will. That is, after all, what we expect from psychotherapy—that the positive changes that occur during the treatment will continue well beyond.

The model of therapy practiced by A Home Within clinicians —"one therapist, one child, for as long as it takes"—is both very traditional and a leap beyond tradition. For one thing, we agree with Winnicott (1986) that many children others see as beyond reach can be helped. For another, we agree with those who do not hold out more limited objectives for our foster child patients than we do for the more advantaged children we treat (Boston & Szur, 1990). We strive to get at the heart and the root of things with our foster child patients, so that they can develop the sturdy understandings and supports they need to live full, good, satisfying lives, believing that nothing less is reasonable or fair (Heineman & Ehrensaft, 2006).

A parallel argument can be me about the role of consultation. Much that we do in consultation groups is similar to traditional ideas—re-cast in a more contemporary, less hierarchical idiom—about how supervision helps therapists develop (Frawley-O'Dea & Sarnat, 2001). Traditional supervision and A Home Within consultation both recognize that effective therapy does not involve applying invariant techniques; that therapy is part science but largely involves intuition and craft. We know that child therapy stirs up a lot in child therapists, which we have to understand intimately if we are to be effective—and, therefore, therapeutic skills are learned through long apprenticeships, in which reviewing one's clinical work with others plays a key role.

However, where supervision is seen as something fundamentally developmental—and, therefore, therapists eventually "graduate" from supervision—A Home Within consultation is based on a lesson we have learned through our pooled experience: thoroughgoing therapeutic work with foster care children is so inherently complex that it needs on-going processing with a group of clinicians to succeed. Similar to the way that foster children live in complex, overlapping systems (biological family, foster family, protective services, court systems, schools, and communities), therapy with foster children needs its own community. Consultation provides that—a collective, shared resource that encourages space for learning.

This means that consultation groups consider together not just what is going on within the foster child patient and between the child and the therapist, but what is going on within the systems in which the child lives as well. It can be tempting to screen out systems issues as "noise" from which the therapy needs to be protected. This is understandable; systems can act bluntly, and can hurt foster children by their actions, sometimes unavoidably, sometimes because they are not sufficiently oriented toward children's emotional realities. But legal, educational, and social-services systems can be understood and helped, the same as children and their parents (Boston & Szur, 1990; Imber-Black, 1988; Rustin, 1998). This means coming to explore, understand, and empathize with the realities, perspectives, and contributions of colleagues in larger systems—to consider this an integral part of the work, not interference (Imber-Black, 1988). And this is something that requires and shapes the work of A Home Within consultation groups.

John came into foster care at the age of ten after he witnessed his father kill his mother. His father was apprehended and was in jail awaiting trial. John and his family were immigrants from West Africa. His foster mother was from the Caribbean. A younger sister was in treatment with another A Home Within therapist in a different consultation group. A brother was in treatment with another therapist in the community.

John, like many children A Home Within clinicians treat, had layered difficulties. Life in his biological family had not been a good-enough time before foster care; it had been disrupted by immigration and contentious because of on-going family arguments and violence. His parents were professionals with solid incomes; his unmarried foster mother could barely make ends meet. There were cultural and religious differences between his biological and foster households. His foster mother's parenting style was more brusque than he readily tolerated. And John had leukemia—in remission, but no one knew for how long.

John's therapist was well trained and experienced. She and I liked and respected each other—a lot. John was the third A Home Within child she had treated. We had a track record together. Our consultation group met weekly and seemed to function well. I admired her sustained commitment.

The therapy with John did not go easily. Both John and his foster mother pushed, sometimes hard, against the ground rules. The foster mother would drop John off on the street in front of the therapist's office—questionable judgment with such a young child, in a busy commercial neighborhood. She often would not pick him up on time; and John would not wait peacefully in the waiting room, when his time was up and the therapist's next patient arrived. The foster mother complained about everything, and often refused to speak with the therapist; she was hostile when she did. The protective services social worker tried to reason with the foster mother, but could not keep her from undermining the therapy.

John seemed to like playing games with the therapist, in both senses of the term—he enjoyed seeing her, and he toyed with her. He wanted more snacks, more time, fewer limits. He was ambivalent about wanting to come, or sometimes wanting to stay.

I felt John's therapist was never far from a sense of despair. She almost constantly questioned whether the therapy was viable, and mostly did not feel John was getting better. I would point out that John's sense of freedom to challenge her reflected his emerging sense of mastery and his feeling of connection to her that, over time, was likely to prove more important than how satisfied his foster mother was with him, or what his grades were in school. The therapist would give thoughtful consideration to what I said, but I never had the sense she was convinced.

We lumbered along. Some potential members of A Home Within could not envision taking enough time away from the demands of practice in a harsh economy to sustain commitment to a weekly consultation group. For stretches of time, we were a group of two, as simultaneously tough and fragile as foster children.

Then we came to a fork in the road. It was time for John's father's trial; justice for John's family depended on his conviction. And the prosecutor informed John's therapist that, in her considered opinion, conviction would likely hinge on John's testimony. The message was delivered not directly, but sheepishly, through John's protective services social worker. The therapist's starting point was that she would not go to court. Like many therapists, she thought doing so had the potential of damaging the therapeutic relationship, and John's all-important sense of the therapeutic safety. John did not want to speak with her about the trial, which felt like proof that her intuition was on target. I assured the therapist—always feeling I sounded too hollow in the way I said it—that I would support her in whatever she decided was right. But I told her I thought we should think about the question together.

In the protective services department with whom we collaborate, social workers often demarcate the good-guy from the bad-guy therapists based on who is willing to show up in court, a miserable but, from their vantage point, all-important experience. Court appearances often involve long waits in the hallway or the back of the courtroom, harsh cross-examination of expert witnesses, and the need to reschedule on short notice. However, children's futures often turn on what happens in court. I felt strongly that we also needed to appreciate that the social worker and the prosecutor were committed professionals, advocating for their understanding of what was in the family's best interest and trying to do their jobs just as we were trying to do ours. John's therapist grasped what I was saying, as I respected what she was articulating with conviction and great clarity; but we could not bridge a gap between our perspectives.

We had good discussions, but things were not moving. I felt something was missing, and did what I had learned to do—I turned to my own consultation group. They know me better than most other people in my life do. And they helped me retrieve the missing link: I was bullied—badly—as a child. I wanted more than anything for someone to stand up for me; so I wanted John's therapist to stand up for him. A grounded but skewed sentiment—I needed to find a vantage point from which I could better appreciate all the relevant sides.

Going back to my colleague with this insight, we were able to work toward some new understandings. John's future would be affected, likely not for the better, if his father was not held accountable for killing his mother. Sometimes, children need their therapists to show the reasonable, calm authority of capable adults—John's therapist could ground herself in this when speaking with him about the trial and model that it was safe for him to speak about the trial with her. Rather than presenting the question of her attendance at the trial in a neutral way whose effect would not really be neutral—it would place the responsibility too squarely on John—she could state her wholehearted willingness to be present in court if that was John's wish. And if she still felt it was too risky for her to show up in court, I would go as a stand-in, so that John would know someone from A Home Within who understood what he was going through was standing up for him.

The sustained consultation group processing bolstered the therapist. When she spoke about the issue again with John, he was clear that he wanted her there on the court day. And the prosecutor decided she needed John's testimony and the therapist's support preparing John to testify—she did not need the therapist herself to testify. What John had said in therapy could stay between him and his therapist, and in our consultation group.

The day John testified, his therapist was a silent presence in the courtroom, in his line of sight. He was a movingly effective witness. John's father was sent to prison. John, after processing his mix of his feelings in subsequent therapy sessions—proof, perhaps, of how much the treatment had helped him—knew that he would be losing a fragile and very ambivalent connection to his father, but felt proud that he had stood up for his mother—as his therapist, in a role as surrogate mother, in a sense, had stood up for him. The outcome evoked in my mind an oddly classical image—the quiet therapist as an even-hovering presence, in favor of truth and development, and consulting to John, as our group had consulted to her.

I hope I have given those who will read this chapter a surer sense of what A Home Within consultation groups can do than I had when I began leading one. The process is as deep and as improvised as a child's play, and sometimes as fragile. But too many—far too many—foster children don't get to play. They can and do find that life-preserving capacity through their therapy with A Home Within.

And far too many therapists don't get the resources and the necessary support of the community we need to do our work. We slide toward a belief that we can make do with less. The work we do in our own home within, our consultation groups, can prove as life-preserving to us as we hope we can be to foster children and those who care for them.

REFERENCES

Alvarez, A. (1992). *Live company: Psychoanalytic psychotherapy with autistic, borderline, deprived and abused children*. New York: Routledge.

Alvarez, A. (2012). *The thinking heart: Three levels of psychoanalytic therapy with disturbed children*. New York: Routledge.

Boston, M., & Szur, R. (Eds.). (1990). *Psychotherapy with severely deprived children, revised edition*. London: Karnac.

Frawley-O'Dea, M. G., & Sarnat, J. (2001). *The supervisory relationship: A contemporary psychodynamic approach*. New York: Guilford.

Heineman, T. V., & Ehrensaft, D. (Eds.). (2006). *Building a home within: Meeting the emotional needs of children and youth in foster care*. Baltimore, MD: Paul Brookes.

Imber-Black, E. (1988). *Families and larger systems: A family therapist's guide through the labyrinth*. New York: Guilford.

Rustin, M. (1998). Dialogues with parents. *Journal of Child Psychotherapy, 24*(2), 233–252.

Winnicott, D.W. (1986). Delinquency as a sign of hope. In D. W. Winnicott, *Home is where we start from: Essays by a psychoanalyst* (pp. 90–100). New York: Norton.

Conclusion

Eight Elements of Relationship-Based Therapy

The stories of the therapists and clients presented in this book illustrate the triumphs, failures, and complexities of providing mental health treatment to traumatized children and youth who spend time in the foster care system. The clinicians of these vulnerable clients center their work on the development and maintenance of healthy relationships. In this chapter we highlight the crucial elements of Relationship-Based Therapy (RBT), paired with examples of each element from the cases presented earlier. Rather than a comprehensive discussion, the summary is intended to provide an overview of the significant factors that contribute to the success of this approach.

A paradox of RBT is that it is at the same time straightforward, drawing heavily on common sense, and also incredibly complex and nuanced. In this chapter we outline the eight essential elements of RBT: (1) Engagement: being fully present in the relationship; (2) Environment: appreciating the context surrounding the relationship; (3) Empathy: imagining the feelings of another; (4) Egocentrism: recognizing the unique make-up of every individual and relationship; (5) Enthusiasm: bringing optimism to difficult realities, (6) Evidence: relying on demonstratively effective approaches; (7) Endurance: remaining open and available; and (8) Extending: appreciating the continuity of relationships. Many of these divisions may seem arbitrary, misrepresenting the complexity of how these elements are intertwined. For example, engagement requires empathy and enthusiasm supports endurance and endurance requires enthusiasm and engagement. Moreover, emotion is infused in all elements. For example, empathy requires an awareness of, and response to, the emotions of another. Throughout, we provide examples of the connection between each element and emotion.

We hope that you will read the pages that follow with an eye to discovering the ways in which you already incorporate RBT into your work and generating ideas about how the eight elements can support your continued clinical efforts. In this chapter we refer to children and youth because the book focuses on our work in the foster care system. However, RBT applies as well to adults and to clients who have not spent time in foster care. The elements described here are fundamental to the building of any therapeutic relationship,

ENGAGEMENT

Clients with a history of hurtful or disappointing relationships often do not enter into new relationships easily. If, as in the case of most foster youth, they have suffered numerous unexpected and unexplained losses—of family members, caseworkers, foster parents, and therapists— they are understandably wary of starting with yet another new person. Some clients, particularly adolescents, may be quite vocal about their expectations of being left. It's not uncommon to hear, "Why should I talk to you? You're just going to leave like all the others." Successful therapeutic relationships require that the therapist be fully engaged in the process of getting to know the client. This includes acknowledging and accepting the client's anxieties about entering a new relationship since, for many, stepping through the door is the hardest part of the therapeutic process.

Engagement Includes Protecting the Integrity of the Therapeutic Process

Too often, therapists face external factors that impede the therapeutic process. Challenges can include a ceiling on financial support, a crisis situation that demands immediate action, or, as we learned in chapter 4, the common revision of an agency motto from do "whatever it takes" for your client to "whatever it takes, so long as it's within our catchment area." In each of these situations, the therapist has a responsibility to make the restrictions clear to the client. The same holds true for interns and others who may only be available for a limited time because of training demands. These situations call for a simple, straightforward explanation of circumstances that may limit the length of the relationship, such as, "I will be at the clinic until next summer," or "We have ten weeks to work together." Conversely, therapists who are working without specific external constraints are in a position to say, "I can't make any promises, but my intention is to be here until our work together is finished."

When delivering information they believe may upset the client, especially if it will confirm a negative expectation, therapists are often tempted to move quickly to try to soften the news. For example, "I will be at the clinic until next summer. Let's think about what we can accomplish in that time." The addition of the second sentence short-circuits the client's chance to experience and process feelings such as anger and disappointment and, understandably, risks sending the message that the therapist really doesn't want to hear anything upsetting.

The over-arching goal of the therapy is to develop a healthy relationship that can provide the foundation for the client to move into other satisfying and growth-promoting relationships; simply accepting all of the emotions that the client brings into the session is the first step toward that goal. Often, sitting quietly and listening to what the client has to say—whether in words or behavior—is the most powerful demonstration of the therapist's engagement with the client in the therapeutic process.

Being Fully Engaged Means Being Attentive to What Might Be Going on in the Mind of the Client

We only know each other by a "meeting of the minds," and the therapist must facilitate this process. Sometimes this can be as simple as asking, "What's on your mind?" or, if the therapist notices a change in facial expression or shift in posture, "What happened just then?" These simple questions show the client that you want to know what he or she is thinking, and that you care. Many youth who have been abused may not make this relational assumption and such a question can be reparative.

Engagement includes expression of the therapist's personal thoughts and feelings only when such disclosures directly benefit the client. Especially for foster youth, who have not had the experience of being kept in mind, it is often remarkable to them that the therapist thinks about them even when they are not in a therapy session. When working with clients who have not had a consistent, caring adult who keeps them in mind, it is very important for therapists to be explicit about the fact that they think about them. This can be a powerful statement, but it can also be simple. The therapist might say, "As I was driving here I was thinking about what we talked about last week and how surprised you were to learn that I think about you even when we're not together. It made me sad to think how lonely that must make you feel." In this context it is important to remember that the therapy is for the benefit of the client and that information about the therapist's thoughts and feelings should be offered only for the purpose of promoting the relationship in a way that will help the client. In the example above, the client's surprise and the therapist's response open the door to a different kind of relationship. The therapist's expression of sadness still relates to the client's experience. This is different from a comment such as, "I was so lonely yesterday and it made me remember how lonely you feel sometimes," which is a statement about the therapist, not the client.

Engagement Requires Anticipation of Closure

Engagement also raises the issue of disengagement and bringing the session to a close. Unlike clients whose experiences and relationships have been relatively predictable, those who have spent time in foster care have often been surprised by people leaving suddenly and never returning. It is both kind and helpful for the therapist to give sufficient warning before the end of a session so that the client doesn't feel cut off or interrupted mid-sentence. Simply telling the client that the session will end in about ten minutes and then in five, allows therapist and client to bring things to an orderly close. Saying, "I know that we're in the middle of something important and I'm sorry to have to interrupt you, but we can talk about it again next week," also reminds the client that the therapist can keep the client in mind until the next session, and that there will indeed be a next session. When therapists mention that the session will be ending, some clients assume that they are just counting down the minutes until they can escape. However, a conversation about ending, and a clear act that indicates a desire to meet again—such as giving the client a business card with the time and date of the next appointment—can serve as a concrete symbol of the continuity of the relationship.

Engagement is a powerful and critical therapeutic tool. For those who have not experienced positive relationships, this process may require time, patience, boundaries, and empathy.

ENVIRONMENT

The success of the therapeutic relationship is, in large measure, influenced by its environment. Therefore, the therapist must assess the environment and, as much as possible, attune the therapy to the surroundings. This requires an awareness of a vast array of factors, including the physical environment of the therapy room, family and peer support, and societal values pertaining to therapy.

The Therapy Room Sets the Stage for Stability and Consistency

Therapists often decorate offices with the goal of creating a pleasant place for clients and themselves. They hang pictures that are soothing, arrange chairs comfortably, and look for ways to ensure warmth and relaxation. One thing many therapists don't realize is the importance of maintaining the environment for clients, not as a place to visit, but as a shared space that also belongs to them. Children may want to leave a toy in a special place, or create a Lego structure that they hope the therapist will save, or, like Michael in chapter 6, transform and control the physical space. When they return to the stable environment, where things remain the same, the knowledge that their trace does not vanish, and that they remain a part of the therapist's world, can help provide a sense of security.

When therapists change the environment, clients notice. This is not to say that change is not acceptable or sometimes appropriate. Many clinicians must provide therapy in a different office each week, or in different community settings. Consequently, the critical principle is to look for ways to ensure environmental stability—be it a consistent meeting place, a seating arrangement, or the presence of a favorite toy. When there is change, the therapist needs to acknowledge it and hold space for the client to express his or her feelings about the change. We know that, too often, foster youth are asked to change without consideration of their feelings. They are sometimes even expected to behave as if the change hadn't happened or was of no consequence. It is our responsibility to help them learn how change can be integrated into their lives in healthy ways.

It Is Important to Keep in Mind the Inherent Power Imbalance in the Therapeutic Relationship

Part of the environment created by the therapist and client involves acknowledgment of power differentials that exist in the relationship. In therapy it is simple: the client is asking for help and the therapist is there to provide it. Unfortunately, embedded in this implicit agreement may be the assumption that something is wrong with the client and the therapist can fix it. For foster youth, this assumption may confirm their belief that they are "broken," leaving them feeling that they have to protect themselves against someone who they fear will see them as damaged or flawed.

Therapists will also see the repercussions of the chronic disempowering of foster youth. Many youth have never had the choice to attend a meeting, to move homes, or to change schools. Rather, they have simply been told what to do, often without input or preparation. When they enter therapy, they are resistant to another adult who will tell them what to do and who will have power over their choices. This was evident when Molly, described in chapter 1, insisted on reading in her first session. Providing clients with choices when appropriate is critical to empowering them to be a part of the therapeutic process.

It is the responsibility of the therapist to be aware of ethical issues related to power, including the many small and seemingly inconsequential ways in which therapists can exploit clients. One common example of this is through timeliness. Many therapists may think that being five minutes late to a session is acceptable. However, therapists who frequently arrive late to sessions announce, by their behavior, that they don't take their clients' time seriously. This is an example of behavior that, at first glance, may seem unimportant, but is actually quite meaningful and therefore entirely unacceptable.

Clinicians working with clients who have been abused or mistreated may sometimes feel as if they are the ones being exploited in the therapeutic relationship. Clients come late, or just don't show up; they disparage the therapist's comments and suggestions; they hurl insults or fall asleep in the session. At these times the clinician must understand that this is the only way that many clients can introduce therapists to their experience and their environment. They may have no other way to tell us about what it is like to feel as if no one cares enough to show up on time, or discounts all of their opinions, or seems not to hear anything they have to say. Therapists who attend to their own feelings of being disregarded, discounted, or exploited will learn something very important about the emotional lives of their clients. Moreover, therapists who are able to use this information to connect with the youth may also develop a deeper understanding of their clients' experiences. For example, if a client consistently arrives late to sessions, the therapist might offer something like, "Maybe without even knowing it, you wanted me to know what it feels like to be waiting and wondering if anyone's going to show up." Rather than telling clients that they need to change their behavior, comments such as this invite them to reflect on their actions in the context of the relationship.

The Adults Who Care for Children and Adolescents Are the Single Most Important Aspect of Their Environment

It is essential that the therapist meet with caregivers to understand their expectations for the therapy, including the extent to which they will lend their support. Support from caregivers includes getting the child to and from sessions on time, keeping the therapist informed of changes in the child's life—including moods and behavior—and meeting with the therapist periodically to collaborate on behalf of the child. This support is imperative, not only for acquiring adequate assessment information, but for generalizing treatment gains beyond the therapy.

When meeting with parents, we must recognize their perceptions of, and experiences with, therapy. If caregivers have been told by a teacher or a caseworker that their child needs to go to therapy and have thus been made to feel as if they are not good parents, the clinician might reasonably expect them to be wary and wanting to keep a distance from the therapist, lest they be judged negatively or be asked to do more when they are already overwhelmed. We see this again and again with Maria, Juan's aunt, in chapter 2. On the other hand, if a child is referred for treatment by caregivers who have themselves had good experiences with therapy, the clinician can reasonably expect that the parents will have some understanding of the process and will be supportive of the relationship. Many foster parents are instructed to take a child to therapy without adequate explanation of the process, desired outcomes, or their role. Therapists must offer information and support if they expect cooperation and collaboration.

It Is Incumbent upon Therapists to Assess Societal Expectations of Therapy That Influence the Client

In some communities psychotherapy is commonplace, while in others people believe that "only crazy people see a shrink." Whether directly or indirectly, attitudes such as these will influence the therapeutic relationship and affect the child's turning toward or away from the therapist as an ally. Especially for adolescents and young adults, their peer relationships will decisively influence the therapeutic relationship. This is particularly true for groups that are easily marginalized and/or mistreated. For example, many foster youth have been traumatized through no fault of their own. However, many of them have also been labeled with behavioral and psychological problems that can imply that they have caused their own difficulties. When referred for therapy, these youth may be unwilling participants and instead, turn to peer groups for affection and acceptance they missed from their families. When assessing environmental influences, keep in mind that we are all part of many, often intertwined, communities, leaving marginalized populations at risk of being stigmatized by different systems simultaneously and repeatedly. A young Hispanic lesbian may face racial prejudice from the larger community and also be ostracized by her devoutly Catholic family who cannot reconcile her homosexuality with their religious beliefs. In situations such as these, the cumulative effect of multiple environmental impingements must be taken into account.

A Careful Consideration of the Therapist's Own Biases Must Be Part of the Environmental Assessment

In any therapeutic relationship, it is necessary that clinicians attend to issues of gender, race, ethnicity, culture, sexual preference, disability, class, religion, and socioeconomic status. When treating clients from the foster care system it is particularly important to keep in mind cultural differences between those who have grown up in a relatively stable family and those whose childhood relationships were characterized by instability and repeated loss. Too often, in this situation, as in others, those from the majority culture assume that those in the minority share their perceptions and values. Isaiah, in chapter 7, made this evident at the start of his work by screening his therapist's attunement to the experiences of minority groups. Assumptions may also be made that those in the majority culture can understand the other person's experience by "putting themselves in his or her shoes." While this is a first step, we must realize that increasing empathy and perspective still does not ensure that we understand in any way the true vantage point of that other person. We need to recognize that cultural competence and understanding is a process. It is not something we can ever completely achieve, but rather something that we must continually strive to attain. We also need to keep in mind that the best way to learn is from the clients themselves.

EMPATHY

The capacity to perceive accurately the feelings of another is a cornerstone of RBT. Empathy, which may emerge from observations or imagination, involves simply comprehending how someone else is feeling in a given situation. For example, if while you are walking you see a man across the street being attacked by a dog, you will almost certainly be able to imagine how the victim feels, not only intellectually, but by your own fear response. The more you learn about this person, including his history and experiences, the better you can imagine what this experience was like for him. Empathy involves a deep understanding—an imagining of what it would be like to be the client, with his/her background and experiences and beliefs.

Empathy Demonstrates the Human Capacity to Construct a "Theory of Mind"

The ability to identify and experience the feelings of another allows therapists to have a much fuller understanding of their clients' experiences than if they relied on cognitive or intellectual capacities alone. A therapist, hearing a young adult describe being punished as a child by being shut in a dark closet, may find herself shuddering, her heart pounding, and palms sweating. She need not have had the experience of being locked in a closet in order to imagine what that must have felt like to a young child. However, the more she gets to know her client and her experiences, the more she can envision the particulars of how the client felt during that experience. This requires that the therapist attempt to see the event not from her own reactions, but the client's. Maybe the therapist would have been scared, but maybe the client was numb because being locked in the closet was a recurring event. To acknowledge this, the therapist could say, "I think that you had been scared so many times that you no longer felt anything when that happened."

Empathic comments allow the client a glimpse into the therapist's mind. They demonstrate that client and therapist have had a "meeting of the minds," acknowledging that the client has successfully conveyed what is in her mind, and that the therapist has thought about what she has said and allowed herself to imagine the experience. Suppose that the therapist had the misfortune of also being locked in a closet as a child and responded, "I know exactly how you felt." Even though this gives the information that therapist and client have a shared experience, this is not an empathic comment because it is about the therapist, not about the client. It is a statement that the therapist was not actually listening to the client. Instead, the story caused the therapist to attend to the memories stored in her own mind, rather than those of her client, resulting in an empathic failure.

Children Who Have Been Mistreated Often Behave as if They Have Limited Capacity for Empathy

To many observers, this behavior is counterintuitive. People often assume that those who have been mistreated will be more sensitive as a result. In fact, though we are hard-wired to be empathically attuned, all neural structures and activity are enhanced or impaired by experience. The child whose parents correctly read and respond to his signals—of excitement, hunger, sadness, or joy—will become increasingly adept at identifying his internal state and, as the neural connections are strengthened, will be able to send progressively clearer and more precise messages about his needs and desires. In turn, he will mirror the attunement of his parents, smiling when they smile at him or joining them in their distress. However, if caregivers are consistently misattuned to a child's signals or respond harshly and without empathy to his distress, the child will mirror their responses. Over time he will do unto others what was done to him—he may become indifferent to or respond cruelly to others' distress. He may greet sadness with laughter rather than a show of sympathy.

Clients Who Have Been Mistreated Do Not Expect to Be Well Treated

For those who have been mistreated, a comment such as, "You must have had a hard day," can be heard as an insult, or a suggestion that the client isn't tough enough to manage. It is essential that therapists remember that victims of maltreatment have lived much of their lives in a traumatized state and are often made anxious by the efforts of those who want to help them. Moreover, this trauma is held in the body, as well as the mind. They may have had little time or space for relaxation or calm reflection. They are used to hearing voices that hurt, rather than help, and words that blame or punish rather than soothe or inspire. The work with Clemee in chapter 9 details this beautifully. In these situations, therapists need to mold the pace of the process to the client's comfort and, in some cases, incorporate relaxation techniques to still their minds to triggers of trauma. Moreover, therapists need to learn to choose their words carefully and be quick to apologize if they have misunderstood or misspoken, since empathy allows us to imagine, but not to know for certain, what it feels like to be standing in another's shoes.

EGOCENTRISM

Although egocentrism has negative connotations, referring to people who think primarily of themsleves, in the context of RBT we use it in two different ways. First, egocentrism refers to the importance of tailoring the therapy to unique needs of every client, putting the client at the center of therapy. It also refers to the fact that trauma results in people living in very self-absorbed, egocentric worlds.

The Experience of Trauma Requires Egocentrism

One of the unfortunate consequences of trauma is a preoccupation with the traumatic events. Sometimes clients ruminate about their traumatic histories, with stories and pictures running endlessly and repetitively through their minds. They often feel completely unable to stop these tormenting images. Understandably, those whose minds are filled with images from the past have difficulty in attending to people and events in their present lives, often giving the impression that they have no interest beyond their internal worlds. While they may act as if they are the center of the world, it is often because they are swirling in the inescapable vortex of their traumatic past. This is evident in nearly every case study in this volume, but is especially clear in Zina's therapy described in chapter 10.

Sadly, abuse, neglect, and repeated abandonment are common among foster youth, often leading to their living in a state of constant, heightened anxiety and egocentrism. Unfortunately, many foster children and youth have endured multiple forms of abandonment, neglect, and abuse—sometimes from a single person and sometimes from many people. The attuned therapist will keep this in mind, perhaps offering comments such as, "I think that sometimes you worry that people will hurt you and sometimes you worry that they will leave you. And sometimes you're not sure which is more frightening."

The attuned therapist will examine what underlies egocentrism rather than making its undoing a treatment goal in and of itself. For example, when individuals attend only to their own experiences, with a concomitant lack of awareness of others, the focus of treatment can quickly turn to decreasing this self-focus and increasing social skills and empathy. However, for those working with traumatized individuals, egocentrism must be seen as a coping skill and something that serves a clear and important purpose in their lives.

Egocentrism Can Challenge Rapport Building

Consideration of the multiple adverse experiences in the lives of foster youth should make clear the necessity of therapy that is tailored to meet the unique needs of each individual. In addition to abuse and abandonment, so many foster youth have also suffered neglect—their needs have simply not been recognized or met. Why, then, would they expect interest or help from a therapist?

This puts therapists who are attempting to form relationships with their clients in an understandably difficult position. They want to engage someone who expects, based on past experiences, that relationships do not meet their needs, are hurtful, and disappear without reason or warning. Why exactly should they take a chance on what we have to offer? Assessing and keeping in mind the needs of the individual client, the therapist is in a position to craft an approach that is "egocentric," that is tailored to the unique needs of the other person in the room, including that person's understandable need to be distrustful for a while.

Therapists must also simultaneously draw on the resources they have developed from being in healthy, sustaining, satisfying relationships. Even therapists who have had more than their share of unhealthy or hurtful relationships must be able to hold the knowledge that relationships can be sources of pleasure and sustenance. It is necessary that they do this while clients gradually come to know that for themselves. This situation is not so different from that of an adult facing a teenager who feels as if the world is coming to an end because of the breakup of a romance; the adult must fully understand the depth and truth of the teen's feelings, while holding the knowledge that the feelings will pass and that the world will not end.

RBT is not a quick or easy solution to overcoming the pain inflicted before or during foster care. It is not a straightforward, linear process. Like development, the building of a relationship can often move two steps forward and then one step back. There is no simple formula, but there are solid guidelines. To state the obvious, no two people are alike and no two relationships, therapeutic or otherwise, will be identical. The therapist is there to offer help and the client is there to receive it. Even though the relationship is not equal, for it to succeed both parties must engage in the process with the shared purpose of improving and enriching the life of the client.

ENTHUSIASM

RBT is hard work, but it is also extremely satisfying work. Human beings are hard-wired to tell stories, and every story is unique. If we are willing to listen genuinely and respectfully we will have the privilege of hearing the amazing stories our clients bring to us. Those working with foster children, youth, and young adults will also hear horrific stories of mistreatment, often leaving them wondering how the person sitting in the room has survived. Regardless, it is our job to show our interest and our enthusiastic desire to hear and appreciate the stories that have shaped our clients into the people that sit in the room with us.

It Is Difficult to Hear Stories That Tear at Our Hearts Day after Day

It is not surprising that therapists get discouraged when they hear tragic stories of abuse and trauma on a regular basis. It is also hard to remain enthusiastic when things seem to move slowly or the client who seemed to be making progress suddenly disappears. Even when the therapist knows that building trust goes slowly and that clients who have been abandoned often leave without warning, feelings of hopelessness and helplessness can and do emerge. Our work is challenging; at times it feels impossible to be present, let alone enthusiastic.

New clinicians who approach their work with eager excitement are particularly vulnerable to feeling as if their enthusiasm is slowly being drowned in a sea of woe, changing regulations, unreturned phone calls, endless paperwork, and little time to think or reflect on all that has come their way. They may find themselves questioning their choice of professions. They may feel more tired than usual, as if they have been overtaken by some low-grade virus that never becomes acute but never disappears. They may complain to colleagues that their supervisors are overly critical and their clients less than appreciative. Or they might find themselves, like Ben's therapist in chapter 11, dreading their meetings as he recited the *Star Wars* story session after session.

And Then Something Shifts

A child who has been withdrawn and emotionally distant tentatively offers to draw a picture and signs it with "love." An adolescent who has shown little interest in school announces that he worked really hard and got a good grade on an exam. A young adult who has been too depressed to do much of anything announces that she has begun a friendship with someone at work. Of course, these changes could be the result of environmental influences, but the therapists might also take them as evidence that the therapeutic relationship is beginning to have positive effects.

Interactions such as these—no matter how small—can renew enthusiasm and remind therapists what initially drew them to the mental health profession. They can bolster a fading sense of competence. However, placing undue reliance on clients' successes or progress poses dangers for therapist and client alike. It leaves therapists vulnerable to losing their confidence when things aren't going so well. Clients, particularly those who, like many foster children, have had to assume responsibility for shoring up fragile parents or caregivers, may quickly surmise that they need "to get better" in order to please their therapist. Success for the sake of the therapist runs counter to the tenets of RBT because it has shifted the focus of the therapy from the emotional life of the client to that of the therapist.

This is not to suggest that Relationship-Based Therapists do not appreciate and enjoy the positive steps in their clients' lives. But they do not look to their clients to sustain them and they do not focus on successes and strengths to the extent that they overlook the real pain and struggles in their clients' lives. Everyone has strengths and weaknesses; the latter are often more difficult to talk about. Many parents don't like to confess that they wanted to—or actually did—hit their child. Children are humiliated when they lose control of bowel or bladder and announce, "I don't want to talk about it." Teens may be embarrassed by their difficulties in understanding their emerging sexuality and bring up their questions and feelings only hesitantly. It is important that there be space for quiet reflection so that difficult topics can be raised at the client's own pace. Therapists who focus primarily on building a safe and trusting relationship with their clients have both the freedom and responsibility to attend to changes in the therapeutic relationship as the primary means of assessing the effectiveness of the therapy.

Curiosity Is a Powerful Tool for Therapists

Curiosity helps the therapist to maintain an enthusiastic interest in what the client brings to the sessions. It also compels the therapist to attend to all of what the client brings—both positive and negative—as well as noting what is missing from the narrative. The therapist's curiosity can also help to spur clients' interest in the workings of their own minds, helping them to build essential self-observational skills. For example, a therapist might comment, "You know, it seems to me that you rarely talk about positive things about yourself, yet you have friends, and people come to you for advice. I wonder what they see in you that you don't talk about." The client might respond with something like, "I thought therapy was only to talk about problems." This gives the therapist an opportunity to extend the conversation into the client's expectations of relationships—in this example, as in the case of many foster kids, that you can only command attention by having problems or being needy, or that resilience doesn't count.

Enthusiasm and curiosity are steadfast therapeutic partners. The mind of the enthusiastic clinician has boundless curiosity and the therapist's curious mind is alive and interested in all that clients bring to the relationship. The therapist's openness to exploration invites a "meeting of the minds" with the client. For clients who have had very few relationships with people genuinely interested in their thoughts and feelings, the therapist's true interest in them can be both terrifying and liberating. The clinician must remember that RBT always offers the possibility of both.

EVIDENCE

Over the last two decades, clinical researchers have provided us with an ever-growing body of evidence supporting the efficacy of different approaches to psychotherapy. This research has spawned attention from policy makers, clinicians, administrators, and insurance companies alike. And it appears that, in many ways, evidence-based practices are the current future of psychotherapy research. However, although these tools have merit, at present they are limited.

There Is a Need for More Research with Foster Youth

The use of evidence-based practices with current and former foster youth has profound limitations. As noted in the introduction, many evidence-based practices have not been tested with foster youth; consequently, we remain unsure whether we can generalize treatments for at-risk and delinquent youth to foster youth—a vulnerable and unique population. Moreover, of the evidence-based practices available, a limited number focus on the therapeutic relationship, despite an understanding that therapeutic rapport is imperative to successful treatment. Rather, these practices allot limited time (e.g., one-three sessions) to "rapport building" without further note of relationship impasses or maintenance. Obviously, we need specific research on evidence-based practices with foster youth, a population for whom, understandably, trust and relationship-building are part of a long and enduring process.

The Research-Informed Clinician

Therapists have a professional and ethical responsibility to remain abreast of advances in their fields and to carefully assess new information as it becomes available. This can be a daunting task, particularly for clinicians working in community-based settings with high demands for client care. Clinicians may also work in sites that require that all staff adhere to a particular theoretical orientation or rely only on interventions that are clearly and succinctly outlined and supported by traditional experimental outcome research. In situations such as these, clinicians may feel that their individual responsibility to remain up-to-date is irrelevant. This is a dangerous position because it assumes that what is happening in the mind of the clinician during the therapy session is of limited value—that the therapist's main challenge is to understand and deliver what other professionals have developed, what clinical researchers have demonstrated to be effective, or what their agency dictates. In other words, the therapist is merely a messenger. It is also dangerous because it assumes that what is happening in the mind of the client is of equally little consequence except to confirm that the message has been received. Clinicians who thoughtlessly implement manualized interventions and procedures effectively remove themselves from the therapeutic relationship and deprive their clients of the most important thing they have to offer—the willingness to know their client's mind.

The Link between Research and RBT

As noted many times over in this volume, evidenced in massive amounts of research on child development, and supported by common sense—caring, stable relationships with adults are vital to healthy development. Moreover, client-therapist rapport is a key mechanism of change. Thus, clinicians who are able to enter into a therapeutic relationship with those whose childhoods lacked continuity and guidance from an adult who cared for and about them, have an enormously important opportunity to demonstrate that relationships can have a positive influence on life. Good relationships help our moods; they offer a chance for give and take; they let us learn about ourselves and others; they let us laugh and cry together; they are the cornerstone to healing; they allow us to lay the foundation on which other healthy relationships can be built. They actually allow us to live, not only healthier and happier, but longer.

RBT does not preclude the therapist using other modalities when indicated. Rather, RBT can act as an underlying assumption that can be melded beautifully with evidence-based techniques. For example, a therapist may rely on play to assist a child who has trouble verbalizing. He might help another client create cognitive strategies for managing depressing thoughts. With another he might suggest tactics for controlling anxiety in an upcoming job interview. Skilled clinicians acquire many therapeutic tools and, with practice, they learn which are most effective with particular clients or in particular situations. Over time, they also learn which are the best fit for who they are and how they approach their work.

The truth of the evidence we gather is not always immediately or easily demonstrated. We form hypotheses and test them, as described in chapter 5 by the therapist who helped the foster parents understand Lucy's behavior as connected to her earlier experiences. This shows the power of wondering and suggesting possibilities rather than asserting our ideas and insisting on the final word. We do this in order to keep both parties engaged in the therapeutic process. It is this meeting of the minds—a process of continually testing, expanding, and refining concepts that makes for lively and enlivening discussion, which lies at the heart of the therapeutic relationship.

ENDURANCE

RBT is not a sprint; it's a cross-county race and you can't know in advance exactly what you'll find along the way. You're never sure of the distance you will cover until you near the finish line. Like long distance runners, therapists must be well prepared and physically, emotionally, mentally fit to build lasting relationships with clients. Nonetheless, therapists too often become so concerned with meeting the needs of their clients that they don't take care of themselves. They forget—or ignore—the basic tenets of good health. They ignore the reality that we cannot do good work when we are emotionally, intellectually, or physically depleted. We need to demonstrate to our clients what it means to take good care of one's self. Our clients learn as much—or more—from our actions as they do from our words.

A Number of Difficulties Can Arise from Therapists' Sense That Their Work Must Rise to the Heroic

The most obvious difficulty that arises from unrealistic therapist self-expectation is that they will inevitably fail and disappoint both their clients and themselves. There is no theoretical orientation or practice that can guarantee success in every situation, even in the hands of the most skilled clinicians or in the most supportive environment. Particularly when working with multiply traumatized clients, we must be aware of our therapeutic limits. We cannot undo the fact of trauma and we do our clients a disservice if we lead them to believe that neglect, abuse, and abandonment do not leave scars. We must balance this knowledge with an optimistic understanding that strength can and does emerge from adversity and that satisfying and productive lives are possible, even in the wake of tragic childhoods.

The Hardships That Our Clients Have Endured Will Inevitably Make Their Way into the Therapeutic Relationship

It is human nature to treat others as we have been treated. Clients who have been mistreated will mistreat others, including their therapists. The healing power of the therapeutic relationship arises from the therapist's capacity to understand this behavior as having to do with past relationships and to respond with compassion rather than with anger or despair. The therapist is in a unique position to break the cycle of mistreatment, but not by meeting anger with anger or withdrawing in response to the client's emotional distance. As shown by so many of the therapists in this book, the therapist must demonstrate a different way of being in a relationship. When the behavior of foster youth is hurtful, too often they are met with a response meant to let them "see how it feels." They already know how it feels to be mistreated! Retaliation for their misbehavior only confirms their belief that people cannot be trusted and relationships offer nothing good.

Another pattern that is common in treatment is that clients don't show up, and yet they keep coming back. Many foster youth will not come to their sessions week after week, or come late, and yet they continue to schedule and show up now and again. For example, a client will not come for the regular Thursday meeting for three weeks, only to show up the fourth week with the expectation that the time is still available. Being able to hold this spot open for a client can be a great show of commitment and promoting trust. It is when we show our clients that we don't give up on them as so many others have, that they can begin to realize that maybe we can be different and maybe, they can look to us for a sustained connection.

Withstanding the Feelings That Traumatized Clients Bring to the Therapy Is Not Easy

Therapists understandably want to withdraw from anger and hurt. This can lead, for example, to their shutting down or acting out their feelings by cancelling or changing sessions for little more than their own convenience. Clinicians need help in managing their feelings in a way that promotes the growth and well being of their clients. They need to take care of themselves and maintain healthy balance so they are available in a therapeutic way for whatever their clients bring into the room—week after week.

Therapists who work extensively with traumatized clients are particularly vulnerable to secondary trauma and may find that they develop symptoms that mimic those of their clients: difficulty sleeping, heightened anxiety, emotional numbness, and preoccupation with the clients' stories, for example. It is important for therapists to remind both themselves and their clients that trauma is held in the body, as well as the mind. In some cases, relaxation techniques can and should be incorporated into the sessions; in other cases, clients may benefit from a reminder that sometimes walking—whether around the block or up and down the stairs of the clinic—can help to still their minds.

The Consultation Groups That Are an Integral Part of A Home Within Can and Should Be Replicated in Other Settings

Therapists working with traumatized populations need the support and understanding of consultants and colleagues. We cannot do this work alone—it is just too hard. All clinicians working in a relationship-based model should have access to a group of like-minded colleagues who can help them endure and understand the complex feelings and behavior their clients bring to the therapy. Without the support of consultants and colleagues, therapists can too easily become overwhelmed, making it impossible for them to think. Sometimes the group is called upon to think when the therapist cannot, as amply demonstrated in chapters 8 and 12. For example, one therapist complained to her consultation group that her client repeatedly cancelled sessions at the last minute. She was angry and discouraged, feeling that her time was being wasted; she wondered if it was even worth continuing. The group was sympathetic to the therapist's feelings and also noted that calling at the last minute was a way of finding out if the therapist was actually there. The therapist then remembered that this client had been locked out of her home many times as a child. With this in mind, she decided that she would call the client the day before their session and remind her that she was planning to see her the next day. The client began attending sessions more regularly and, when she needed to cancel or change an appointment, calling in advance. This was the first step toward her being able to recognize this pattern in her relationships.

This example demonstrates how the capacity to think can be obscured by feeling mistreated and how it can be restored by feeling understood. With the help of the group, the therapist was able to use her feelings creatively to help her client. This closely parallels the process by which parents of young children help them manage feelings that threaten to overwhelm them. For example, when a toddler panics at the sight of a scratch on his knee, the reasonable parent neither rushes him off to the emergency room nor ignores his distress. Instead she sympathetically reassures him that it's a small scratch, cleans it, and finds a bandage—sometimes two or three, if that's what it takes to bring the panic under control.

Instances such as this are repeated thousands of times over in healthy parent-child relationships. Through them children learn that they can count on adults to help them and that life's hurts can often—though not always—be soothed. They learn to distinguish between small and large injuries—both physical and emotional—and to respond appropriately. Those who have not had these comforting childhood experiences can easily be confounded and respond to an inadvertent slight as if it were an insult and appear to barely notice a truly aggressive comment. And, like the patient parent, the therapist will soon learn that interventions will need to be repeated many times over to be truly helpful.

Effective therapy demands endurance—both the capacity to withstand difficult thoughts and feelings in the moment and the willingness to withstand them over and over and over again until the therapy draws to a natural close. We usually know that we cannot care well for others unless we take good care of ourselves, but sometimes we forget. What we need to remember is that taking care of ourselves is part of our commitment to our clients.

EXTENDING

The interpersonal aspect of the therapeutic relationship will, inevitably, draw to a close. At some point therapist and client will stop meeting. For those who have spent time in foster care and lived through so many relationships that ended unexpectedly and abruptly, it is exceedingly important that the conclusion of therapy, if at all possible, be planned and include input from the client about how and when the sessions will stop. While there are many ways that therapy can end badly, there is no single right way to manage the final stage of therapy.

In an Ideal World, the Therapeutic Work Continues until Client and Therapist Agree That It Is Time for It to End

However, we live in an imperfect world and there are external factors that often determine the length of the therapy. As noted at the beginning of this chapter, therapy may be limited for financial reasons, insurance limits, or agency policies requiring a pre-determined number of sessions. Clients seeing interns will usually only have access to their therapist for the training period, though sometimes therapy can be continued in a different setting as the intern moves toward licensure. When this isn't possible or when insurance or finances limit the length of treatment, therapy should include a planned termination.

Unplanned Endings Call for Creative Thinking

The most painful endings are those that replicate earlier losses and come without warning as, for example, when a parent or other caregiver suddenly decides that the therapy must end. Even when the therapist is able to argue for a few additional sessions, the decision is rarely revocable. When it becomes clear that the end has come despite the therapist's best efforts, he should assist with a transfer to a new therapist, if appropriate. If it is impossible to have even a few termination sessions, at the very least, the therapist should make every effort to bring closure by sending a note along with a small memento of the time spent together. In one instance a teenager was suddenly moved from one foster home to another about fifty miles distant with no one willing to provide transportation so that she could say a proper "goodbye." Her therapist copied and laminated one of the collages they had worked on together and sent it to her with a note that she would keep the original in her office as her reminder of the time they had spent together. Phone calls and/or e-mails can also help to bring closure, when face-to-face meetings aren't possible.

Sometimes Therapy Ends in Fits and Starts

One young man kept regular appointments for about a year before his attendance became sporadic. He would leave a message saying that he wanted to set up an appointment, sometimes changing his mind when the therapist returned his call and sometimes attending a session. This continued for several months. In one phone call the therapist commented, "It seems like you're sometimes not sure if you want to come in or not." He replied, "I think I don't need to come in any more, but I don't want any session to be the last one." The therapist reminded him that he had an open-door policy and the client could always return. "Okay, then why don't I come next week and it will be the next-to-last session. We just won't schedule the last one," was his response. The therapist agreed to this plan, pleased that the client could move on, comforted by carrying the possibility of one (or more) sessions with him.

In the example above, the client was able to explain his behavior. Sometimes clients disappear without explanation. In those cases the therapist can only speculate about the reasons. We know that some clients can't imagine that someone would notice their absence, let alone miss them, while others stay away because they can't imagine anything other than a painful separation. These endings are often very difficult for therapists, who understand that bringing closure to activities and relationships can be satisfying and make the transition to life's next chapter easier.

Foster youth often have little experience with smooth transitions, as is painfully clear in Lilly's story in chapter 3. Children like Lilly are often expected to say "hello" to a new foster home before they have had time to say "goodbye" to the last. This is especially important to keep in mind if therapists are beginning work with clients who have been transferred from another clinician. Therapists are often so eager to begin building a relationship with new clients that they overlook their need to mourn the loss of the previous therapist. Particularly in settings staffed by interns, loss will be at the center of the therapeutic relationship. The client who has been left by one therapist will have trouble embracing the second and may not even try with the third. However, there is no chance of forming a meaningful relationship unless the therapist acknowledges the pain of these losses and tries to help the client bear the grief.

One of the Ways We Manage Grief Is by Carrying Those We Have Loved and Lost with Us

Whether we lose someone to death or through the vagaries of life, the internalized relationship does not end, unless it has been so brief or inconsequential that we have not taken it in. A successful therapeutic relationship, like the gains made as a result, will extend well beyond the interpersonal interactions on which it was built. A young child needs to be in proximity to her mother to feel her comfort, but as she grows she can call on the soothing maternal presence she carries within her. Clients in a new relationship with a therapist require frequent and regular contact in order to be able to draw on the therapist's strength. It is only over time that they can internalize that strength and make it their own. At the beginning of a therapy that stretched over several years a young woman called her therapist several times a week in a state of panic. Brief phone contact usually calmed her, but did not sustain her for more than a few days. After some months, if the therapist didn't reach her when returning a call and left a message, those calls would sometimes not be returned. The client explained that hearing the message was enough. Still later, the client described that in states of anxiety she would sometimes listen to the therapist's outgoing message to calm herself. Finally, although her anxiety had diminished significantly, in those moments when she felt it building she was able to simply think about her therapist in order to restore calm.

One of the most important pieces of work in the final phase of therapy is helping clients recognize the ways in which the relationship and therapeutic gains now belong to them. They can get along without us precisely because they have us with them. We live in A Home Within them.

SUMMARY

"What good are you? What I need is a mother!" That was the opening salvo of an adolescent meeting her therapist for the first time. Whether spoken or unspoken, this is the fundamental question that therapists working with parentless children must continually grapple with; we cannot afford to forget it. We need to keep in mind, hard as it is, that our connection to our clients cannot ever fill the void created by parental absence. We must also never forget that the therapist's task is not to fill the void, but to help the children, teens, and young adults who come to us for help, recognize their losses, and mourn them as best they can.

Those who have spent time in foster care have every reason to be sad and angry. We are charged with knowing that for and with them. If we are to work effectively, we must acknowledge that trauma cannot be undone, but can be overcome. As we have repeatedly heard in the stories in this volume, the traumatic histories that foster youth bring to treatment tempt both clients and therapists to turn away from the pain of the past—to move quickly toward the present and the future. If we give in to this temptation then we doom our clients to repeating their pasts in their future relationship. If they have been abused or abandoned, they risk becoming embroiled in abusive and unstable relationships. Neglected children, as adults, will find themselves unable to care fully for themselves or others. Therapists cannot replace parents, nor should they try. However, they can offer a turning point through a relationship that refuses to repeat the past and holds a vision for a different future. Through a healthy, caring, lasting therapeutic relationship foster youth can come to know that relationships hold the possibility for growth, pleasure, respect, and love.

Index

About the Editors and the Contributors

ABOUT THE EDITORS

Toni V. Heineman, DMH, is executive director and founder of A Home Within. Dr. Heineman is a clinical psychologist who has been in private practice treating children, adults, and families in the San Francisco Bay area for over thirty years. Dr. Heineman has taught and supervised interns, graduate students, and psychiatric residents and presented at numerous local and national professional meetings. She was awarded a Draper Richards Social Entrepreneur Fellowship, the Social Entrepreneur Award from the Manhattan Institute, and a 2008 Purpose Prize.

June M. Clausen, PhD, is chair and professor of psychology at the University of San Francisco (USF). Dr. Clausen directs the Foster Care Research Group, a team of undergraduate and graduate social scientists that conducts outcome evaluation on all the clinical and outreach programs of A Home Within. In addition to her research activities and her university administrative responsibilities, Dr. Clausen teaches several undergraduate psychology courses at USF. She also maintains a clinical practice in San Jose, CA, in which she provides evaluation, consultation, and treatment for child and adult survivors of trauma.

Saralyn C. Ruff, PhD, oversees the Fostering Relationships program of A Home Within, dedicated to improving mental health services for foster youth by providing research and theory-based resources and training to staff. Dr. Ruff also teaches in the psychology department at the University of San Francisco and practices as a clinician in San Francisco, CA.

ABOUT THE CONTRIBUTORS

Paula Lorig Ammerman, PhD, is faculty at the Chicago Institute for Clinical Social Work where she also has a private psychotherapy and clinical consultation practice in Chicago. She has been a volunteer with A Home Within since 2006.

Tali Barr, PhD, studied art and philosophy at Hebrew University in Jerusalem, Israel, and moved to the United States to finish her MFA at the San Francisco Art Institute. She received her PhD from the California School of Professional Psychology in 1997. She is the author of *Fishing with a Straight Hook* and several other papers on both art and psychology. Tali has a private practice in Berkeley and remains an active artist.

German Cheung, PsyD, is a clinical psychologist working psychoanalytically with children and adults. He works in private practice and at Richmond Area Multi-Services, Inc. (RAMS), a community mental health agency in San Francisco. German's clinical interests include treating: traumatized, emotionally disturbed, and severely mentally ill children and adults; multicultural and immigration-related issues; and, psycho-spiritual conflicts. Cheung supervises staff at RAMS and serves as an adjunct faculty at both California School of Professional Psychology-Hong Kong and Alliant International University.

Daria Dato, LCSW, is in private practice in Dallas, Texas. She has taught and mentored undergraduate social work students at Texas Woman's University. Daria's interests include integrating psycho-educational and psychodynamic modalities in psychotherapy. Theoretically, she is interested in relational psychotherapy from an attachment theory perspective.

Heidi L. Haddad, LCSW, has been working with children, youth, couples, and families for more than twelve years, both domestically and internationally, in a variety of non-profit settings. Heidi provides mediation specialized in family and co-parenting issues. In 2010, she opened Head and Heart Therapy, a private practice providing individual, family and group psychotherapy. Heidi is also the cofounder and codirector of Goddess Grrrl, a nonprofit organization dedicated to increasing the social, emotional, and mental health skills of girls aged ten to eighteen years.

John Lundin, PsyD, is a psychologist with a private practice in Oakland, California. He has a background in work with foster children and specializes in treating children and adults suffering from anxiety and relationship issues.

He is also a teacher, supervisor, and speaker on various topics related to child development and parenting.

Deborah Offner, PhD, is a clinical psychologist who divides her time between The Commonwealth School in Boston and private practice in Newton, Massachusetts. She is a candidate in psychoanalysis at PINE (Psychoanalytic Institute of New England). Deborah's interests include adolescent development, the effects of emotional distress on academic performance, and the application of psychological principles in educational settings. Deborah joined the Boston Chapter of A Home Within at the time of its inception in 2010.

Sharif Okasha, PsyD, is a licensed clinical psychologist practicing in San Francisco. He maintains a private practice where he works with children and adults in individual and family therapy. In addition to his private practice, he serves as a supervisor, clinician, and program manager at a community mental health clinic.

Claudia Rose, MSW, has worked with children, adolescents and families for over twenty years as a caseworker, psychotherapist, and clinical supervisor specializing in the fields of grief/loss, trauma, and foster care. She graduated in 1996 from The University of Chicago's School of Social Service Administration. She is also a graduate of the Child and Adolescent Psychoanalytic Psychotherapy program of the Chicago Institute for Psychoanalysis. She is currently employed as a Research Analyst at NORC at the University of Chicago, a non-profit social science academic research center, working with adolescent males in the juvenile justice system.

Elsa Rosenberg, MS, is a licensed marriage and family therapist and has been practicing in San Francisco, California, for over twenty years. She is affiliated with the San Francisco Center for Psychoanalysis, The Psychotherapy Institute in Berkeley, California, and is a member of local and state professional associations. Elsa primarily sees adult individuals and couples for psychodynamic psychotherapy and volunteers as an A Home Within clinician.

Richard Ruth, PhD, is associate professor of clinical psychology at The George Washington University and a member of the faculty and steering committee of the Child and Adolescent Psychotherapy Program at the Washington School of Psychiatry. He is in private practice as a psychologist and psychoanalyst in Wheaton, Maryland. His particular interests are in cross-cultural assessment and treatment, disability, trauma, and LGBT issues. He is clinical director of the Montgomery County, Maryland, chapter of A Home Within.

Wendy von Wiederhold, PhD, has been involved with A Home Within for the past sixteen years, first as a clinician, then as the clinical director of the San Francisco chapter and for the past five years as the program director, overseeing the local chapters and starting new chapters across the country. Dr. von Wiederhold teaches adolescent and infant development and is in private practice in San Francisco and in St. Helena specializing in the psychodynamic treatment of adolescents, adults and couples.

www.ingramcontent.com/pod-product-compliance
Ingram Content Group UK Ltd.
Pitfield, Milton Keynes, MK11 3LW, UK
UKHW040910190926
475560UK00008B/72

9 780765 709820